It's another great book from CGP...

GCSE Extension Science is all about **understanding how science works**. And not only that — understanding it well enough to be able to **question** what you hear on TV and read in the papers.

But don't panic. This book includes all the **science facts** you need to learn, and shows you how they work in the real world. It even includes a **free** Online Edition you can read on your computer or tablet.

How to get your free Online Edition

Just go to **cgpbooks.co.uk/extras** and enter this code...

2271 7460 7476 2565

By the way, this code only works for one person. If somebody else has used this book before you, they might have already claimed the Online Edition.

CGP — still the best! ☺

Our sole aim here at CGP is to produce the highest quality books — carefully written, immaculately presented and dangerously close to being funny.

Then we work our socks off to get them out to you — at the cheapest possible prices.

Contents

Published by CGP

From original material by Richard Parsons.

Editors:
Luke Antieul, Katie Braid, Emma Elder, Ben Fletcher, David Hickinson, Edmund Robinson, Helen Ronan, Hayley Thompson, Jane Towle, Karen Wells and Dawn Wright.

Contributors:
Mike Bossart, Barbara Mascetti and Adrian Schmit.

ISBN: 978 1 84762 859 6

With thanks to Philip Dobson, Ian Francis and Ann Shires for the proofreading.
With thanks to Jan Greenway, Laura Jakubowski and Laura Stoney for the copyright research.

Printed by Elanders Ltd, Newcastle upon Tyne.
Clipart from Corel®

The Scientific Process

You need to know a few things about how the world of science works — both for your <u>exams</u> and your <u>controlled assessment</u>. Investigate these next few pages and you'll be laughing all day long on results day.

Scientists Come Up with *Hypotheses* — Then *Test* Them

About 100 years ago, we thought atoms looked like this.

1) Scientists try to <u>explain</u> things. Everything.
2) They start by <u>observing</u> or <u>thinking about</u> something they don't understand — it could be anything, e.g. planets in the sky, a person suffering from an illness, what matter is made of... anything.
3) Then, using what they already know (plus a bit of insight), they come up with a <u>hypothesis</u> — a possible <u>explanation</u> for what they've observed.
4) The next step is to <u>test</u> whether the hypothesis might be <u>right or not</u> — this involves <u>gathering evidence</u> (i.e. <u>data</u> from <u>investigations</u>).
5) To gather evidence the scientist uses the hypothesis to make a <u>prediction</u> — a statement based on the hypothesis that can be <u>tested</u> by carrying out <u>experiments</u>.
6) If the results from the experiments match the prediction, then the scientist can be <u>more confident</u> that the hypothesis is <u>correct</u>. This <u>doesn't</u> mean the hypothesis is <u>true</u> though — other predictions based on the hypothesis might turn out to be <u>wrong</u>.

Scientists *Work Together* to Test Hypotheses

Then we thought they looked like this.

1) Different scientists can look at the <u>same evidence</u> and interpret it in <u>different ways</u>. That's why scientists usually work in <u>teams</u> — they can share their <u>different ideas</u> on how to interpret the data they find.
2) Once a team has come up with (and tested) a hypothesis they all agree with, they'll present their work to the scientific community through <u>journals</u> and <u>scientific conferences</u> so it can be judged — this is called the <u>peer review</u> process.
3) Other scientists then <u>check</u> the team's results (by trying to <u>replicate</u> them) and carry out their own experiments to <u>collect more evidence</u>.
4) If all the experiments in the world back up the hypothesis, scientists start to have a lot of <u>confidence</u> in it.
5) However, if another scientist does an experiment and the results <u>don't</u> fit with the hypothesis (and other scientists can <u>replicate</u> these results), then the hypothesis is in trouble. When this happens, scientists have to come up with a new hypothesis (maybe a <u>modification</u> of the old explanation, or maybe a completely <u>new</u> one).

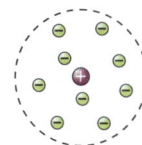

Scientific Ideas *Change* as *New Evidence* is Found

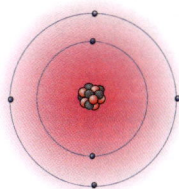

And then we thought they looked like this.

1) Scientific explanations are <u>provisional</u> because they only explain the evidence that's <u>currently available</u> — new evidence may come up that can't be explained.
2) This means that scientific explanations <u>never</u> become hard and fast, totally indisputable <u>fact</u>. As <u>new evidence</u> is found (or new ways of <u>interpreting</u> existing evidence are found), hypotheses can <u>change</u> or be <u>replaced</u>.
3) Sometimes, an <u>unexpected observation</u> or <u>result</u> will suddenly throw a hypothesis into doubt and further experiments will need to be carried out. This can lead to new developments that <u>increase</u> our <u>understanding</u> of science.

You expect me to believe that — then show me the evidence...

If scientists think something is true, they need to produce evidence to convince others — it's all part of <u>testing a hypothesis</u>. One hypothesis might survive these tests, while others won't — it's how things progress. And along the way some hypotheses will be disproved — i.e. shown not to be true.

Scientific Information and Development

Sadly, <u>science isn't</u> always as <u>straightforward</u> as you might think. Here are a few reasons why...

Scientific Information Isn't Always Very Good Quality

1) Scientific information can be presented by a person who is <u>biased</u>.

2) When a person is biased, it means that they <u>favour</u> a <u>particular interpretation</u> of the evidence for a reason that's <u>incorrect</u> or <u>unrelated</u> to the scientific information. Bias can be <u>intentional</u> or <u>unintentional</u>.

3) A person who is intentionally biased might <u>misrepresent</u> the evidence — give the true facts, but present them in a way that makes them <u>misleading</u>. This might be to persuade you to agree with them...

> **EXAMPLE**
>
> **Scientists say 1 in 2 people are of above average weight** ⬅ Sounds like we've got a big weight problem. It's a <u>scientific analysis</u> of the facts, and almost certainly <u>true</u>.
>
> But an <u>average</u> is a kind of '<u>middle value</u>' of all your data. Some readings are <u>higher</u> than average (about <u>half</u> of them, usually). Others will be <u>lower</u> than average (the other half).
>
> So the above headline (which made it sound like we should all <u>lose</u> weight) could just as accurately say: ➡ **Scientists say 1 in 2 people are of below average weight**

4) A person who is intentionally biased might also give scientific information <u>without any evidence</u> to back it up. This might be because there's <u>no evidence</u> to support what they're saying, or it could be that the person is just <u>ignoring</u> the evidence that exists (e.g. because it contradicts what they're saying).

5) Information that isn't backed up with any <u>evidence</u> could just be an <u>opinion</u> — you've got <u>no way</u> of telling whether it's <u>true or not</u>.

Society Influences the Development of Science

1) The question of whether something is <u>morally</u> or <u>ethically</u> right or wrong can't be answered by experiments — there is <u>no "right" or "wrong" answer</u>.

2) The best we can do is get a <u>consensus</u> from society — a <u>judgement</u> that <u>most people</u> are more or less happy to live by. <u>Science</u> can provide <u>more information</u> to help people make this judgement, and the judgement might <u>change</u> over time. But in the end it's up to <u>people</u> and their <u>conscience</u>.

3) In an ideal world, the <u>best decision</u> about any moral or ethical dilemma would have the <u>best outcome</u> for the <u>majority of people</u> involved.

Other Factors Can Affect Scientific Development Too

Economic factors:
- <u>Companies</u> very often won't pay for research unless there's likely to be a <u>profit</u> in it.
- Society can't always <u>afford</u> to do things scientists recommend (e.g. investing heavily in alternative energy sources) without <u>cutting back elsewhere</u>.

Social factors: Decisions based on scientific evidence affect <u>people</u> — e.g. should fossil fuels be taxed more highly (to invest in alternative energy)? Should alcohol be banned (to prevent health problems)? <u>Would the effect on people's lifestyles be acceptable...?</u>

Cultural factors: Cultural feelings can sometimes affect whether <u>research</u> is <u>carried out</u> or <u>given funding</u>, e.g. some people are against research which involves animal testing.

It's a scientific fact that the Moon's made of cheese...

Whenever you're given any kind of scientific information just stop for a second and ask yourself how <u>convincing</u> it really is — think about the <u>evidence</u> that's been used (if any) and the way that the information's been <u>presented</u>.

Planning Investigations

That's all the dull stuff about the world of science over — now onto the hands-on part. The next few pages show how <u>practical investigations</u> should be carried out — by both <u>professional scientists</u> and <u>you</u>.

To Make an Investigation a *Fair Test* You Have to *Control the Variables*

An important part of planning an investigation is making sure it's a <u>fair test</u>.

1) In a lab experiment you usually <u>change one variable</u> and <u>measure</u> how it affects the <u>other variable</u>.

> **EXAMPLE:** you might change only the angle of a slope and measure how it affects the time taken for a toy car to travel down it.

2) To make it a fair test <u>everything else</u> that could affect the results should <u>stay the same</u> (otherwise you can't tell if the thing that's being changed is affecting the results or not — the data won't be reliable).

> **EXAMPLE** continued: you need to keep the slope length the same, otherwise you won't know if any change in the time taken is caused by the change in angle, or the change in length.

3) The variable that you <u>change</u> is called the <u>independent</u> variable.

4) The variable that's <u>measured</u> is called the <u>dependent</u> variable.

5) The variables that you <u>keep the same</u> are called <u>control</u> variables.

> **EXAMPLE** continued:
> Independent = angle of slope
> Dependent = time taken
> Control = length of slope

6) Because you can't always control all the variables, you often need to use a <u>control experiment</u> — an experiment that's kept under the <u>same conditions</u> as the rest of the investigation, but doesn't have anything done to it. This is so that you can see what happens when you don't change anything at all.

The *Equipment* Used has to be *Right for the Job*

1) The measuring equipment you use has to be <u>sensitive enough</u> to accurately measure the chemicals you're using, e.g. if you need to measure out 11 ml of a liquid, you'll need to use a measuring cylinder that can measure to 1 ml, not 5 or 10 ml.

2) The <u>smallest change</u> a measuring instrument can <u>detect</u> is called its **RESOLUTION**. E.g. some mass balances have a resolution of 1 g and some have a resolution of 0.1 g.

3) You should also be able to <u>explain why</u> you've chosen each bit of kit.

Experiments Must be *Safe*

1) Part of planning an investigation is making sure that it's <u>safe</u>.

2) There are lots of <u>hazards</u> you could be faced with during an investigation, e.g. <u>radiation</u>, <u>electricity</u>, <u>gas</u>, <u>chemicals</u> and <u>fire</u>.

3) You should always make sure that you <u>identify</u> all the hazards that you might encounter.

4) You should also come up with ways of <u>reducing the risks</u> from the hazards you've identified.

5) One way of doing this is to carry out a <u>risk assessment</u>:

> For an experiment involving a <u>Bunsen burner</u>, the risk assessment might be something like this:

> <u>Hazard:</u> Bunsen burner is a fire risk.
> <u>Precautions:</u>
> • Keep flammable chemicals away from the Bunsen.
> • Never leave the Bunsen unattended when lit.
> • Always turn on the yellow safety flame when not in use.

Hazard: revision boredom. Precaution: use CGP books

Wow, all this even before you've started the investigation — it really does make them run more smoothly though.

Getting the Data Right

There are a few things that can be done to make sure that you get the best results you possibly can.

Trial Runs Help Figure out the Range and Interval of Variable Values

1) Before you carry out an experiment, it's a good idea to do a trial run first — a quick version of your experiment.

2) Trial runs help you work out whether your plan is right or not — you might decide to make some changes after trying out your method.

3) Trial runs are used to figure out the range of variable values used (the upper and lower limit).

4) And they're used to figure out the interval (gaps) between the values too.

> Slope example from previous page continued:
> - You might do trial runs at 20, 40, 60 and 80°. If the time taken is too short to accurately measure at 80°, you might narrow the range to 20-60°.
> - If using 20° intervals gives you a big change in time taken you might decide to use 10° intervals, e.g. 20, 30, 40, 50...

Data Should be as Reliable and Accurate as Possible

1) Reliable results are ones that can be consistently reproduced each time you do an experiment. If your results are reliable they're more likely to be true, so you can make valid conclusions from them.

2) When carrying out your own investigation, you can improve the reliability of your results by repeating the readings and calculating the mean (average). You should repeat readings at least twice (so that you have at least three readings to calculate an average result).

3) To make sure your results are reliable you can also take a second set of readings with another instrument, or get a different observer to cross check.

4) Checking your results match with secondary sources, e.g. studies that other people have done, also increases the reliability of your data.

5) You should also always make sure that your results are accurate. Really accurate results are those that are really close to the true answer.

6) You can get accurate results by doing things like making sure the equipment you're using is sensitive enough (see previous page), and by recording your data to a suitable level of accuracy. For example, if you're taking digital readings of something, the results will be more accurate if you include at least a couple of decimal places instead of rounding to whole numbers.

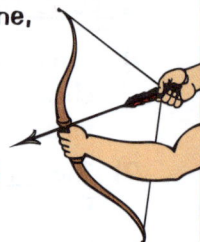

You Can Check For Mistakes Made When Collecting Data

1) When you've collected all the results for an experiment, you should have a look to see if there are any results that don't seem to fit in with the rest.

2) Most results vary a bit, but any that are totally different are called anomalous results.

3) They're caused by human errors, e.g. by a whoopsie when measuring.

4) The only way to stop them happening is by taking all your measurements as carefully as possible.

5) If you ever get any anomalous results, you should investigate them to try to work out what happened. If you can work out what happened (e.g. you measured something wrong) you can ignore them when processing your results.

Reliable data — it won't ever forget your birthday...

All this stuff is really important — without good quality data an investigation will be totally meaningless. So give this page a read through a couple of times and your data will be the envy of the whole scientific community.

Presenting and Interpreting Data

The fun doesn't stop once you've collected your data — it then needs to be <u>presented</u>...

Data <u>Needs to be</u> <u>Organised</u> <u>and</u> <u>Processed</u>

1) <u>Tables</u> are dead useful for <u>organising data</u>.

2) When you draw a table <u>use a ruler</u> and make sure <u>each column</u> has a <u>heading</u> (including the <u>units</u>).

3) Problem is, <u>raw data</u> generally just ain't that useful. You usually have to <u>process</u> it in some way.

4) A couple of the most simple calculations you can perform are the <u>mean</u> (average) and the <u>range</u> (how spread out the data is).

Different Types <u>of Data</u> Should be <u>Presented</u> in <u>Different Ways</u>

1) You'll have to <u>choose</u> the best way to present your data.

2) If the independent variable is <u>categoric</u> (comes in distinct categories, e.g. blood types, metals) you should use a <u>bar chart</u> or a <u>pie chart</u> to display the data.

3) If the independent variable is <u>continuous</u> (numerical data that can have any value within a range, e.g. length, volume, time) you should use a <u>line graph</u> to display the data.

Here are a few useful tips for drawing line graphs:

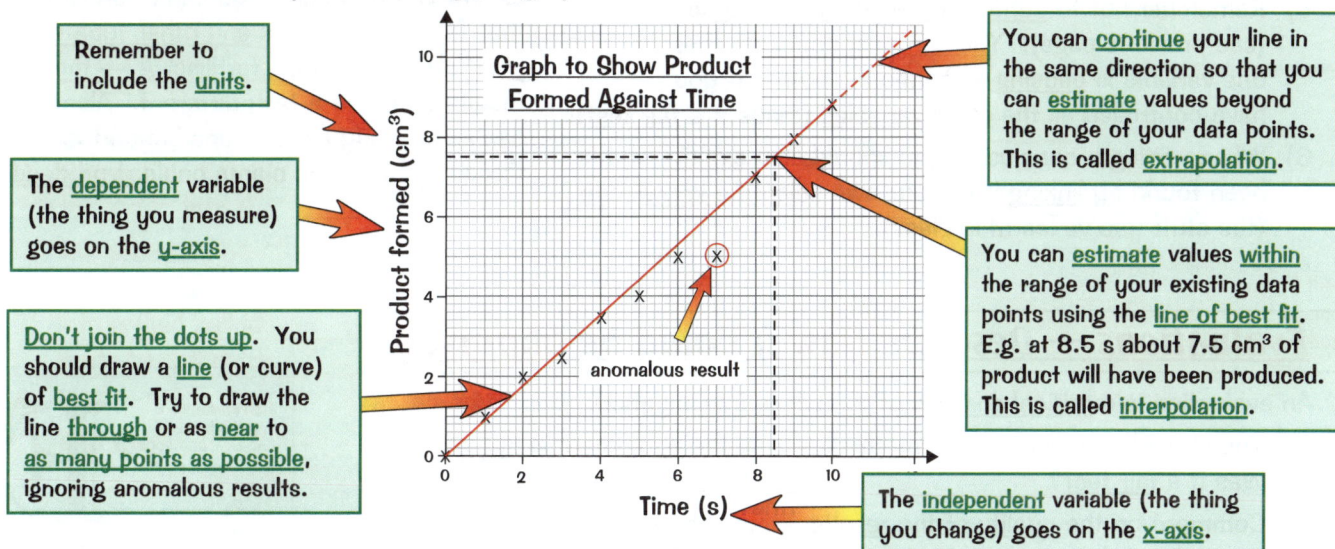

Remember to include the <u>units</u>.

The <u>dependent</u> variable (the thing you measure) goes on the <u>y-axis</u>.

Don't join the dots up. You should draw a <u>line</u> (or curve) of <u>best fit</u>. Try to draw the line <u>through</u> or as <u>near</u> to as many points as possible, ignoring anomalous results.

Graph to Show Product Formed Against Time

Product formed (cm^3)

anomalous result

Time (s)

You can <u>continue</u> your line in the same direction so that you can <u>estimate</u> values beyond the range of your data points. This is called <u>extrapolation</u>.

You can <u>estimate</u> values <u>within</u> the range of your existing data points using the <u>line of best fit</u>. E.g. at 8.5 s about 7.5 cm^3 of product will have been produced. This is called <u>interpolation</u>.

The <u>independent</u> variable (the thing you change) goes on the <u>x-axis</u>.

Line Graphs <u>Can Show</u> Relationships <u>in Data</u>

1) Line graphs are great for showing relationships <u>between two variables</u>.

2) Here are the <u>three</u> different types of <u>correlation</u> (relationship) shown on line graphs:

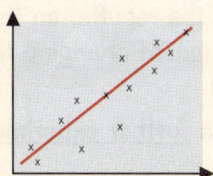

<u>POSITIVE</u> correlation — as one variable <u>increases</u> the other <u>increases</u>.

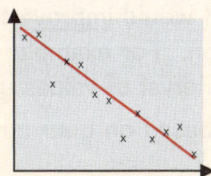

<u>INVERSE</u> (negative) correlation — as one variable <u>increases</u> the other <u>decreases</u>.

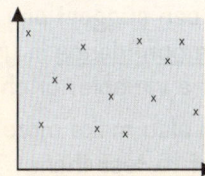

<u>NO</u> correlation — there's <u>no relationship</u> between the two variables.

3) You've got to be careful not to <u>confuse correlation</u> with <u>cause</u> though. A <u>correlation</u> just means that there's a <u>relationship</u> between two variables. It <u>doesn't mean</u> that the change in one variable is <u>causing</u> the change in the other (there might be <u>other factors</u> involved).

Concluding and Evaluating

At the end of an investigation, the conclusion and evaluation are waiting. Don't worry, they won't bite.

A Conclusion is a Summary of What You've Learnt

1) Once all the data's been collected, presented and analysed, an investigation will always involve coming to a conclusion.

2) Drawing a conclusion can be quite straightforward — just look at your data and say what pattern you see.

EXAMPLE: The table on the right shows the heights of pea plant seedlings grown for three weeks with different fertilisers.

Fertiliser	Mean growth (mm)
A	13.5
B	19.5
No fertiliser	5.5

CONCLUSION: Fertiliser B makes pea plant seedlings grow taller over a three week period than fertiliser A.

3) However, you also need to use the data that's been collected to justify the conclusion (back it up).

EXAMPLE continued: Fertiliser B made the pea plants grow 6 mm more on average than fertiliser A.

4) There are some things to watch out for too — it's important that the conclusion matches the data it's based on and doesn't go any further.

5) Remember not to confuse correlation and cause (see previous page). You can only conclude that one variable is causing a change in another if you have controlled all the other variables (made it a fair test).

6) When writing a conclusion you should also explain what's been found by linking it to your own scientific knowledge (the stuff you've learnt in class).

EXAMPLE continued: You can't conclude that fertiliser B makes any other type of plant grow taller than fertiliser A — the results could be totally different. Also, you can't make any conclusions beyond the three weeks — the plants could drop dead.

Evaluations — Describe How it Could be Improved

An evaluation is a critical analysis of the whole investigation.

1) You should comment on the method — was the equipment suitable? Was it a fair test?

2) Comment on the quality of the results — was there enough evidence to reach a valid conclusion? Were the results reliable, accurate and precise?

3) Were there any anomalies in the results — if there were none then say so.

4) If there were any anomalies, try to explain them — were they caused by errors in measurement? Were there any other variables that could have affected the results?

5) When you analyse your investigation like this, you'll be able to say how confident you are that your conclusion is right.

6) Then you can suggest any changes that would improve the quality of the results, so that you could have more confidence in your conclusion. For example, you might suggest changing the way you controlled a variable, or changing the interval of values you measured.

7) You could also make more predictions based on your conclusion, then further experiments could be carried out to test them.

8) When suggesting improvements to the investigation, always make sure that you say why you think this would make the results better.

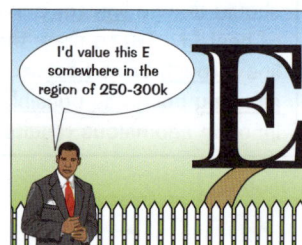

I'd value this E somewhere in the region of 250-300k

Evaluation — in my next study I will make sure I don't burn the lab down...

I know it doesn't seem very nice, but writing about where you went wrong is an important skill — it shows you've got a really good understanding of what the investigation was about. It's difficult for me — I'm always right.

Controlled Assessment

At some point you'll have to do the <u>controlled assessment</u>. Here's a bit about it, but make sure you can recite all the stuff we've covered in this section first — it'll really help you out.

There are *Three Parts* to the *Controlled Assessment*

(1) ### Research and Collecting Secondary Data

For Part 1 you'll be given some material to introduce the task and a <u>research question</u>. You'll need to read this through and then:

1) Carry out <u>research</u> and collect <u>secondary data</u> (data that other people have collected, rather than data you collect yourself).

2) Show that you considered all the <u>different sources</u> you could have used (e.g. books, the Internet) and <u>chose</u> the ones that were <u>most suitable</u>. You also need to explain <u>why</u> you chose those sources.

3) Write a <u>full list</u> (bibliography) of all the sources you used.

4) <u>Present</u> all the data you collected in an <u>appropriate</u> way, e.g. using tables.

(2) ### Planning and Collecting Primary Data

For Part 2 you'll be given some more <u>information</u> to get your head around. Read this through and then:

1) Come up with a <u>hypothesis</u> based on the information you've been given.

2) <u>Plan</u> an experiment to test your hypothesis. You'll need to think about:
   - What <u>equipment</u> you're going to use (and <u>why</u> that equipment is <u>right for the job</u>).
   - What <u>measurements</u> you're going to take of the <u>dependent variable</u>.
   - How you're going to <u>minimise errors</u> so that your results are <u>accurate</u> and <u>reliable</u>.
   - What <u>range</u> of values you will use for the <u>independent variable</u>.
   - What <u>interval</u> you will use for the <u>independent variable</u>.
   - What variables you're going to <u>control</u> (and <u>how</u> you're going to do it).
   - How many times you're going to <u>repeat</u> the experiment.

There's lots of help on all of these things on pages 3-6.

3) <u>Explain</u> all the choices you made when planning the experiment.

4) Write a <u>risk assessment</u> for the experiment.

5) <u>Carry out</u> the experiment to collect <u>primary data</u>, taking any <u>precautions</u> from the risk assessment.

6) <u>Present</u> all the data you collected in an <u>appropriate</u> way, e.g. using tables.

(3) ### Analysis and Evaluation

For Part 3 you'll have to complete a <u>question paper</u> which will ask you to do things like:

1) <u>Process</u> (e.g. using a bit of maths) and <u>present</u> (e.g. using graphs) <u>both</u> the primary and secondary data you collected in Part 1 and Part 2 in the most <u>appropriate</u> way.

2) <u>Analyse</u> and <u>interpret</u> the data to identify any <u>patterns</u> or <u>relationships</u>.

3) <u>Compare</u> your primary and secondary data to look for similarities and differences.

4) Write a <u>conclusion</u> based on all the data you collected and back it up with your own <u>scientific knowledge</u>. Say whether the <u>secondary data</u> you collected <u>supports</u> the conclusion.

5) Look back to your <u>hypothesis</u> and say whether the data <u>support</u> the hypothesis or not.

6) <u>Evaluate</u> the <u>methods</u> you used to collect the data and the <u>quality of the data</u> that was collected.

7) Say how <u>confident</u> you are in your <u>conclusion</u> and make <u>suggestions</u> for how the investigation could be <u>improved</u>. You'll also need to say <u>why</u> your suggestions would be an improvement.

Read this through and your assessment will be well under control...

You could use this page like a tick list for the controlled assessment — to make sure you don't forget anything.

Bones and Cartilage

Bones and joints are pretty darned important — without them you wouldn't be able to move around at all.

If You Didn't Have a Skeleton, *You'd be* Jelly-like

1) The job of a skeleton is to support the body and allow it to move — as well as protect vital organs.
2) Fish, amphibians, reptiles, birds and mammals are all vertebrates — they all have an internal skeleton including a backbone. Some animals (e.g. insects) have an external skeleton — their skeleton is on the outside of their bodies.
3) An internal skeleton has certain advantages compared to an external skeleton:

   - It can easily grow with the body.
   - It's easy to attach muscles to it.
   - It's more flexible than an external skeleton.
   - It gives the body support and provides a framework.

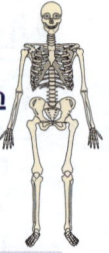

Bones *are* Living Tissues...

Bones are a lot cleverer than they might look...

1) Bones are made up of living cells — so they grow, and can repair themselves if they get damaged.

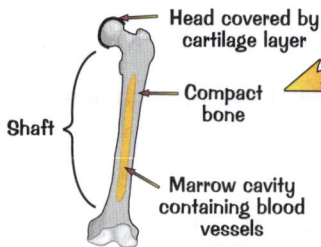

Head covered by cartilage layer
Compact bone
Shaft
Marrow cavity containing blood vessels

2) Long bones (e.g. the big one in your thigh) are actually hollow — this makes them lighter than solid bones of the same size (and stronger than solid bones of the same mass). This makes movement far more efficient.

3) The hole in the middle of some long bones is filled with bone marrow. Bone marrow is a spongy substance that makes new blood cells — meaning your bones are actually a kind of blood factory.

...That Start Off Life as Cartilage

1) Bones start off as cartilage in the womb. Cartilage is living tissue that looks and feels a bit rubbery. It can grow and repair itself too (although not as easily as bone).

2) As you grow, a lot of your cartilage is replaced by bone. Blood vessels deposit calcium and phosphorus in the cartilage — which eventually turns it into bone. This process is called ossification.

3) You can tell if someone is still growing by looking at how much cartilage is present — if there's a lot, they're still growing.

4) Even when you're fully grown, the ends of bones remain covered with cartilage (to stop bones rubbing together at joints — see next page).

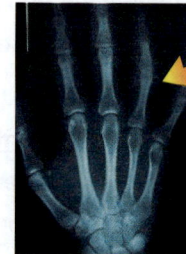

Bones show up on an X-ray, but cartilage doesn't.

X-rays can also show where fractures are.

Bones and Cartilage Can Get Damaged

1) Cartilage and bone are both made up of living tissue, and so can get infected.

2) Even though bones are really strong, they can be fractured (broken) by a sharp knock. Elderly people are more prone to breaking bones as they often suffer from osteoporosis — a condition where calcium is lost from the bones. (Osteoporosis makes the bones softer, more brittle and more likely to break — it can be treated with calcium supplements.)

3) A broken bone can easily injure nearby tissue — so you shouldn't move anyone who might have a fracture. That's especially true for someone with a suspected spinal fracture (broken back) — moving them could damage their spinal cord (basically an extension of the brain running down the middle of the backbone). Damage to the spinal cord can lead to paralysis.

What do skeletons say before eating?... bone appetit...

Bones are all too easily thought of as just organic scaffolding. They're pretty amazing really, and painful if you break one. But bones usually mend pretty easily — if you hold them still, a break will knit itself together.

Joints and Muscles

Like it says in the song, the knee bone's connected to the thigh bone. And it's done with a <u>joint</u>. Read on.

Joints Allow the Bones to Move

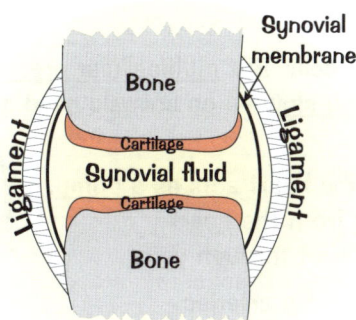

1) <u>Synovial joints</u> (e.g. the knee) are the <u>main type</u> of joint in the body.

2) The bones at a synovial joint are <u>held together</u> by <u>ligaments</u>. Ligaments have a high <u>tensile strength</u> (i.e. you can pull them and they don't snap easily), but are pretty <u>elastic</u> (stretchy).

3) The ends of bones are covered with <u>cartilage</u> to stop the bones <u>rubbing</u> together. And because cartilage can be slightly compressed, it can act as a <u>shock absorber</u>.

4) The <u>synovial membrane</u> releases <u>synovial fluid</u> to <u>lubricate</u> the joints, allowing them to move more easily.

5) Different kinds of joints move in different ways. For example...

BALL AND SOCKET

...like the <u>hip</u> or <u>shoulder</u>.

The joint can move in <u>all directions</u>, and can also <u>rotate</u>.

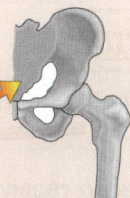

HINGE

...like the <u>knee</u> or <u>elbow</u>.

The joint can go <u>backwards and forwards</u>, but not side-to-side.

Muscles Pull on Bones to Move Them

1) Bones are attached to muscles by <u>tendons</u>.

2) Muscles move bones at a joint by <u>contracting</u> (becoming <u>shorter</u>). They can only <u>pull</u> on bones to move a joint — they <u>can't</u> push.

3) This is why muscles usually come in <u>pairs</u> (called <u>antagonistic pairs</u>). When <u>one muscle</u> in the pair contracts, the joint moves in <u>one direction</u>. When the <u>other muscle</u> contracts, it moves in the <u>opposite</u> direction.

① **Arm bends**

humerus

Biceps contracts

Triceps relaxes

radius

ulna

② **Arm straightens**

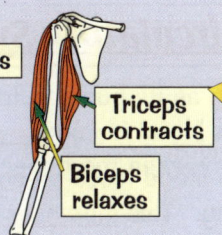

Triceps contracts

Biceps relaxes

4) The <u>biceps</u> and <u>triceps</u> are an antagonistic pair of muscles. When the <u>biceps</u> contracts it pulls the lower arm <u>upwards</u>. This bends the arm. And when the <u>triceps</u> contracts the lower arm is pulled back <u>down</u>. This straightens the arm.

5) Together, they make the arm work as a <u>lever</u>, where the <u>elbow</u> is the <u>pivot</u> (<u>fulcrum</u>).

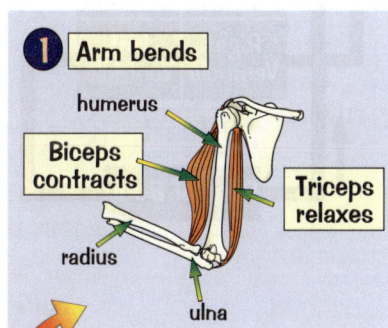

What's a skeleton's favourite instrument?... a trom-bone...

Different joints have different <u>ranges of movement</u>. And if you do something that makes the bone move further than its range of movement (like fall on it), then you could <u>dislocate</u> it. Painful. Make sure you learn the different parts of the <u>synovial joint</u>, as well as exactly what each bit does.

Circulatory Systems

Ah, the circulatory system — my heart's all of a flutter just thinking about it...

Lots of Animals Need a Blood Circulatory System

1) All living cells need to be supplied with materials like oxygen and glucose.
   They also need to get rid of waste materials like carbon dioxide.

2) In single-celled organisms these materials just diffuse in and out of the cell. But multicellular organisms like animals are much larger. Diffusion through all the cells would be too slow — so animals need a blood circulatory system to transport materials efficiently around their bodies.

3) In any circulatory system (so this goes for humans, dogs, fish, etc.), the heart acts as a pump. The heart contracts, pushing blood round the body. Blood flows away from the heart along arteries, through capillaries at the organs, and then back to the heart through veins.

4) As blood travels round the body through blood vessels it loses pressure. So arteries have the highest pressure, veins have the lowest and capillaries are in between.

Humans Have a Double Circulatory System

1) Animals with gills (e.g. fish), have a single circulatory system — one circuit of blood vessels from the heart.

2) For this, you need a two-chambered heart — one chamber to receive blood and one to pump blood out to the gills and the rest of the body.

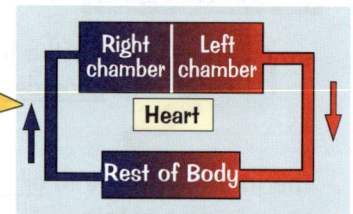

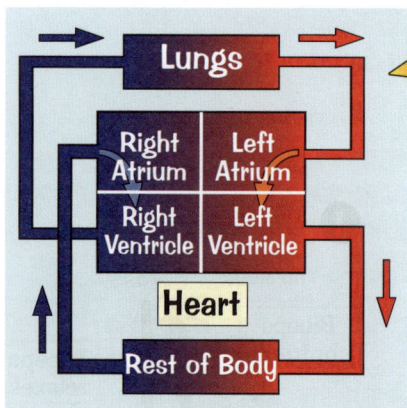

3) Humans (and other mammals) have a double circulatory system. It has two circuits from the heart — one to the body and the other to the lungs.

4) In a double circulatory system, you need a four-chambered heart This allows the blood to be pumped separately to the lungs and the body, which is important for maintaining a high pressure (see below).

5) Unborn babies don't need a double-circulatory system. They get their oxygen from their mother via the placenta, so their blood doesn't need to travel to the lungs. As a result, all unborn babies have a 'hole in the heart' (a gap between the atria), which allows blood to bypass the lungs. It closes soon after birth.

(See page 13 for more on different types of hole in the heart.)

Blood is Under a Higher Pressure In a Double Circulatory System

1) In animals with a single circulatory system, the blood loses pressure as its pumped to the gills and then around the rest of the body. This means the overall pressure of the blood is fairly low.

2) In a double circulatory system, blood pressure is much higher. The blood loses pressure in the lungs, but returns to the heart before being pumped to the rest of the body. This increases the pressure of the blood going to the body.

3) Keeping the blood at a higher pressure allows materials to be transported around the body more quickly.

The heart — it's all just pump and circumstance...

In the exam you might be asked to interpret data on pressure changes in the arteries, veins and capillaries. Remember that pressure goes from high to low in the alphabetical order of their names — so arteries have the highest pressure, then capillaries have medium pressure and veins have the lowest pressure. Simple.

The Cardiac Cycle and Circulation

The chambers of the heart work together to pump blood around your body — and you need to know how.

The Cardiac Cycle is How the Heart Contracts

1) The heart pumps blood around the body by contracting and relaxing the atria and ventricles in sequence.

2) Blood is prevented from flowing in the wrong direction through the heart by the atrio-ventricular and semilunar valves.

3) The sequence of events in one complete heartbeat is called the cardiac cycle:

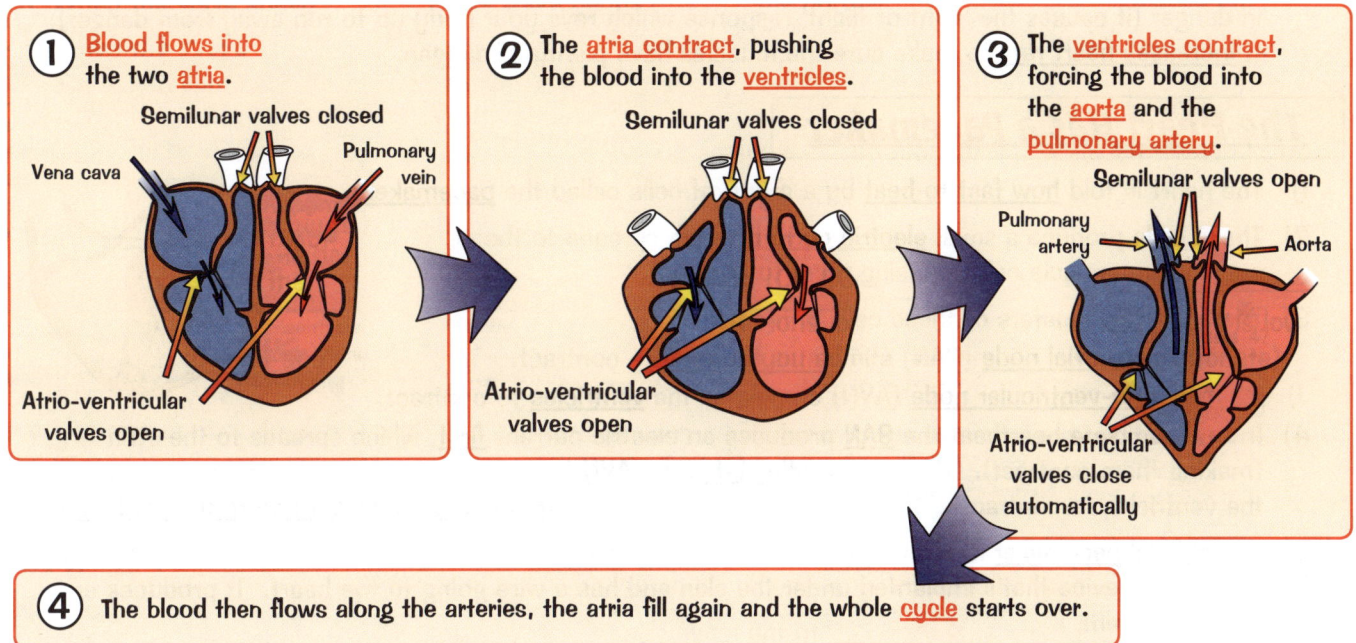

① Blood flows into the two atria.

Semilunar valves closed

Vena cava

Pulmonary vein

Atrio-ventricular valves open

② The atria contract, pushing the blood into the ventricles.

Semilunar valves closed

Atrio-ventricular valves open

③ The ventricles contract, forcing the blood into the aorta and the pulmonary artery.

Semilunar valves open

Pulmonary artery

Aorta

Atrio-ventricular valves close automatically

④ The blood then flows along the arteries, the atria fill again and the whole cycle starts over.

We Haven't Always Known This Much About the Heart

CLAUDIUS GALEN (ancient Greece).
1) He cut up animals to study them, and so knew about chambers in the heart.
2) He thought arterial blood was made by the heart, while blood in veins was made by the liver, sucked through veins by the heart and consumed by the organs.

WILLIAM HARVEY (1578-1657).
Before Harvey, scientists still believed more or less the same as Galen. Harvey changed all this. He showed that:
- the heart valves stopped the back flow of blood,
- the heart is a pump (rather than something that sucks),
- the pulse is caused by the heart pumping blood into the arteries,
- the same blood was circulated around the body over and over again — not manufactured and consumed.

Blood vessels — a vampire's favourite type of ship...

If you're given data in the exam on the cardiac cycle, don't panic — so long as you understand how the heart pumps blood around the body, you'll be just fine. And no matter how bad it looks, at least it isn't in Greek...

Heart Rate

The heart has a regular beat — and this page explains why. So keep reading...

Heart Rate Changes *According to Activity*

1) When you exercise, your muscles need more oxygen to work harder, so you need to breathe faster. Your heart also pumps faster to deliver more oxygenated blood to your muscles. (And when you stop exercising your heart gradually returns to normal.)

What happens is that your muscles produce more carbon dioxide — this change is detected by the brain, which tells your body to breathe faster.

2) Hormones can also affect your heart rate, e.g. adrenaline is released when you get a shock or you're in danger (it causes the 'fight or flight' response which revs your body up to run away from danger). It increases heart rate to make sure the muscles have plenty of oxygen.

The Heart Has a Pacemaker

1) The heart is told how fast to beat by a group of cells called the pacemakers.

2) These cells produce a small electric current which spreads to the surrounding muscle cells, causing them to contract.

3) There are two clusters of these cells in the heart:
   - The sino-atrial node (SAN) stimulates the atria to contract.
   - The atrio-ventricular node (AVN) stimulates the ventricles to contract.

SAN

electrical impulses

AVN

4) In one complete heartbeat the SAN produces an electric current first, which spreads to the atria (making them contract). The current stimulates the AVN to produce an electric current (causing the ventricles to contract). This process ensures that the atria always contract before the ventricles.

5) An artificial pacemaker is often used to control heartbeat if the pacemaker cells don't work properly. It's a little device that's implanted under the skin and has a wire going to the heart. It produces an electric current.

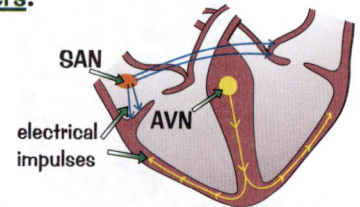

ECGs and Echocardiograms Measure the Heart

Doctors can measure how well the heart is working (heart function) in two main ways.

1) Electrocardiogram (ECG) — showing the electrical activity of the heart. They can show:
   - heart attacks — e.g. if you're having a heart attack, or are about to have one,
   - irregular heartbeats and general health of the heart.

This is what a healthy person's ECG looks like...

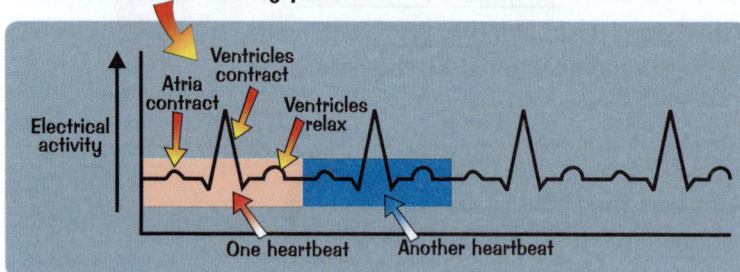

Electrical activity

Atria contract

Ventricles contract

Ventricles relax

One heartbeat   Another heartbeat

...and here are some unhealthy ones.

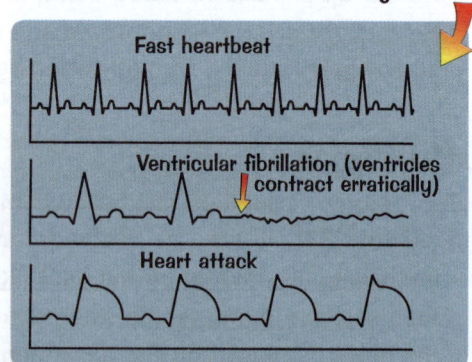

Fast heartbeat

Ventricular fibrillation (ventricles contract erratically)

Heart attack

2) Echocardiogram — an ultrasound scan of the heart, which can show:
   - an enlarged heart — this could indicate heart failure,
   - decreased pumping ability — this could indicate a disease called cardiomyopathy,
   - valve function — torn, infected or scarred heart valves can cause problems.

A stitch — the best running pacemaker in the world...

In the exam you might be asked to interpret an ECG — they look scary but they're not too difficult... If a peak is missing, then that part of the heart isn't contracting. If the peaks are close together, the heart's beating faster. But if everything is going haywire, then it could be a heart attack or fibrillation.

Module B5 — The Living Body

Heart Disease

Some types of heart disease are getting more common — but there are new ways of treating them...

There are Three Main Ways Your Heart Can Go Wrong

1) HOLE IN THE HEART

- A hole in the heart is a gap in the wall separating either the two ventricles or the two atria.
- It allows blood to move directly from one side of the heart to the other. This allows deoxygenated and oxygenated blood to mix, which reduces the amount of oxygen in the blood being pumped to the body.
- A hole in the heart sometimes needs to be corrected by surgery.

All unborn babies have a hole in the heart, which usually closes up after birth — see page 10 for more.

2) VALVE DAMAGE

- The valves in the heart can be damaged or weakened by heart attacks, infection or old age.
- The damage may cause the valve not to open properly, causing high blood pressure. It may even allow blood to flow in both directions rather than just forward. This means that blood doesn't circulate as effectively as normal.
- Severe valve damage can be treated by replacing the valve with an artificial one.

3) CORONARY HEART DISEASE (CHD)

- Coronary heart disease is when the coronary arteries supplying blood to the heart muscle get blocked by fatty deposits.
- This reduces blood flow to the heart muscle and often results in a heart attack.
- It can be treated by a coronary bypass operation, where a piece of blood vessel is taken from another part of the body and inserted to 'bypass' the blockage.

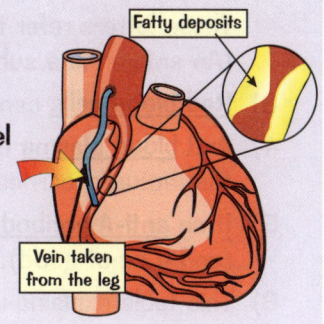

Fatty deposits

Vein taken from the leg

You can have surgery to put a lot of heart problems right. For example...

- You can have a heart transplant — an entirely new heart from a donor.
- You can also get new bits fitted, such as valves and pacemakers (see below).
- You can get a heart assist device — this takes over the pumping duties of a failing heart. This 'buys time' while the patient waits for a transplant.

Artificial Parts Can Be Used Instead of Heart Transplants

1) The main advantage of using artificial parts (valves and pacemakers) is that rejection isn't normally a problem. They're usually made from metals or plastics, which the body can't recognise as foreign in the same way as it does with living tissue.

2) Replacing a valve is a much less drastic procedure than a transplant, and inserting a pacemaker only involves an overnight stay in hospital.

3) However, the main disadvantage is that the new valves and pacemakers might not last very long and need replacing as a result.

See page 15 for more on organ rejection.

There's no treatment for a broken heart...

Heart disease is serious stuff, but scientists have developed lots of ways of treating it. Heart transplants have been an option since the 1960s and today artificial devices can also be used to keep the old tickers working.

Blood Clotting and Transfusions

If you get a cut, you don't want all your blood to drain away — this is why clotting is so handy. Sometimes injuries are so bad you lose a lot of blood and you need to replace it — that's where transfusions come in.

Blood Sometimes Doesn't Clot Properly

1) When you're injured, your blood clots to prevent too much bleeding. A clot is a mesh of protein fibres (called fibrin fibres) that 'plugs' the damaged area. Clots are formed by a series of chemical reactions that take place when platelets in your blood are exposed to damaged blood vessels.

PLATELETS
These are small fragments of cells that help blood clot.

2) Too little clotting could mean you bleed to death (well, you're more likely to get loads of bruises). Too much clotting can cause strokes and deep vein thrombosis (DVT).

3) People who are at risk of stroke and DVT can take drugs to reduce their risk. Warfarin, heparin and aspirin all help prevent the blood from clotting.

4) Haemophilia is a genetic condition where the blood doesn't clot easily because a clotting factor can't be made by the body — this missing clotting factor can be injected.

Blood Type is Important in Transfusions

1) If you're in an accident or having surgery, you may lose a lot of blood — this needs to be replaced by a blood transfusion, using blood from a blood donor. But you can't just use any old blood...

2) People have different blood groups or types — you can be any one of: A, B, O or AB. These letters refer to the type of antigens on the surface of a person's red blood cells. (An antigen is a substance that can trigger a response from a person's immune system.)

3) Red blood cells can have A or B antigens (or neither, or both) on their surface.

4) And blood plasma can contain anti-A or anti-B antibodies. (Plasma's the pale liquid in blood that actually carries all the different bits — e.g. the blood cells, antibodies, hormones, etc.)

5) If an anti-A antibody meets an A antigen, the blood clumps together. This is known as agglutination (and it's not good). The same thing happens when an anti-B antibody meets a B antigen.

6) This table explains which blood groups can donate blood to which other blood groups.

Blood Group	Antigens	Antibodies	Can give blood to	Can get blood from
A	A	anti-B	A and AB	A and O
B	B	anti-A	B and AB	B and O
AB	A, B	none	only AB	anyone
O	none	anti-A, anti-B	anyone	only O

For example, if your blood group is type O, your blood can be given to anyone — there are no antigens on your blood cells, so any anti-A or anti-B antibodies have nothing to 'attack'. You can only receive blood from other type O people though — your antibodies would attack the antigens in type A, B or AB blood.

I think I need an information transfusion... from this book to my brain...

You might get asked a question on who can donate blood to whom in the exam. Just look at what blood type the donor is and think about what antigens and antibodies they have in their blood. It's hard, and you need to think carefully about it (I do anyway), but it does make sense.

Transplants and Organ Donation

If an organ is severely damaged, it can be removed and replaced by one from someone else — this known as an organ transplant. Unfortunately though, it's not as simple as just whacking in a new kidney...

Organs Can Come From Living or Dead Donors

1) Living donors can donate whole (or parts of) certain organs. For example, you can live with just one of your two kidneys and donate the other, or you can donate a piece of your liver.

2) Organs from people who have recently died can also be transplanted.

3) To be an organ donor, a person must meet certain criteria...

> All donors must be:
> * Relatively young so that the organ is as fit and healthy as possible.
> * A similar body weight to the patient needing the transplant, so the organ is a good 'fit'.
> * A close tissue match to the patient to prevent problems with rejection (see below).
>   For a living donor, this usually means being a close family member of the patient.

> Living donors must be over the age of 18.

> Donors who have died must have done so very recently — this is because organs only stay usable for a few hours outside the body.
> Close relatives of the dead donor must give their permission.

4) Success rates of transplants depend on a lot of things — e.g. the type of organ (e.g. the heart is riskier than a kidney), the age of the patient, the skill of the surgeon, etc.

Transplants Can Be Rejected

1) One of the main problems with organ transplants is that the patient's immune system often recognises the new organ as 'foreign' and attacks it — this is called rejection.

2) To reduce the chances of this happening, the donor should have a similar tissue type to the patient (i.e. have similar antigens on their cell surfaces). This is what's meant by being a 'close tissue match'.

3) Doctors use immuno-suppressive drugs that suppress the patient's immune system to help stop the donor organ being rejected — but it leaves the patient more vulnerable to infections.

There are Ethical Issues Surrounding Organ Donation

1) Some people think for religious reasons that a person's body should be buried intact (so giving organs is wrong). Others think life or death is up to God (so receiving organs is wrong).

2) Others worry that doctors might not save them if they're critically ill and their organs are needed for transplant. There are safeguards in place that should prevent this though.

3) There are also worries that people may get pressured into being a 'living donor' (e.g. donating a kidney to a close relative). But doctors try to ensure that it's always the donor's personal choice.

I think I need a brain transplant to learn all this lot...

Did you know that if you transplant a piece of a liver it can actually grow back to normal size within a few weeks. Impressive. Changing the subject slightly... one donor (if they're dead) can donate several organs — e.g. their heart, kidneys, liver, lungs, pancreas... And on top of that, other tissues (e.g. skin, bone, tendons, corneas...) can also be donated. It's absolutely amazing really, when you think about it.

Organ Donation and Organ Replacement

Organ transplants can save lives — but there are more people who need replacement organs than there are donors. Sometimes mechanical replacements can be used instead — but they're not perfect, either...

There Are Problems With the Supply of Donor Organs

1) The UK has a shortage of organs available for donation...

   - You can join the NHS Organ Donor Register to show you're willing to donate organs after you die. However, doctors still need your family's consent before they can use the organs for a transplant.
   - Some people say it should be made easier for doctors to use the organs of people who have died. One suggestion is to have an 'opt-out' system instead — this means anyone's organs can be used unless the person has registered to say they don't want them to be donated.

2) The shortage of donors means that a person needing a transplant usually has to wait for an organ to become available.

3) The wait can last a long time because the organ donor must meet so many different criteria (see previous page).

You Can Get Mechanical Replacements for Organs

1) Sometimes, temporary mechanical replacements for organs can be used to keep someone alive. This could be for anything from a few hours (e.g. during an operation), to several months or even years (e.g. if they're waiting for a suitable organ donor).

2) Mechanical replacements can be used inside or outside of the body. Here are a few examples of mechanical replacements used outside of the body...

   ### HEART-LUNG MACHINES
   These keep a patient's blood oxygenated and pumping during heart or lung surgery.

   ### KIDNEY DIALYSIS MACHINES
   These can filter a patient's blood (e.g. while they wait for a kidney transplant).

   ### MECHANICAL VENTILATORS
   These are used to push air in and out of a patient's lungs if they stop breathing.

3) There are problems in using mechanical replacements though, e.g.

   - They usually need a constant power supply.
   - They're often large and difficult to move around.
   - They must be made from materials that won't harm the body and won't degrade (i.e. break down or rust).
   - Even if they're made from the right materials, they can occasionally cause inflammation or allergic reactions in the patient.

I haven't got an organ to donate — but I've got a piano...

Organ donation can save lives, but some people feel strongly about what happens to their body after they die — and you need to make sure you can discuss the advantages and disadvantages of an organ register in the exam. Mechanical replacements don't raise so many ethical issues, but they're not perfect — and you need to know why.

The Respiratory System

The <u>respiratory system</u> is the posh name for the <u>breathing system</u> — all things to do with the lungs.

We Need to Take In Oxygen and Remove Carbon Dioxide

1) When we breathe, we <u>take in oxygen</u> for respiration and <u>release carbon dioxide</u>.

2) Carbon dioxide is a <u>waste product</u> of respiration. At a <u>high level</u>, CO_2 is <u>toxic</u> — which is why it must be <u>removed</u> from the body through breathing.

3) When the <u>brain</u> detects a <u>rise</u> in the CO_2 level in the blood, it responds by <u>increasing</u> the <u>rate of breathing</u>.

Ventilation (Breathing) Uses Muscles

Inspiration (or Breathing In)...

1) Your <u>intercostal</u> muscles (between the ribs) and <u>diaphragm</u> (the muscle beneath the lungs) <u>contract</u>, and <u>increase</u> the <u>volume</u> of the thorax (the bit of your body containing your lungs).

2) This expands the <u>lungs</u> and <u>decreases</u> the <u>pressure</u> inside them, which draws air <u>in</u>.

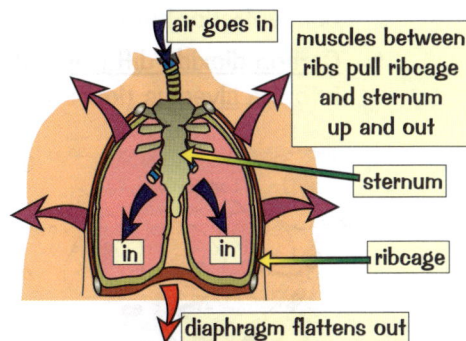

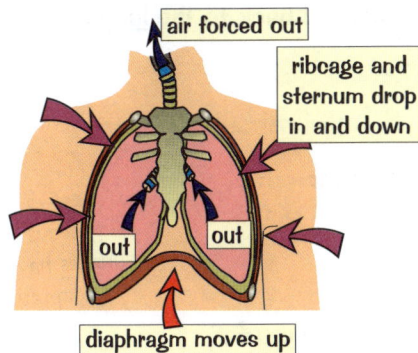

air goes in

muscles between ribs pull ribcage and sternum up and out

sternum

ribcage

in | in

diaphragm flattens out

air forced out

ribcage and sternum drop in and down

out | out

diaphragm moves up

...and Expiration (or Breathing Out)

1) <u>Intercostals</u> and <u>diaphragm relax</u>.

2) The thorax volume <u>decreases</u>.

3) This <u>increases</u> the pressure in the lungs and air is forced <u>out</u>.

Lung Capacity Can be Measured with a Spirometer

Doctors measure lung capacity using a machine called a <u>spirometer</u> — it can help <u>diagnose</u> and <u>monitor lung diseases</u>.

The patient breathes into the machine (through a tube) for a few minutes, and the volume of air that is breathed in and out is measured and plotted on a graph (called a <u>spirogram</u>) — like this one...

1) The <u>total volume of air</u> you can fit in your lungs is your <u>total lung capacity</u> (usually about 6 litres).

2) The volume of air you breathe in (or out) in <u>one normal breath</u> is called your <u>tidal air</u>.

3) Even if you try to breathe out really hard there's always <u>some air left</u> (just over a litre) in your lungs to make sure that they <u>stay open</u> — this is called the <u>residual air</u>.

4) Total lung capacity minus residual air gives you <u>vital capacity air</u> — the amount of usable air (or the <u>maximum</u> volume of air that can be breathed <u>in</u> or <u>out</u>).

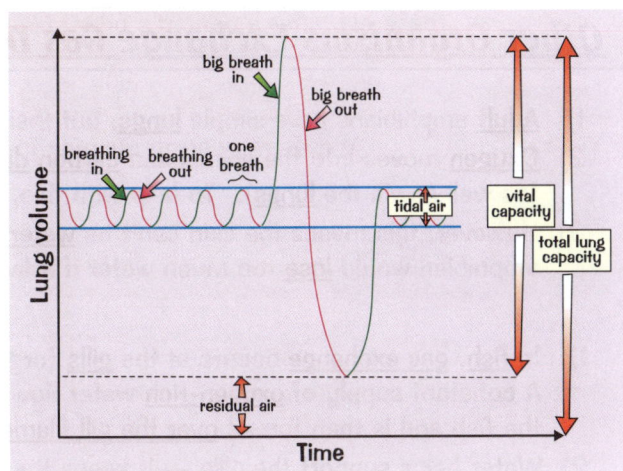

big breath in

big breath out

breathing in | breathing out | one breath

Lung volume

tidal air

vital capacity

total lung capacity

residual air

Time

Spirograms... aren't they those fancy drawing machines...

If the values on a spirogram are <u>low</u> the person might have a <u>lung disease</u>. If the <u>tidal volume</u> increases (i.e. if they're <u>breathing deeper</u>), then they're probably <u>exercising</u>. Simple really.

More on the Respiratory System

All living organisms need to exchange gases for respiration — but they do it in very different ways...

In Humans, Gaseous Exchange Happens in the Lungs

1) The lungs contain millions of little air sacs called alveoli
   — these air sacs are where gas exchange takes place.

2) The blood passing next to the alveoli has just returned to the lungs from the rest of the body, so it contains lots of carbon dioxide and very little oxygen. As a result:
   - Oxygen diffuses out of the alveolus (an area of high O_2 concentration) into the blood (an area of low O_2 concentration).
   - Carbon dioxide diffuses out of the blood (high concentration) into the alveolus (low concentration) to be breathed out.

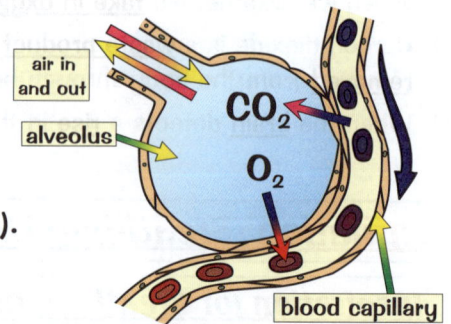

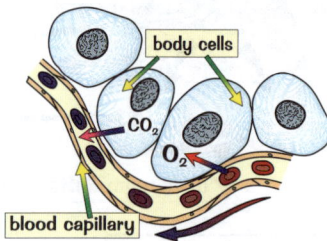

3) When the blood reaches body cells which need oxygen it is released from the red blood cells (where there's a high concentration) and diffuses into the body cells (where the concentration is low).

4) At the same time, carbon dioxide diffuses out of the body cells (where there's a high concentration) into the blood (where there's a low concentration). It's then carried back to the lungs.

The Alveoli Are Adapted for Gas Exchange

To make gaseous exchange as efficient as possible the alveoli have:
- a very large surface area to increase the rate of diffusion,
- a moist surface to help oxygen and carbon dioxide dissolve,
- a permeable surface to help gases exchange easily,
- a thin lining (only one cell thick) so gases don't have to diffuse very far,
- a good blood supply.

All gaseous exchange surfaces have similar adaptations.

Other Organisms Exchange Gas Differently...

1) Adult amphibians have simple lungs, but their skin also plays an important part in gaseous exchange.

2) Oxygen moves into the animal and carbon dioxide moves out through their permeable skin (as well as via the lungs). To help with this, an adult amphibian's skin has to be kept moist.

3) However, this means the skin can't be waterproof. This lack of waterproofing means the amphibian would lose too much water if it lived in a dry environment — it must have a moist habitat.

1) In fish, gas exchange occurs at the gills (organs at the sides of the head). A constant supply of oxygen-rich water flows through the open mouth of the fish and is then forced over the gill filaments when the mouth closes.

2) Water helps support the gills — it keeps the gill filaments separated from each other. If fish weren't in water their gills would stick together and they would suffocate (which is why fish can only breathe when they're in water).

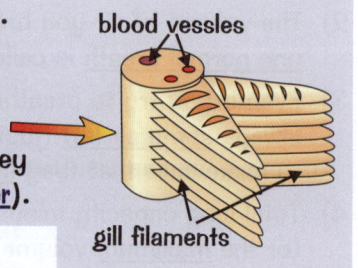

What did the fish say when it swam into a wall? Dam...

It's not the most interesting stuff but you need to learn this page — or you'll be a fish out of water on exam day.

Lung Disease

Without your lungs you'd be stuffed, so it's a good thing they've got ways of protecting themselves from little nasties like dust and microbes. Even so, your lungs are still susceptible to diseases.

Cilia and Mucus Protect the Lungs

1) The human respiratory tract consists of the trachea (windpipe) and bronchi (tubes to the lungs).

2) It's lined with mucus and cilia (little hairs), which catch dust and microbes before they reach the lungs.

3) The cilia beat, pushing microbe-filled mucus out of the lungs as phlegm.

4) Sometimes the microbes get past the body's defences and cause infection. The lungs are particularly prone to infections because they're a dead end — microbes can't easily be flushed out.

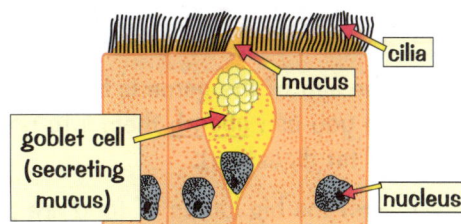

Ciliated cells in the trachea and bronchi.

Lung Disease Can be Caused by Lots of Things

INDUSTRIAL MATERIALS

E.g. asbestos. Asbestos can cause a disease called asbestosis — this is where inflammation and scarring in the lungs limits gas exchange. Asbestos used to be used as an insulator in roofs, floors, furnaces, etc. Its use is more tightly controlled now.

GENETIC CAUSES

E.g. cystic fibrosis is an inherited lung condition. A single defective gene causes the lungs to produce a really thick, sticky mucus that clogs up the bronchioles (small tubes in the lungs) — this makes breathing difficult and can lead to life-threatening infections.

LIFESTYLE CAUSES

E.g. smoking can cause lung cancer. This is where cells divide out of control, forming a tumour and reducing the surface area in the lungs.

ASTHMA

1) Asthmatics' lungs are overly sensitive to certain things (e.g. pet hair, pollen, dust, smoke...).

2) When they encounter these things the muscles around the bronchioles contract, constricting the airways.

3) The lining of the airways becomes inflamed and fluid builds up in the airways, making it hard to breathe (an asthma attack).

4) Symptoms of an attack are:
   - difficulty breathing,
   - wheezing,
   - a tight chest.

5) When symptoms appear a muscle relaxant drug is inhaled (from an inhaler) to open up the airways.

6) Some people also take drugs to stop attacks happening in the first place (but there's no actual cure.)

Stop huffing and puffing and just LEARN it..

There are lots of different types of lung disease, and some of them, like asthma, can be managed quite easily. Lung cancer on the other hand is pretty nasty — but you can lower your chances of getting it by not smoking. Make sure you learn the examples on this page and way the lungs protect themselves from disease for the exam.

Digestion

Digestion is the breaking down of the nutrients in your food, so that they can be absorbed.
There are two types of digestion — physical and chemical.

Big Molecules are Broken Down into Smaller Ones

1) The aim of the game is break down the large insoluble molecules in food into small soluble molecules so you can absorb them into your blood plasma or lymph (a type of fluid that carries the products of fat digestion).

2) First the big lumps of food are physically digested — this basically means chewing them in the mouth, then churning them about in the stomach. Physical digestion allows food to pass easily through the digestive system and provides a larger surface area for chemical digestion (the next step).

3) Chemical digestion involves enzymes — biological catalysts that speed up reactions. Digestive enzymes break down molecules that are too big to pass through cell membranes.

There are Three Main Types of Digestive Enzyme

1 CARBOHYDRASES break down big carbohydrates (e.g. STARCH) into SIMPLE SUGARS.

The breakdown of starch is a two-step process:

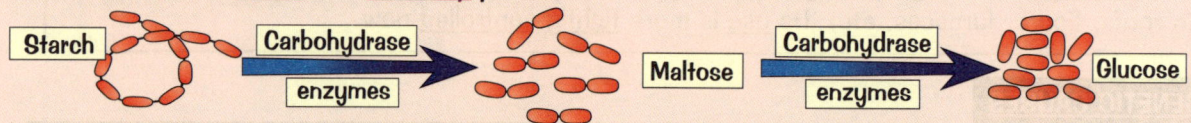

Starch → Carbohydrase enzymes → Maltose → Carbohydrase enzymes → Glucose

They're active in two places: 1) The mouth
2) The small intestine

2 PROTEASES break down PROTEINS into AMINO ACIDS.

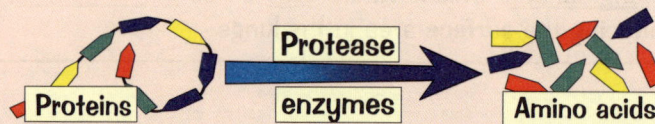

Proteins → Protease enzymes → Amino acids

They're active in two places: 1) The stomach
2) The small intestine

3 LIPASES break down FATS into FATTY ACIDS and GLYCEROL.

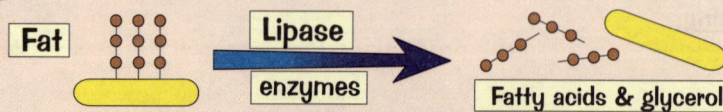

Fat → Lipase enzymes → Fatty acids & glycerol

They're active in the small intestine.

Now get digesting those facts...

Revision is a lot like digestion if you think about it — you break down the big topics into manageable chunks and then absorb the information. Imagine if you could eat this book and absorb all the facts in one sitting... it'd make life easier. But it probably wouldn't be as tasty as scoffing baked beans on toast. Mmmm toast...

More on Digestion

Phew. That last page on digestion was so much <u>fun</u>, I just thought, "What the heck, let's have another". So here you have it. Read on and <u>enjoy</u>...

Enzymes *Need the* Right Conditions *to* Function Properly

1) The <u>pH</u> in the <u>stomach</u> is very <u>acidic</u> (about pH 1-2). It's maintained at this level to provide the <u>optimum pH</u> for <u>protease enzymes</u> to work.

2) Other enzymes have <u>higher optimum pHs</u>. The pH in the <u>mouth</u> and <u>small intestine</u> is <u>alkaline</u> or <u>neutral</u> so that the enzymes there can function properly.

Bile *Improves* Fat Digestion

1) <u>Bile</u> is made in the <u>liver</u> and stored in the <u>gall bladder</u>.

2) It helps <u>fat digestion</u> in the <u>small intestine</u> by breaking the fat down into <u>tiny droplets</u>. This is called <u>emulsification</u> and it gives a much <u>bigger surface area</u> of fat for the <u>lipase</u> enzymes to work on.

3) Bile is also <u>alkaline</u>, so it <u>neutralises acid</u> from the stomach to make the <u>conditions right</u> for enzymes in the small intestine to work.

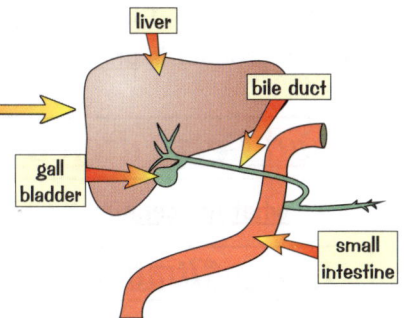

liver

bile duct

gall bladder

small intestine

Food Molecules *Are* Absorbed *into the* Blood *by* Diffusion

1) Glucose and amino acids are <u>small enough</u> to <u>diffuse</u> into the <u>blood plasma</u>.

The products of <u>fat</u> digestion can't get into the blood plasma so they diffuse out of the gut (intestines) and into a fluid called <u>lymph</u>, in the <u>lymphatic system</u>. From here they're <u>emptied into the blood</u>.

2) The <u>nutrients</u> then <u>travel</u> to where they're needed, and then <u>diffuse out again</u>, e.g. <u>glucose</u> travels to <u>muscles</u> for <u>respiration</u> during exercise.

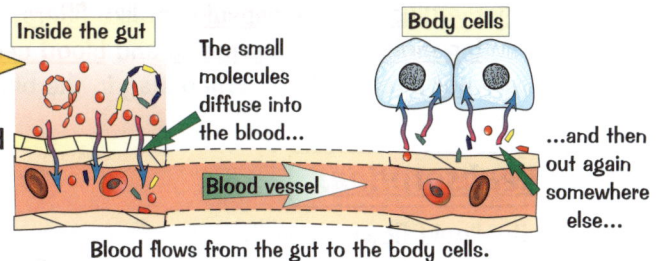

Inside the gut

Body cells

The small molecules diffuse into the blood...

Blood vessel

...and then out again somewhere else...

Blood flows from the gut to the body cells.

The Small Intestine *is* Adapted *for* Absorption *of* Food

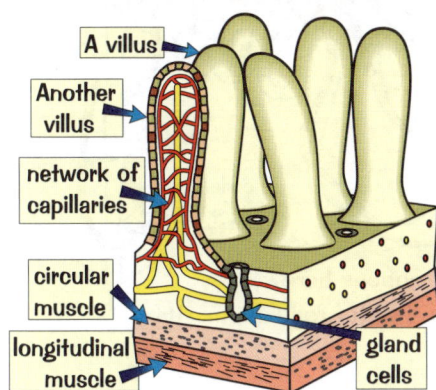

A villus

Another villus

network of capillaries

circular muscle

longitudinal muscle

gland cells

1) The small intestine is very <u>long</u>, so there's time to break down and absorb the food before it reaches the end.

2) There's a really <u>big surface area</u> for absorption, because the walls of the small intestine are covered in <u>millions and millions</u> of tiny little projections called <u>villi</u>.

3) Each <u>cell</u> on the surface of a villus also has its own <u>microvilli</u> — little projections that increase the surface area even more.

4) Villi have a <u>single permeable</u> layer of surface cells (which form a <u>thin lining</u>) and a very <u>good blood supply</u> to allow <u>quick absorption</u>.

You don't have to bust a gut to revise this page...

Just think. That lovely piece of <u>toast</u> you had for breakfast this morning will be making its way through your digestive system as we speak. Eventually it'll end up in the <u>perfectly adapted</u> small intestine, where all the tiny toasty molecules will be absorbed into your bloodstream by <u>diffusion</u> through the <u>villi</u>. Amazing really.

The Kidneys

The kidney is involved in excretion (the removal of waste products from the body).

The Kidneys are Excretion Organs

The kidneys perform three main roles:

1) Removal of urea from the blood. Urea is produced in the liver from excess amino acids.

2) Adjustment of salt levels in the blood.

3) Adjustment of water content of the blood.

They do this by filtering stuff out of the blood under high pressure, and then reabsorbing the useful things. The end product is urine.

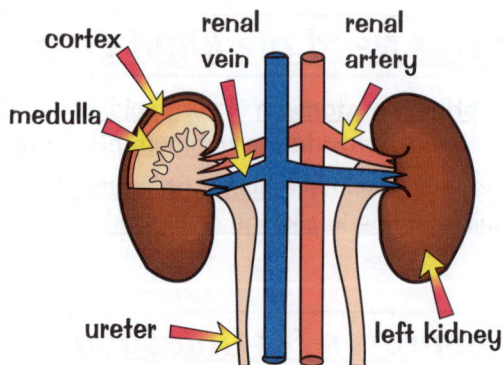

Blood Gets Filtered in the Nephrons (Kidney Tubules)

Here's what happens as the blood passes through the kidneys...

1) Ultrafiltration:

1) A high pressure is built up which squeezes water, urea, salts and glucose out of the blood and into the capsule (see diagram below right).

2) Membranes between the blood vessels in the glomerulus and the capsule act like filters, so big molecules like proteins and blood cells are not squeezed out. They stay in the blood.

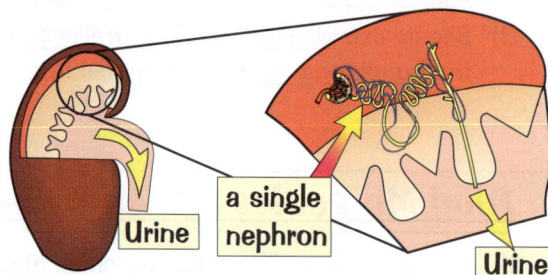

2) Reabsorption:

As the liquid flows along the nephron, useful substances are selectively reabsorbed:

1) All the sugar is reabsorbed. (This involves the process of active transport against the concentration gradient.)

2) Sufficient salt is reabsorbed (again, using active transport). Excess salt is not.

3) Sufficient water is reabsorbed, according to the level of the hormone ADH (see next page).

Enlarged View of a Single Nephron:

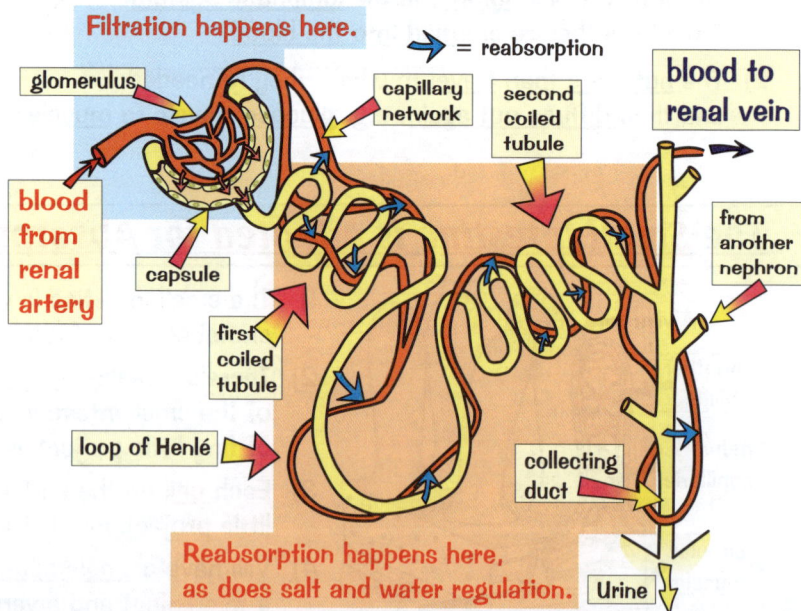

3) Release of wastes:

Urea, excess salt and excess water are not reabsorbed. These continue out of the nephron, into the ureter and down to the bladder as urine.

Reabsorb those facts and excrete the excess...

On average, the kidneys filter 1500 litres of blood a day (you only have 4-6 litres of blood in your body — it just goes through the kidneys about 300 times). And the kidneys excrete 1.5 litres of urine a day — so that's 547.5 litres of wee a year... that's five baths full... not that I'm suggesting you put it there.

Waste Removal

Waste removal isn't the easiest or most interesting topic in the world, I admit — but you do need to know it...

Water Content is Controlled by the Kidneys

It's important to keep a constant concentration of water molecules in the blood plasma. This prevents too much water moving into or out of the tissues by osmosis. It also keeps the blood pressure constant.

1) The amount of water reabsorbed in the kidney nephrons is controlled by a hormone called anti-diuretic hormone (ADH). ADH makes the nephrons more permeable so that more water is reabsorbed back into the blood.

2) The brain monitors the water content of the blood and instructs the pituitary gland to release ADH into the blood according to how much is needed.

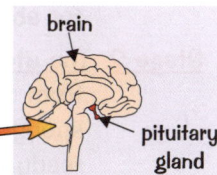

3) The whole process of water content regulation is controlled by a mechanism called negative feedback. This means that if the water content gets too high or too low a mechanism will be triggered that brings it back to normal.

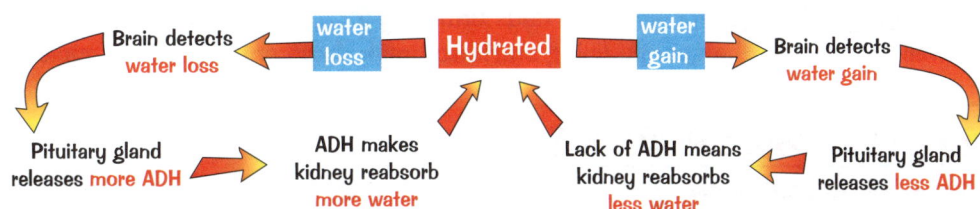

Brain detects water loss — water loss — Hydrated — water gain — Brain detects water gain

Pituitary gland releases more ADH — ADH makes kidney reabsorb more water — Lack of ADH means kidney reabsorbs less water — Pituitary gland releases less ADH

Your Urine isn't Always the Same

The amount and concentration of urine is controlled by ADH. It depends on three main things:

1) HEAT — When it's hot you sweat (which evaporates, cooling down the skin). Sweat contains water, so... sweating causes water loss.

This causes the release of ADH into the blood so that the kidneys will reabsorb more water. This leaves only a small amount of excess water that needs to be got rid of — so only a small amount of quite concentrated urine will be produced.

2) EXERCISE — Exercise makes you hot, so you sweat to cool down. This produces the same effect as heat — a concentrated, small volume of urine.

3) WATER INTAKE — Not drinking enough water will produce concentrated urine (since there'll be little excess water to 'dilute' the other wastes). Drinking lots of water will produce lots of dilute urine.

Dialysis Filters the Blood Mechanically

1) Patients who have kidney failure can't filter their blood properly — but a dialysis machine can be used to filter their blood for them.

2) Dialysis has to be done regularly to keep dissolved substances at the right concentrations, and to remove waste.

3) Dialysis fluid has the same concentration of sodium and glucose as blood plasma (which means those aren't removed from the blood).

4) The barrier is permeable to things like ions and waste substances, but not big molecules like proteins (just like the membranes in the kidney). So.. the waste substances (such as urea) and excess water from the blood move across the membrane into the dialysis fluid.

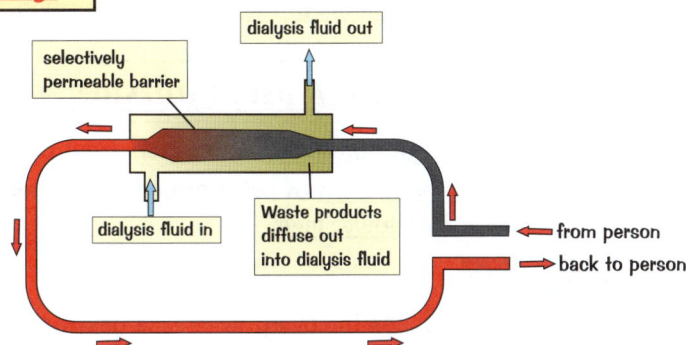

Simon says touch urea... actually don't...

Kidney failure patients often have high blood pressure because diseased kidneys can't control the water content of the blood. This excess water is removed during dialysis (up to 5 litres of fluid can be removed in one session).

The Menstrual Cycle

The monthly <u>release of an egg</u> from a woman's ovaries is part of the <u>menstrual cycle</u>.

The Menstrual Cycle Has Four Stages

Stage 1 <u>Day 1 — menstruation starts</u>. The uterus lining breaks down for about four days.

Stage 2 <u>The uterus lining builds up again</u>, from day 4 to day 14, into a thick spongy layer full of blood vessels, ready to receive a fertilised egg.

Stage 3 <u>An egg develops and is released</u> from the ovary at day 14 — this is called <u>ovulation</u>.

Stage 4 <u>The wall is then maintained</u> for about 14 days until day 28. If no fertilised egg has landed on the uterus wall by day 28, the spongy lining starts to break down and the whole cycle starts again.

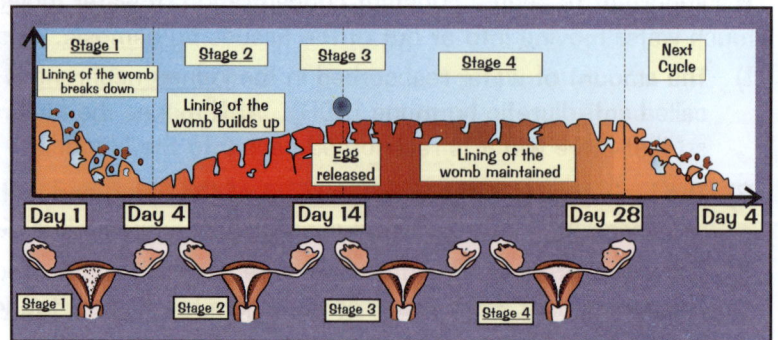

It's Controlled by Four Hormones

1. FSH (follicle-stimulating hormone)

1) Produced in the <u>pituitary gland</u>.
2) Causes an <u>egg to develop</u> in one of the ovaries.
3) <u>Stimulates</u> the <u>ovaries</u> to produce <u>oestrogen</u>.

2. Oestrogen

1) Produced in the <u>ovaries</u>.
2) Causes the lining of the uterus to <u>repair</u> (thicken and grow).
3) <u>Stimulates</u> the production of <u>LH</u> (which causes the release of an egg) and <u>inhibits</u> production of <u>FSH</u>.

3. LH (luteinising hormone)

1) Produced by the <u>pituitary gland</u>.
2) Stimulates the <u>release of an egg</u> at day 14 (<u>ovulation</u>).
3) Indirectly <u>stimulates progesterone</u> production.

4. Progesterone

1) Produced in the <u>ovaries</u>.
2) <u>Maintains</u> the lining of the uterus. When the level of progesterone <u>falls</u>, the lining <u>breaks down</u>.
3) <u>Inhibits</u> the production of <u>LH</u>.

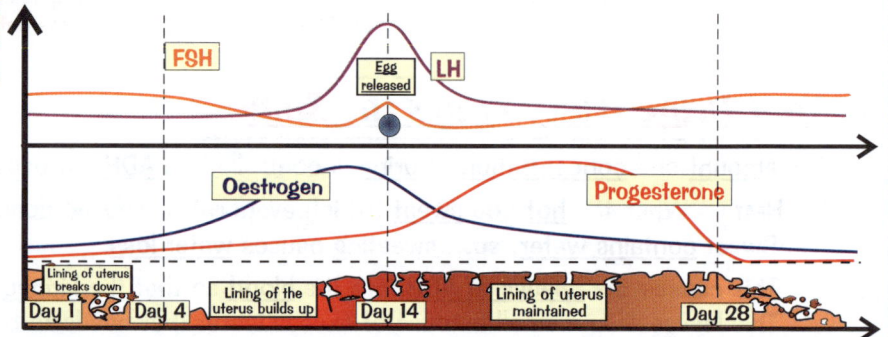

Negative Feedback Mechanisms Affect Hormone Production

1) The <u>production of hormones</u> in the menstrual cycle is controlled by <u>negative feedback</u>.
2) When the <u>concentration</u> of one hormone becomes <u>too high</u>, the release of another hormone will return it to a <u>lower level</u>.

Example 1:

1) <u>FSH</u> stimulates the ovary to release <u>oestrogen</u>.
2) Oestrogen <u>inhibits</u> the release of <u>FSH</u>.

So when there's lots of FSH, oestrogen is released and FSH production is inhibited. This causes the FSH level to <u>fall</u>.

Example 2:

1) <u>LH</u> indirectly stimulates the production of <u>progesterone</u>.
2) Progesterone <u>inhibits</u> the release of <u>LH</u>.

When there's lots of LH, progesterone is released. LH production is inhibited and the LH level <u>falls</u>.

Which came first — the chicken or the luteinising hormone...

You need to know <u>what hormone does what</u> for the exam — and where negative feedback comes in. So learn it.

Controlling Fertility

The artificial use of sex hormones like oestrogen and FSH can be used to control human fertility.

Female Hormones Can Be Used to Reduce Fertility For Contraception

1) Contraceptives like the pill contain oestrogen — this prevents the release of an egg (ovulation).

2) This may seem kind of strange (since naturally oestrogen helps stimulate the release of eggs). But if oestrogen is taken every day to keep the level of it permanently high, it mimics pregnancy and inhibits the release of FSH. After a while egg development and production stop and stay stopped.

Infertility Can be Treated in Different Ways

1) ARTIFICIAL INSEMINATION (AI) — this is where a man's sperm is placed into a woman's uterus without having sex. It's used if there's some kind of problem with the sperm reaching the egg, or if the man suffers from certain kinds of infertility. Sperm from a donor can also be used if necessary.

2) FSH INJECTIONS — some women have very low levels of the hormone FSH, so their eggs don't develop properly and they can't get pregnant. FSH injections can increase fertility by stimulating egg production — making fertilisation more likely.

3) IN VITRO FERTILISATION (IVF) — this is where a woman's eggs are fertilised outside the body. The woman is given hormones to stimulate egg production. Several eggs are then collected and mixed with the man's sperm, and a few fertilised eggs are implanted back into the woman's uterus.

So... for IVF you need sperm, eggs and a healthy uterus. Any of these can come from someone else:

• Some women can't produce eggs. But they can still have a baby by using donated eggs.

• Some women can produce eggs but always miscarry. The couple's fertilised eggs can be implanted into another woman (called a surrogate mother), who gives birth to their baby.

4) OVARY TRANSPLANTS — some women don't have ovaries (e.g. due to surgery for ovarian cancer) or they have damaged ones that don't produce any eggs (again, often due to cancer treatment). A relatively new (and rare) way to treat this is to transplant a healthy ovary donated by someone else.

Not Everyone Agrees with Infertility Treatment

Infertility treatment can give an infertile couple a child — a pretty obvious benefit. But some people argue against using some of these fertility treatments, either for ethical or practical reasons.

1) In IVF not all the fertilised eggs are implanted back into the woman. Some people think that throwing away these extra fertilised eggs (embryos) is denying a life and so morally wrong.

2) IVF increases the chance of multiple pregnancies (e.g. twins). This can be a danger to the mother's health and possibly a financial burden to the parents.

Foetuses Can be Screened to See If They're Healthy

1) Doctors can screen a foetus for genetic disorders before it's born. They can check for various problems, e.g. Down's syndrome and cystic fibrosis.

2) The main screening method is amniocentesis — where doctors use a long needle to remove some of the fluid that surrounds the baby. This contains skin cells from the baby, and the chromosomes in these can be analysed.

3) Like with infertility treatments, there are ethical issues surrounding screening. For example...

• If the foetus has a genetic defect, the parents may consider whether or not to continue the pregnancy.

• Foetal screening like amniocentesis can increase the risk of miscarriage.

Too many initials to learn — FSH, AI, IVF, CIA, DVD...

Foetal screening isn't done on every pregnant woman — just those at risk of having babies with genetic defects.

More on Growth

Growth is pretty important. Without growth, we'd still be an egg-sperm fusion, and that's about it.

Growth is Influenced by Many Things

Growth happens when cells divide (by mitosis — producing new cells identical to the originals).

1) The size an adult reaches is mainly due to genetic factors, but it can be influenced by external factors.

E.g., **1. Diet** is important, especially for children who are growing. A poor diet, particularly if it's low in proteins (needed to make new cells) or minerals (for bone growth), may mean that a child doesn't grow as much as its genes would allow.

2. Exercise can also affect growth. Exercise builds muscle, and weight-bearing exercise can increase bone mass. Exercise also stimulates the release of growth hormone.

> Human growth hormone is produced by the pituitary gland (see page 23).
> It stimulates the growth of the whole body, but especially growth of the long bones.

2) Sometimes hormonal or genetic factors affect growth. Gigantism (extreme height) is often the result of a tumour of the pituitary in childhood, which causes too much growth hormone to be produced. Dwarfism (extreme short stature) is caused by genetic factors, and results in stunted bone growth.

A Baby's Growth is Monitored

1) Different parts of a baby (and foetus) grow at different rates, e.g. a baby's head grows relatively quickly.

2) A baby's growth is regularly monitored after birth to make sure it's growing normally and provide an early warning of any growth problems. Three measurements are taken — length, mass and head size. These results are plotted on average growth charts, like this...

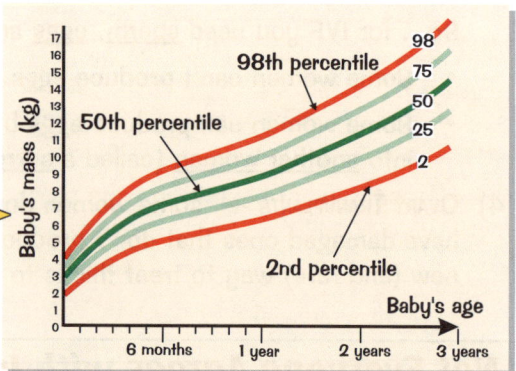

3) The chart shows a number of 'percentiles'. E.g. the 50th percentile shows the mass that 50% of babies will have reached at a certain age.

4) Babies vary in size, so doctors aren't usually concerned unless a baby's size is above the 98th percentile or below the 2nd percentile, or if there's an inconsistent pattern (e.g. a very small baby with a very large head).

Growth charts can pick up things like obesity, malnutrition, dwarfism, water on the brain, and so on.

People Live Longer Than They Used To

Life expectancy in the UK has increased loads over the last century...
There are many reasons for this, such as:

1) medical advances mean previously fatal conditions can be treated,

2) places of work and housing are much safer and healthier,

3) people are better off and can afford a healthier diet and lifestyle,

4) there's less industrial disease.

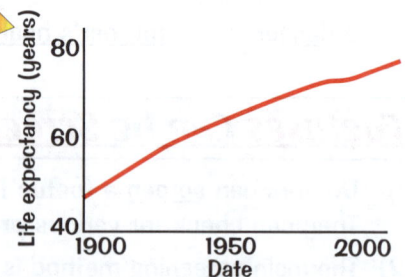

There are problems that come with people living longer, however.
(No one's saying it's a bad thing — only that we need to think about it...)

1) The population grows, leading to possible shortages of housing and more environmental pollution.

2) The number of older people increases, and the state might not be able to give pensions to everyone.

3) Older people have more medical problems and need more care, increasing costs to the taxpayer.

From cell division to babies to old-age pensioners — what a page...

It's a big worry, this whole people living longer lark. By the time you're a senior citizen, you'll have to work until you're in your 70s as there just won't be enough money to give everyone pensions. Poor you.

Revision Summary for Module B5

It's the end of the section. And that can only mean one thing. Yep... it's time for a good ol' revision summary. That's right — it's time to see how much you've learnt. Which had better be everything, frankly — or you're going to have to go back and learn the stuff again — properly, this time.
So heads down, eyes open — and get ready to see how much revision you need, or don't need, to do...

1) List three advantages of an internal skeleton over an external skeleton.
2) Why is it unwise to move someone with a broken bone?
3) Sketch and label a diagram of a synovial joint.
4) What happens to the lower arm when the triceps contracts?
5) Describe the circulatory system of humans. How is it different from the circulatory system of fish?
6) Explain why the blood is under higher pressure in a double circulatory system.
7) Describe the sequence of events in the cardiac cycle.
8) Name three contributions Harvey made to our understanding of the circulatory system.
9) Name the two clusters of pacemaker cells in the heart. What do they do?
10) What does ECG stand for? Describe what a healthy person's ECG should look like.
11) Explain what's going wrong if someone has a hole in the heart.
12) Give one advantage and one disadvantage of the use of heart pacemakers and heart valves over heart replacement.
13) What exactly is happening when blood clots?
14) Explain what would happen if a person with type A blood was given a transfusion of type B blood.
15) To be a living donor, you must meet four criteria. What are they?
16) Describe two problems with organ transplants.
17) Give three ethical reasons why some people are concerned about organ transplants.
18) Suggest three problems in the supply of donor organs.
19) Describe what happens to the pressure and volume in the lungs when you breathe in and out.
20) What machine would a doctor use to measure lung capacity? Why would you want to measure it?
21) Describe how gaseous exchange occurs in human alveoli.
22) Explain why fish gills only work in water.
23) Explain how cilia and mucus protect the lungs.
24) List the four main causes of lung disease. Which of these is the most likely to result in lung cancer?
25) Give two functions of physical digestion.
26) Name three types of digestive enzyme and state the name of the type of molecule they break down.
27) Describe how stomach pH aids digestion.
28) Give three ways that villi are adapted to aid digestion.
29) Describe the three main roles of the kidneys.
30) Explain how a kidney works.
31) Describe three things that affect the amount and concentration of urine produced.
32) How does a dialysis machine work? Which substances does it remove from the blood?
33) Which four hormones control the menstrual cycle? What exactly do they do?
34) How does negative feedback control the concentration of hormones in the menstrual cycle?
35) Describe four types of fertility treatment.
36) List three reasons why people may argue that fertility treatment is wrong.
37) Name a method of foetal screening.
    Explain two ethical issues to do with foetal screening.
38) How can diet and exercise affect a person's growth?
39) What three measurements do doctors make to check a baby is growing normally?
40) Why are people living longer these days? What problems is this trend likely to cause?

Module B6 — Beyond the Microscope

Bacteria

Bacteria may be very small, but they're mightily important and may well crop up in your exam. So read on...

Bacterial Cells are Usually Smaller and Simpler than Animal Cells

1) Bacterial cells have a cell wall to help them keep their shape and stop them from bursting.

2) They have a strand of DNA in the cytoplasm that controls the cell's activities and replication. Some also have several small loops of DNA called plasmids.

3) They sometimes have a flagellum (tail) to help them move.

4) They come in 4 shapes: rods, curved rods, spheres and spirals.

5) Bacteria can consume a huge range of organic nutrients from their surroundings. This provides them with energy. Some types of bacteria can even produce their own nutrients.

6) This means that different bacteria can survive in almost any habitat, e.g. soil, water, air, the human body and food.

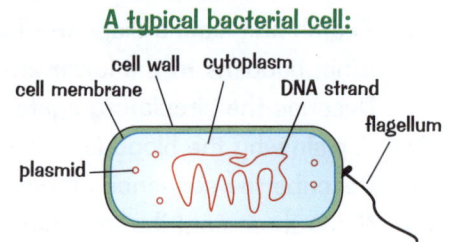

A typical bacterial cell:

cell membrane   cell wall   cytoplasm   DNA strand   flagellum   plasmid

Bacteria Reproduce by Asexual Reproduction

1) Bacteria reproduce by asexual reproduction — they're clones of each other. They reproduce by a process called binary fission (a posh way of saying 'they split in two').

2) Bacteria reproduce very quickly. If disease-causing bacteria enter your body, they can reproduce and cause disease before your body has a chance to respond.

3) Bacteria reproduce faster when it's warm and there's a good source of nutrients. This is why it's important to store food carefully. E.g. If you leave some meat on a warm kitchen top, bacteria on the meat will reproduce very quickly and cause it to spoil (go off). In a fridge, the cold temperature would slow down the bacteria's reproduction and it wouldn't spoil as quickly.

Aseptic Technique Should be Used for Culturing Bacteria

1) You can culture (grow) bacteria on an agar plate — a Petri dish containing agar jelly. Bacteria can be transferred to the plate from a sample using a wire inoculation loop.

2) When you culture bacteria, it's important to use aseptic technique to protect yourself from infection and to stop the agar from being contaminated by other microbes. This involves:
   - Wearing gloves and keeping long hair tied back (so it doesn't fall in your culture).
   - Sterilising equipment before and after use — e.g. passing the inoculation loop through a Bunsen burner flame to kill any unwanted bacteria on it.
   - Sealing the dish once you've transferred the bacteria onto it.
   - Disposing of cultures safely after use — usually done by pressure sterilising in an autoclave.

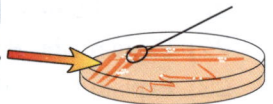

We Can Use Bacteria to Make Useful Things Like Yoghurt

1) The equipment is sterilised to kill off any unwanted microorganisms.

2) Then the milk is pasteurised (heated up to 72 °C for 15 seconds) — again to kill off any unwanted microorganisms. Then the milk's cooled.

3) A starter culture of Lactobacillus bacteria is added. The mixture is incubated (heated to about 40 °C) in a vessel called a fermenter. The bacteria break down the lactose sugar in the milk into lactic acid. The lactic acid causes the milk to clot and solidify into yoghurt.

4) A sample is taken to make sure it's at the right consistency. Then flavours (e.g. fruit) and colours are sometimes added and the yoghurt is packaged.

Yoghurt — bacteria and gone-off milk... mmm...yummy...

Bacteria are also used to make cheese, vinegar, silage (for animal feed) and compost (for your garden). Bacteria that can make Belgian chocolates, caviar and profiteroles haven't been discovered yet.

Microorganisms and Disease

There are different kinds of microorganism, e.g. bacteria, viruses, fungi and protozoa. Some are useful, while others are pretty harmful if you get infected. This page focuses on the nasty ones...

Viruses Can Only Reproduce Inside Living Cells

1) Viruses aren't cells. They're usually no more than a protein coat around a strand of genetic material.
2) They can only reproduce inside living cells, so they must infect other organisms in order to multiply.
3) Viruses can infect plant, animal and bacterial cells.
4) A particular type of virus will only attack specific cells.

Here's how a virus reproduces:

1) The virus attaches itself to a specific host cell and injects its genetic material into the cell.

2) The virus then uses the host cell to make the components of new viruses.

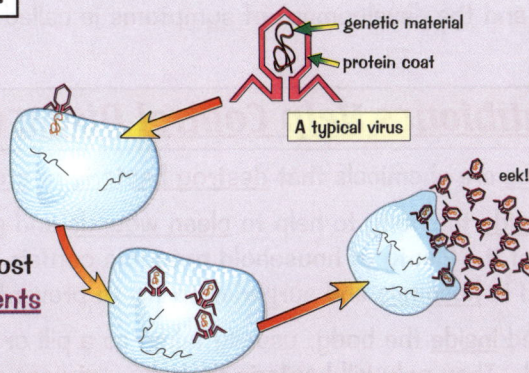

genetic material
protein coat
A typical virus
eek!

3) This eventually causes the host cell to split open — releasing the new viruses.

Different Diseases Can Be Transmitted in Different Ways

1) IN FOOD — e.g. food poisoning. You can get ill from eating food that's been contaminated with bacteria. It can be prevented by good hygiene and by making sure food is properly cooked before it's eaten.
2) IN WATER — e.g. cholera. You can get infected with cholera by drinking water that's been contaminated with sewage (nice). It isn't a big problem in the developed world, but it kills many people in developing countries where sanitation is poor. Good sanitation can prevent cholera and other waterborne diseases.
3) BY AIRBORNE DROPLETS — e.g. influenza (flu). Flu and other viruses can be spread via the tiny airborne droplets released when you cough or sneeze. Sneezing into a tissue, washing your hands properly and disinfecting contaminated surfaces can all help to prevent the spread of flu.
4) THROUGH CONTACT — e.g. athlete's foot. The fungus which causes athlete's foot can be spread by people walking in bare feet on damp floors in places like showers and bathrooms. You can prevent it by washing your feet regularly and by not walking around bare foot. Disinfecting surfaces also helps.

Poor Sanitation is Linked to a High Incidence of Disease

1) The incidence of a disease is the number of new cases that occurs in a population in a certain time.
2) Good sanitation and public health measures are linked to a low incidence of disease. A clean water supply, good sewage works, public health education and clean hospitals prevent the spread of disease. E.g. government campaigns to educate people about how influenza is spread are designed to help lower the incidence of flu.
3) Poor sanitation is linked with a high incidence of disease. E.g. a high incidence of food poisoning and cholera might be caused by a lack of clean water or a rubbish sewage system.
4) Developing countries are less likely to be able to afford good sanitation and public health measures.

Incidence of revision is increasing due to exams...

You could be asked to interpret data on the incidence of disease in the exam. Don't panic — just remember that poor sanitation and a lack of public health measures often contribute to a high incidence of disease.

Treating Infectious Diseases

You probably don't need telling that this page is important — some of the ideas here can literally save lives.

There Are Four Stages in an Infectious Disease

1. Firstly the microorganism enters the body — e.g. through the nose or mouth.

2. Once the microorganism is in the body, it reproduces rapidly, producing many more microorganisms.

3. The microorganisms then produce toxins (poisonous substances) which damage cells and tissues.

4. The toxins cause symptoms of infection, e.g. pain, diarrhoea and stomach cramps. Your immune system's reaction to the infection can also cause symptoms, e.g. fever. The time between exposure to the microorganism and the development of symptoms is called the incubation period.

Antiseptics and Antibiotics Help Control Diseases

1) Antiseptics and antibiotics are chemicals that destroy bacteria or stop them growing.

2) Antiseptics are used outside the body to help to clean wounds and surfaces. They're used to prevent infection rather than treat it. Plenty of household products contain antiseptics, e.g. bathroom cleaners. Antiseptics are also used in hospitals and surgeries to try to prevent infections like MRSA.

3) Antibiotics are drugs used inside the body, usually taken as a pill or injected. They're used to treat patients who are already infected. They only kill bacteria though — viruses aren't affected by them.

Bacteria Can Evolve and Become Resistant to Antibiotics...

1) Random mutations in bacterial DNA can lead to changes in the bacteria's characteristics. Sometimes, they mean that the bacteria are less affected by a particular antibiotic.

2) Bacteria with these genes are better able to survive and reproduce in a host who's being treated to get rid of the infection.

3) This leads to the gene for antibiotic resistance being passed on to lots of offspring — it's just natural selection. The gene spreads and becomes more common in a population of bacteria over a period of time.

4) Bacteria that are resistant to antibiotics (e.g. MRSA) are definitely bad news as they cause infections that are very hard to treat.

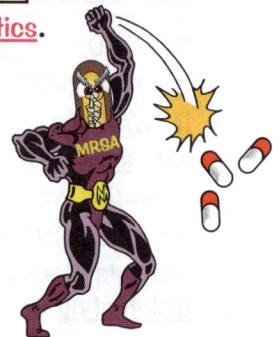

...So Do Everyone a Favour and Always Finish Your Antibiotics

1) The more often antibiotics are used, the bigger the problem of antibiotic-resistance becomes.

2) It's important that doctors only prescribe antibiotics when it's really necessary:

> It's not that antibiotics actually cause resistance, but they do create a situation where naturally resistant bacteria have an advantage and so increase in numbers. If they won't do you any good, it's pointless to take antibiotics — and it could be harmful for everyone else.

3) It's also important that you take all the antibiotics a doctor prescribes for you:

> Lots of people stop bothering to take their antibiotics as soon as they feel better, but this can increase the risk of antibiotic resistant bacteria emerging — so you must complete the dose.

Coughs and sneezes spread diseases but antibiotic resistance is scarier...

Worrying stuff, but hold your horses — there's a whole other page on infectious diseases coming right up...

More on Infectious Diseases

Bacteria and viruses are always waiting to pounce as soon as you let your guard down... Bloomin' microbes.

Diseases Often Spread Rapidly After Natural Disasters

Natural disasters like earthquakes and hurricanes can damage the infrastructure of an area, and completely disrupt health services. In these conditions disease can spread rapidly among the population.

1) Some natural disasters damage sewage systems and water supplies. This can result in contaminated drinking water containing the microorganisms that cause diseases like cholera.

2) People can become displaced when their homes are destroyed. They might move into temporary camps, with large numbers of other people and poor sanitation. In these conditions, diseases could spread easily.

3) Health services can be disrupted by damaged transport links — allowing infections to spread rapidly.

4) Electricity supplies are also often damaged by natural disasters. This means that food goes off quickly because refrigerators can't work — this can lead to an increase in food poisoning.

Pasteur, Lister and Fleming All Improved Disease Treatment

Louis Pasteur (1822-1895) came up with the germ theory of disease

Until the 19th century people didn't understand how diseases were caused or spread. People used to think that diseases spontaneously appeared from nowhere. The scientist Louis Pasteur argued that there are microbes (also called 'germs' or 'microorganisms') in the air which cause disease and decomposition.

Pasteur carried out experiments to prove this theory, e.g.

1) He heated broth in two flasks, both of which were left open to the air. However, one of the flasks had a curved neck so that bacteria in the air would settle in the loop, and not get through to the broth.

2) The broth in the flask with the curved neck stayed fresh, proving that it was the microbes and not the air causing it to go off.

Flask 1: Air and microbes get in

Flask 2: Air gets in, but microbes can't

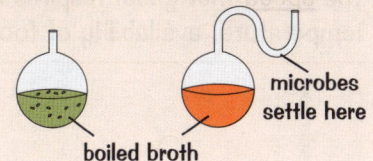

microbes settle here

boiled broth

Joseph Lister (1827-1912) was the first doctor to use antiseptics in surgery

1) When Lister first started working as a surgeon, hospital conditions were pretty unhygienic. Nearly half of patients undergoing surgery died from infections of their wounds, known as 'hospital gangrene' or 'sepsis'.

2) Lister's observations of wounds led him to think sepsis was a type of decomposition. He knew about Pasteur's work on microbes in the air. He realised he needed to kill microbes that were getting into wounds from the air.

3) Lister began to treat and dress wounds using the antiseptic carbolic acid. This killed the bacteria in the wounds and prevented sepsis. Gradually, Lister's techniques were taken up by the rest of the medical profession.

Alexander Fleming (1881-1955) discovered the antibiotic penicillin in 1928 — by accident

1) Fleming was clearing out some plates containing bacteria. He noticed that one of the plates of bacteria also had mould on it and the area around the mould was free of the bacteria.

2) He found that the mould (called *Penicillium notatum*) on the plate was producing a substance that killed the bacteria — this substance was penicillin.

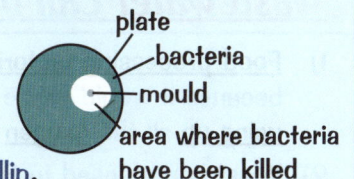

plate
bacteria
mould
area where bacteria have been killed

After Fleming there was no more phlegm-ing...

Fleming used to paint pictures using highly pigmented (coloured) bacteria. At first you wouldn't be able to see the picture. But as the bacteria grew, the picture would gradually appear... What a guy.

Yeast

This page is all about <u>yeast</u> — a type of <u>fungus</u> and a pretty useful <u>microorganism</u>.

Yeast Can Respire Anaerobically or Aerobically

1) When yeast <u>respires anaerobically</u> (without oxygen) it produces ethanol, carbon dioxide and energy. This process is called <u>fermentation</u>. Here is the equation for fermentation:

$$\text{glucose} \rightarrow \text{ethanol} + \text{carbon dioxide} \;(+\; \text{energy})$$
$$C_6H_{12}O_6 \rightarrow 2C_2H_5OH + 2CO_2 \;(+\; \text{energy})$$

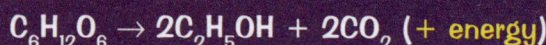

Ethanol is a type of alcohol.

The fermentation process is used to make <u>beer</u> and <u>wine</u> (see next page).

2) Yeast can also respire <u>aerobically</u> (with oxygen). This releases <u>more energy</u> than anaerobic respiration. Aerobic respiration is the same for yeast as it is for plants and animals:

$$\text{glucose} + \text{oxygen} \rightarrow \text{carbon dioxide} + \text{water} \;(+\; \text{energy})$$

3) Whether the yeast respire aerobically or anaerobically depends on <u>whether there is oxygen present</u>. If <u>oxygen is present</u> it respires <u>aerobically</u>. If <u>oxygen runs out</u> it switches to <u>anaerobic respiration</u>

4) Yeast prefer to respire aerobically (because it releases more energy),so <u>fermentation only takes place</u> in the <u>absence</u> of <u>oxygen</u>.

Yeast's Growth Rate Varies Depending on the Conditions

1) The faster yeast <u>respires</u>, the faster it's able to <u>reproduce</u>.

2) The <u>speed</u> that yeast respires and reproduces (its <u>growth rate</u>) <u>varies</u>. It's <u>growth rate</u> is controlled by temperature, availability of food, pH and how quickly waste products can be removed.

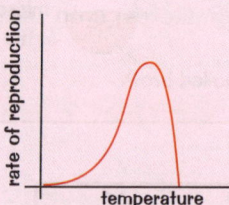

1) Yeast reproduces <u>faster</u> when it's <u>warmer</u> (growth rate <u>doubles</u> for every <u>10 °C</u> rise in temperature until the optimum is reached). But if it's too hot the yeast <u>dies</u>.

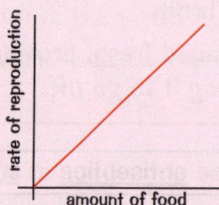

2) The <u>more food (glucose)</u> there is, the <u>faster</u> the yeast reproduces.

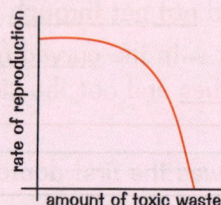

3) Build-up of <u>toxic waste</u> products, e.g. ethanol, <u>slows down reproduction</u>.

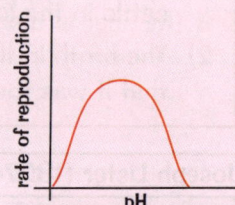

4) The <u>pH</u> has to be <u>just right</u>. Too high or low a pH slows down reproduction.

3) Yeast also <u>reproduces faster</u> in the <u>presence of oxygen</u>. This is because it's able to respire <u>aerobically</u>, giving it <u>more energy</u> for reproduction.

4) One way of <u>measuring</u> how fast the yeast is reproducing is to measure <u>how much glucose (sugar) it breaks down</u>. The <u>faster</u> the yeast reproduces, the <u>more glucose</u> will be broken down.

Wastewater Can be Cleaned Up with Yeast

1) <u>Food-processing factories</u> need to get rid of <u>sugary water</u>. They can't just release it into waterways because it would cause pollution. <u>Bacteria</u> in the water would feed on the sugar and reproduce quickly, <u>using up</u> all the <u>oxygen</u> in the water. Other organisms in the water that <u>need oxygen</u> (like fish) <u>die</u>.

2) <u>Yeast</u> can be used to <u>treat the contaminated water</u> before it's released — it uses up the sugar in respiration.

At yeast it's an easy page...

You might get asked to <u>interpret data</u> on the <u>breakdown of sugar</u> by yeast in different conditions, e.g. changing the temperature, the absence of O_2. Just remember — the <u>faster it reproduces</u>, the <u>more sugar</u> it breaks down.

Brewing

Yeast is used to ferment sugar into alcohol as part of the brewing process.

We Use Yeast for Brewing Beer and Wine

1 Firstly you need to get the sugar out of the barley or grapes:

BEER
- Beer is made from grain — usually barley.
- The barley grains are allowed to germinate for a few days, during which the starch in the grains is broken down into sugar by enzymes. Then the grains are dried in a kiln. This process is called malting.
- The malted grain is mashed up and water is added to produce a sugary solution with lots of bits in it. This is then sieved to remove the bits.
- Hops are added to the mixture to give the beer its bitter flavour.

WINE
The grapes are mashed and water is added... a bit simpler than beer making.

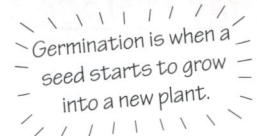

Germination is when a seed starts to grow into a new plant.

2 Yeast is added and the mixture is incubated (kept warm). The yeast ferments the sugar into alcohol. The fermenting vessels are designed to stop unwanted microorganisms and air getting in (to make sure that the yeast respire anaerobically).

- The rising concentration of alcohol (ethanol) in the fermentation mixture due to anaerobic respiration eventually starts to kill the yeast. As the yeast dies, fermentation slows down.
- Different species of yeast can tolerate different levels of alcohol. Some species can be used to produce strong wine and beer with a high concentration of alcohol.

3 The beer and wine produced is drawn off through a tap. Sometimes chemicals called clarifying agents are added to remove particles and make it clearer.

4 The beer is then pasteurised — heated to kill any yeast left in the beer and completely stop fermentation. Wine isn't pasteurised — any yeast left in the wine carry on slowly fermenting the sugar. This improves the taste of the wine. Beer also tastes better if it's unpasteurised and aged in the right conditions. But big breweries pasteurise it because there's a risk unpasteurised beer will spoil if it's not stored in the right conditions after it's sold. Finally the beer is casked and the wine is bottled ready for sale.

Distillation Increases the Alcohol Concentration

1) Sometimes the products of fermentation are distilled to increase the alcohol content. This produces spirits, e.g. if cane sugar is fermented and then distilled, you get rum.

2) Distillation is used to separate the alcohol out of the alcohol-water solution that's produced by fermentation.

3) The fermentation products are heated to 78 °C, the temperature at which the alcohol (but not the water) boils and turns into vapour.

4) The alcohol vapour rises and travels through a cooled tube which causes it to condense back into liquid alcohol and run down the tube into a collecting vessel.

5) The distillation of alcohol is a commercial process that can only be done on licensed premises — you're not allowed to do it in your garden shed.

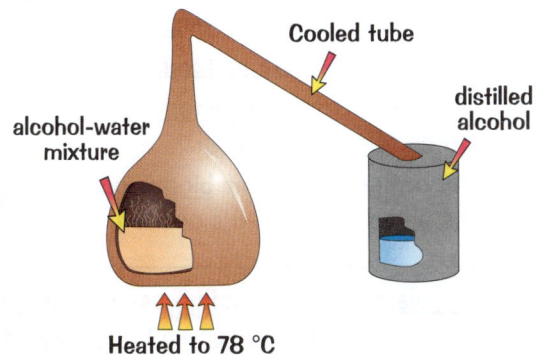

Cooled tube / distilled alcohol / alcohol-water mixture / Heated to 78 °C

A-wop-bop-aloobop alop-bam-brew...♪

You can ferment pretty much any kind of fruit to make alcohol, e.g. cider is made from fermented apples. The sugar that yeast feeds on is naturally found in the fruit — you just have to mash them to get it out.

Biofuels

Biofuels could be hugely underlined important in the future, as fossil fuel supplies run out. You need to know about them.

Energy Can be Transferred from Biomass

Biomass is living or recently-dead organic material, e.g. plant matter. It's also a store of energy. The energy stored in biomass can be transferred into more useful forms, e.g.

- Fast growing trees can be burnt, releasing heat.
- Biomass can be fermented by yeast and bacteria to create products such as biogas, which can be used as fuel (see below).

It's better to burn fast growing trees than slow growing ones because they can be replaced quickly and easily.

Biogas is Made Mainly of Methane

1) Biogas is usually about 70% methane (CH_4) and 30% carbon dioxide (CO_2). It also contains traces of hydrogen, nitrogen and hydrogen sulfide.

2) Biogas containing more than 50% methane burns easily, but if it contains around 10% methane it can be explosive.

3) Biogas is made by bacteria in a digester (see below). The bacteria's respiration produces methane.

Ka-boom

Biogas Can be Used as Fuel

1) Biogas can be burned to power a turbine, which can be used to generate electricity. This is especially useful for producing electricity in remote areas with no mains supply.

2) Biogas can be burned to heat water and produce steam to heat central heating systems.

3) It can also be used as a fuel for cars and buses.

Biogas is Made by Anaerobic Fermentation of Waste Material

1) Biogas can be made from plant waste and animal poo in a simple fermenter called a digester. Sludge waste, e.g. from sewage works or sugar factories, is used to make biogas on a large scale.

2) Several different types of bacteria are used to produce biogas. Some decompose the organic matter and produce waste, then another type decompose that waste, and so on, until you get biogas. This process is a type of fermentation — it involves the breakdown of substances without oxygen.

3) Biogas digesters need to be kept at a constant warm temperature (30-40 °C). This is the optimum temperature for the bacteria's respiration. Any cooler and the bacteria don't produce biogas as fast. Any hotter and the bacteria will be killed. The conditions in the digester also need to be anaerobic.

4) The diagram on the right shows a simple biogas generator. It needs to have the following:

- An inlet for waste material to be put in.
- An outlet for the digested material to be removed through.
- An outlet so that the biogas can be piped to where it's needed.

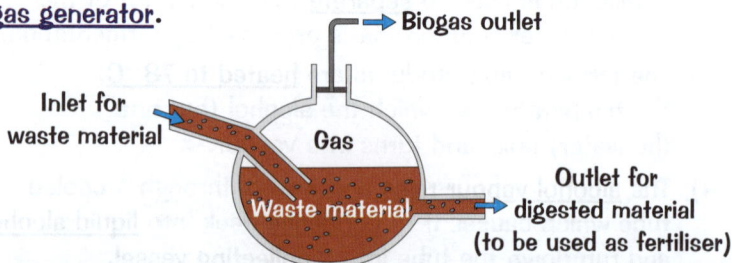

Biogas outlet

Inlet for waste material

Gas

Waste material

Outlet for digested material (to be used as fertiliser)

Large-scale biogas production uses a continuous flow method — organic waste is continuously fed into the digester, and the biogas and solid digested material are continuously removed at a steady rate.

You can make biogas too — just eat some lentils...

Biogas isn't always a good thing — if it's released somewhere it shouldn't be it can cause problems. Methane is sometimes released from landfill sites and it can set alight and burn, or even explode. This can make a site unusable for many years, so a new site for dumping rubbish has to be found.

More on Biofuels

Biogas is better for the environment than burning fossil fuels. It's <u>sustainable</u> (unlike fossil fuels) and it's a <u>relatively clean fuel</u> — releasing fewer pollutants when burnt than oil and coal.

Biofuels Have Their Advantages...

1) One big advantage of biofuels over fossil fuels is that they can be produced in a <u>sustainable</u> way. The <u>crops</u> which are <u>decomposed</u> to <u>make biogas</u> can be <u>replaced quickly</u> with new plants. In contrast, there is a <u>finite</u> supply of <u>fossil fuels</u> like coal and crude oil — they will <u>run out</u> eventually.

2) Another advantage is that the plants grown to make biogas <u>photosynthesise</u>. This <u>removes CO_2</u> (a <u>greenhouse gas</u>) from the atmosphere and can <u>balance out</u> the <u>release of CO_2</u> from <u>burning the biogas</u>. However this is <u>only true</u> if:

   - The biofuels are <u>burnt</u> at the <u>same rate</u> that the new biomass is <u>produced</u>.
   - Areas of land are <u>cleared</u> to grow biomass <u>without burning other vegetation</u>. When the vegetation is <u>burnt</u> it releases more <u>CO_2</u> into the atmosphere.

   This is good because increasing greenhouse gas levels are causing <u>global warming</u>.

3) Biogas is a <u>cleaner fuel</u> than <u>diesel</u> or <u>petrol</u>. Burning these fossil fuels <u>produces particulates</u>, which can cause lung disease. Burning biogas <u>doesn't produce particulates</u>.

...And Their Disadvantages

1) Biogas <u>doesn't contain</u> as much <u>energy</u> as the same volume of <u>natural gas</u> (from underground supplies) because it's more dilute.

I think we're gonna need more sticks.

2) <u>Large areas</u> of land are sometimes <u>cleared</u> of vegetation to create space to produce biofuels. As well as increasing greenhouse gas levels, this can create huge problems for ecosystems:

   - <u>Habitat loss</u> — as plants are cleared, the <u>habitats</u> of many plant and animal species are <u>destroyed</u>.
   - <u>Extinction of species</u> — the loss of habitats and a change in food availability might mean that some species are <u>die out</u> in the area. This is <u>bad news</u>.

Ethanol Can be Used as a Biofuel

1) <u>Ethanol</u> can be burnt as <u>fuel</u>. It's a <u>cleaner fuel</u> than petrol or diesel, producing <u>fewer pollutants</u>.

2) <u>Ethanol</u> is a <u>renewable resource</u>. It is produced by using yeast to <u>ferment glucose</u> (see page 32). Materials like <u>sugar cane</u>, <u>corn</u> and <u>barley</u> can be used as a source of glucose in ethanol production.

3) <u>Cars</u> can be adapted to run on a <u>mixture of ethanol and petrol</u> — known as '<u>gasohol</u>'. Gasohol is a mixture of about 10% ethanol and 90% petrol.

4) Using gasohol <u>instead of pure petrol</u> means that <u>less crude oil</u> is being used up (petrol is refined from crude oil, which is a non-renewable energy source).

5) Another advantage is that the <u>growth of crops</u> for ethanol production means that <u>CO_2</u> is being <u>absorbed</u> from the atmosphere in photosynthesis. This goes some way towards balancing out the release of CO_2 when the gasohol is burnt.

6) Some countries, such as <u>Brazil</u>, have made extensive use of gasohol. It's most <u>economically viable</u> in areas where there is <u>plenty of sugar cane</u> (e.g. tropical countries) and <u>not a lot of oil</u>.

You'd be a bio-fool not to learn this page...

Biogas probably isn't, sadly, the solution to <u>all</u> the world's energy needs. Some countries consume more energy than they could possibly get from biogas (because they <u>don't have the land</u> to grow enough crops).

Soils

I expect that you were hoping to discover that soil is just wet dirt. Unfortunately that's not quite correct. There's actually quite a bit you need to know — so knuckle down and get this page learnt, pronto.

Different Soils Contain Different Particles

1) Sandy soils are made up of large mineral particles. Because the particles are so large, they leave large pores (gaps) in the soil — this means that sandy soils often have a high air content and are very permeable (water can pass through them easily).

2) Clay soils are mostly made up of tiny particles. The small particles can pack tightly together and leave very small pores in the soil — so clay soils usually have a low air content and low permeability. They tend to retain more water than sandy soils because the water molecules cling to the small particles.

3) Loam soils contain a mixture of sand and clay particles. Their properties depend on the relative amounts of the different types of particles.

4) Most soils also contain humus — decomposed, dead organic matter. Humus helps to support soil life (see next page).

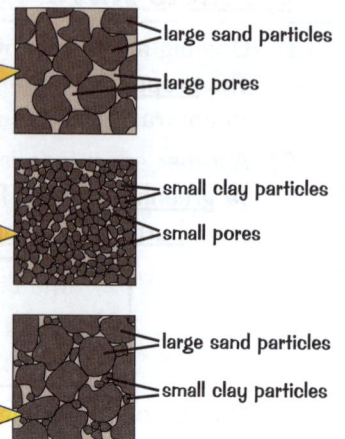

— large sand particles
— large pores

— small clay particles
— small pores

— large sand particles
— small clay particles

You Can Do Experiments to Work Out the Structure of a Soil Sample

You Can Measure The Water and Humus Content...

1) Take the mass of a small sample of soil.

2) Heat the sample to 105 °C until it reaches a constant mass — this will boil off all the water in the soil.

3) Take the mass of the soil sample again — The difference between the first and second reading is equal to the mass of water from the original soil sample.

4) Heat the soil sample to 550 °C for two hours — this will burn all the humus from the soil sample.

5) Take the mass of the soil sample for a third time. The difference between the second and third reading is equal to the mass of humus in the original soil sample.

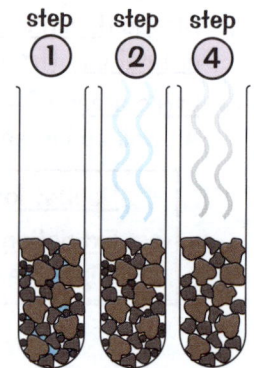

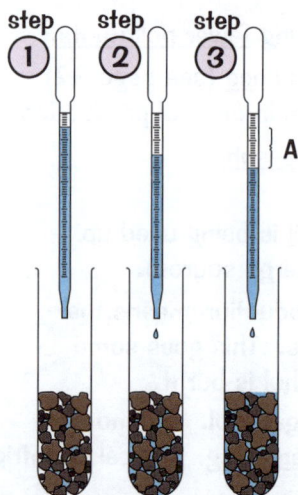

step 1 step 2 step 4

step 1 step 2 step 3

A

... As Well As The Air Content

1) Loosely pack a sample of soil into a beaker or test tube and measure the volume of soil.

2) Fill up a pipette (or measuring cylinder) with a known volume of water and gradually add it to the beaker, letting it seep down into the soil sample.

3) Continue doing this until the water comes up to the top of the soil sample.

4) To find out how much water you added, subtract the volume of water left in the pipette from the volume you started with.

5) As the water has replaced the air in the soil, the volume of water added is the same as the volume of air that was in the sample to begin with. This is shown as 'A' on the diagram.

My friend eats humus and pitta bread for lunch every day — gross...

You might get asked to explain the results of experiments like these in the exam. Don't panic though — just apply what you've learnt on this page and you'll be fine. The important thing to remember is that particle size will affect both the permeability and air content of a soil. Humus content also affects air content (see next page).

Life in the Soil

As well as bits of rock, water and air, soil is teeming with life — which is what this page is all about.

Soil is Full of Living Things

1) Soil may not look all that exciting, but it's pretty important to us. Plants need it for anchorage (to stop them falling over) and for a supply of minerals and water. And animals need plants for food and oxygen.

2) Soil is an ecosystem in itself, containing complex food webs. Herbivores (plant-eaters), carnivores (meat-eaters) and detritivores (which feed on dead organisms) are all found in the soil.

3) There are several other types of organism that live in the soil — microscopic protozoans, fungi, nematode worms and bacteria.

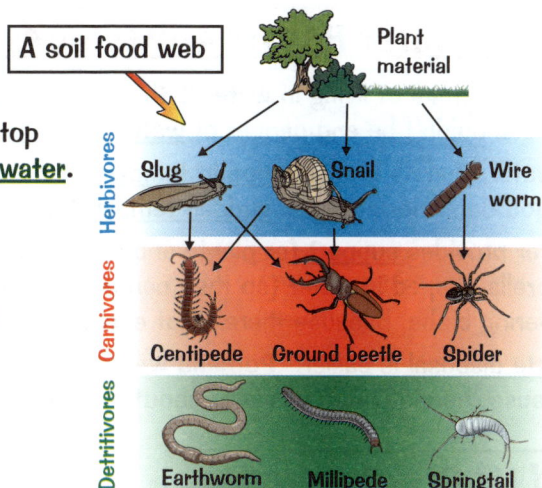

A soil food web

Plant material

Herbivores: Slug, Snail, Wire worm

Carnivores: Centipede, Ground beetle, Spider

Detritivores: Earthworm, Millipede, Springtail

Soil Can Only Support Life If The Conditions Are Spot On

1) In order for a soil to support life, it must contain water and oxygen. All living things need water to carry out reactions in their cells, and cannot survive without it. Almost everything needs oxygen too, for respiration. For example, the roots of plants need to get oxygen from the soil so they can respire.

2) The presence of humus (see previous page) also helps to support life in the soil:

- As organic material is slowly broken down by decomposers, minerals and nutrients are released into the soil. These compounds can then be used by other organisms.
- Humus also increases the air content of the soil, making more oxygen available to the organisms that live there.

Earthworms Help Keep Soil Healthy and Fertile

Charles Darwin, more famous for his theory of natural selection, spent an awful lot of his time studying worms. He observed them closely and experimented on them to see what sort of food they ate and how they behaved. He discovered these reasons why worms are good for soil structure and fertility:

What's worse than biting into an apple and finding a worm?

... studying soil.

1) Earthworms bury leaves and other organic material in the soil, where bacteria and fungi can decompose them.
2) Their burrows allow air to enter the soil (aeration) and water to drain through it. Aeration provides the soil organisms with oxygen, but drainage is important, too — if the soil is waterlogged, there's less oxygen available.
3) They mix up the soil layers, distributing the nutrients more equally.
4) Soil in earthworm poo is less acidic than the soil they eat. This can help to neutralise soil acidity (although worms tend to avoid very acidic soils). Acidic soils are less fertile than neutral or alkaline soils.

Farmers and gardeners can buy earthworms (from worm farms) and add them to their soil to improve it.

Reading this page opens up a whole can of — well... worms...

Well, that page was a bit livelier. You might be one of those people that loves bugs and creepy crawlies, but all this worm business gives me the heebie jeebies. Those little rascals might be great for the soil but they freak me out. I'm not as bad as my friend though — he's afraid of butterflies — now that's just plain weird.

Life in Water

Life in water is very different from life on land...

Living in Water Has Its Advantages...

1) One advantage of living in water is that there's a plentiful supply of water... unsurprisingly. There shouldn't be any danger of water shortage or dehydration (unless a drought makes streams dry up).

2) In water, there's less variation in temperature. Water doesn't heat up or cool down as quickly as air, so you don't normally get sudden temperature changes — which water life can find difficult to withstand.

3) Water provides support for plants and for animals that have no skeletal system. E.g. jellyfish are umbrella-shaped in water (so they can swim) but if they get washed up on a beach they end up as quivering blobs, because there's not enough support... and then you stand on them. Ouch.

4) Waste disposal is easier. Poo and wee are easily dispersed. The loss of water in wee doesn't matter because there's plenty of water about to make up for it.

...and Its Disadvantages

1) Water is more resistant to movement than air, so animals living in water have to use more energy to move about. Think how much effort it takes to walk in the sea compared to walking on the beach.

2) Aquatic animals have to be able to control the amount of water in their body (water regulation). This is because the water an animal lives in has a different concentration of solutes from the animal's cells. If the animal couldn't regulate water, water molecules would enter or leave the animal's cells by osmosis to even up the solute concentrations. This would cause damage to the cells. E.g.

> • If the animal lived in salt-water its cells would probably contain a lower solute concentration than the surrounding water. If the animal wasn't able to regulate water, then water molecules would leave its cells by osmosis, causing them to shrivel and die.
>
> • If the animal lived in freshwater, its cells would probably contain a higher solute concentration than the surrounding water. If the animal wasn't able to regulate water, then water molecules would enter its cells by osmosis, causing them to swell and burst.

Amoebas Regulate Water Content Using Contractile Vacuoles

Most single-celled organisms, like amoebas, only have a cell membrane between them and the surrounding water. So they regulate their water content like this:

Amoebas regulate water with a contractile vacuole which collects the water that diffuses in by osmosis. The vacuole then moves to the cell membrane and contracts to empty the water outside the cell.

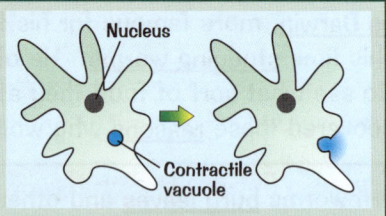

Nucleus

Contractile vacuole

Plankton are Microscopic Organisms That Live in Water

1) Plankton are microscopic organisms that live in fresh and salt water. There are two types:

   • Phytoplankton are microscopic plants.
   • Zooplankton are microscopic animals. Zooplankton feed on phytoplankton.

2) Phytoplankton photosynthesise and are the main producers in aquatic food webs, so they're very important in both freshwater and salt-water ecosystems.

"Waiter, do you have frog's legs?" — "No, I always walk like this"...

Some organisms (mainly insects and amphibians) spend part of their life cycle in water and part on land to exploit both habitats. The two environments provide different challenges, so the different parts of the life cycle often have different body forms (e.g. tadpole and frog).

More on Life in Water

There are monsters in the water. Millions of them. They're only tiny, mind...

Plankton Populations Vary According to the Season

1) Photosynthesis is affected by temperature, light intensity and the availability of minerals like nitrates. These factors vary at different depths and in different seasons, causing the rate of photosynthesis to vary too.
   - During the winter months and in deep water, light intensity and temperature are low. Mineral concentration on the other hand is relatively high. In these conditions, light intensity and temperature limit the rate of photosynthesis.
   - During the summer and near the water's surface, light intensity and temperature are higher but mineral concentration is much lower. Mineral concentration limits the amount of photosynthesis.

2) Phytoplankton populations usually increase between late spring and late summer. This is called an algal bloom (phytoplankton are a type of algae). An algal bloom makes the water go all green and murky. The increase is due to longer, sunnier days in summer:
   - More light is available for photosynthesis and the energy is used for growth.
   - Temperatures increase, causing both photosynthesis and growth rates to increase.
   - The population of zooplankton also increases because there is more phytoplankton to feed on.

There are Different Types of Food Web in the Oceans

1) Most ocean food webs are 'grazing food webs' — this means that they begin with a living producer. (A producer is any organism which can produce its own food.)

2) Producers in ocean food webs are often phytoplankton. But in deep water where light can't penetrate, photosynthesis can't take place. In these places some grazing food webs are supported by bacterial producers that rely on sulfur from deep sea vents (instead of sunlight).

3) In other deep-sea food webs, animals often feed on dead, decomposing material that has slowly fallen from nearer the surface. This 'marine snow' is the major source of nutrients for these food webs.

There are Several Causes of Water Pollution

1) Fertilisers and Sewage

Pollution of water by fertilisers and sewage causes eutrophication.

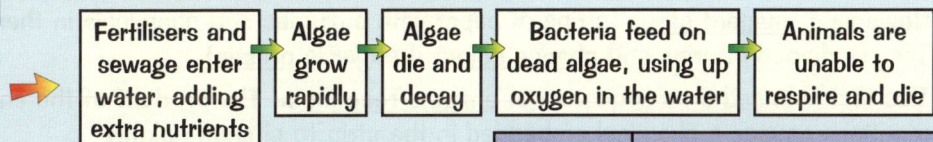

| Fertilisers and sewage enter water, adding extra nutrients | → | Algae grow rapidly | → | Algae die and decay | → | Bacteria feed on dead algae, using up oxygen in the water | → | Animals are unable to respire and die |

Some organisms are particularly sensitive to the level of oxygen in the water. These species are used by scientists to indicate how polluted the water is (the less oxygen, the more polluted). For this reason they're called indicator species.

Pollution level	Indicator species
Clean	Stonefly nymph, Mayfly nymph
Low	Freshwater shrimp, Caddis fly larva
High	Bloodworm, Waterlouse
Very high	Rat-tailed maggot, sludgeworm

Species that are sensitive to different pHs can also be used as indicator species. By seeing which species live in a particular area, scientists can make a pretty good estimate of the pH.

2) Industrial Chemicals and Pesticides

Chemicals which have caused water pollution include pesticides like DDT (used to kill lice and mosquitoes) and industrial chemicals like PCBs (used as coolants and electrical insulators). If water is polluted by these, they are taken up by organisms at the bottom of the food chain. They aren't broken down by the organisms, so when they're eaten the chemical is passed on. The concentration of the chemical increases as it is transferred up the food chain — because each organism eats many of the organisms below it. Organisms at the top of the food chain, e.g. whales, accumulate a huge dose and may die.

Mouldy pizza — indicator species for dirty bedrooms...

You might be asked to interpret marine food webs in the exam. Think about how organisms in the food chain will be affected by an increase/decrease of plankton. If their food source decreases, so will their population.

Enzymes in Action

Enzymes are molecules made of protein, which speed up (catalyse) chemical reactions in living organisms.

Enzymes are Used in Biological Washing Powder...

1) Some stains are caused by soluble chemicals and so they wash out easily in water. Stubborn stains contain insoluble chemicals like starch, proteins and fats. They don't wash out with just water.

2) Non-biological washing powders (detergents) contain chemicals that break up stains on your clothes.

3) Biological washing powders contain the same chemicals as non-biological ones, but also contain a mixture of enzymes which break down the stubborn stains.

Stain	Sources of stain	Enzymes	Product
Carbohydrate	Jam, chocolate	Amylases	Simple sugars
Lipid (fats)	Butter, oil	Lipases	Fatty acids and glycerol
Protein	Blood, grass	Proteases	Amino acids

The products of these enzyme-controlled reactions are soluble in water and so can be easily washed out of clothes.

4) Biological washing powders usually work best at moderate wash temperatures because the enzymes are denatured (destroyed) by high temperatures. However, some newer powders contain enzymes that are more resistant to heat and so can be used with a hotter water temperature.

5) Biological washing powders might not work very well in acidic or alkaline tap water. This is because the enzymes can be denatured by extremes of pH.

6) You can buy special stain removers (e.g. for wine, blood or oil). Some of these are just special solvents, but some contain specific enzymes that will break down the stain.

...and in Medical Products...

1) Diabetes is diagnosed by the presence of sugar in the urine. Many years ago, doctors actually used to taste patients' urine to test for sugar... yuk. Later they tested the urine for sugar using Benedict's solution. When it's heated, the solution changes colour from blue to orange if sugar is present. This test relies on chemical properties (not enzymes).

2) Nowadays, reagent strips (strips of paper with enzymes and chemicals in them) are used. They're dipped in urine and change colour if sugar is present.

3) This test is based on a sequence of enzyme reactions. The product of the enzyme-controlled reactions causes a chemical embedded in the strip to change colour.

4) There are similar strips which can be used to test blood sugar levels (see next page).

...and in the Food Industry

Low-Calorie Food	1) Table sugar (sucrose) is what you normally sweeten food with at home. 2) In the food industry an enzyme called sucrase (or invertase) is used to break down sucrose into glucose and fructose. Glucose and fructose are much sweeter than sucrose. 3) This means you can get the same level of sweetness using less sugar. This helps to make low-calorie food sweeter without adding calories.
Cheese	The enzyme rennet is used to clot milk in the first stages of cheese production.
Juice Extraction	The enzyme pectinase is used in fruit juice extraction. It breaks down pectin (a part of the cell wall in apples and oranges), causing the cell to release its juice.

Stubborn stains — not just dirty, but grumpy...

Not everyone can use biological washing powders. Some of the enzymes remain on the clothes and can irritate sensitive skin, making it sore and itchy. People with sensitive skin have to use non-biological powders.

More Enzymes in Action

When enzymes are used to speed up reactions, they end up <u>dissolved in the mixture</u> with the substrates and products — and can be <u>difficult to remove</u>. One way to avoid this is to <u>immobilise</u> the enzymes...

Immobilising Enzymes Makes Them Easier to Remove

1) Many industrial processes use <u>immobilised enzymes</u>, which <u>don't</u> need to be <u>separated out</u> from the mixture after the reaction has taken place.

2) Enzymes can be immobilised in different ways. One way is to encapsulate them in <u>alginate beads</u> (alginate is a gel-like substance). The beads are formed by mixing the enzyme with <u>alginate</u>, then dropping the mixture into a <u>calcium chloride solution</u>.

3) The immobilised enzymes are <u>still active</u> and still help speed up reactions.

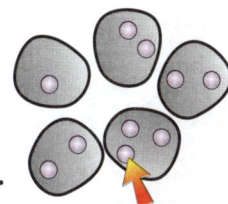

enzyme molecule encapsulated within a bead of alginate

> **Advantages of Immobilising Enzymes**
> 1) The enzymes <u>don't contaminate</u> the product.
> 2) Immobilised enzymes in alginate beads can be used in <u>continuous flow processing</u> (see below).

Immobilised Enzymes Can be Used to Make Lactose-Free Milk

1) The sugar <u>lactose</u> is naturally found in <u>milk</u> (and yoghurt). It's broken down in your digestive system by the <u>enzyme lactase</u>. This produces <u>glucose</u> and <u>galactose</u>, which are then <u>absorbed</u> into the blood.

2) Some people <u>lack the enzyme lactase</u>. If they drink milk the lactose isn't broken down and <u>gut bacteria ferment it</u>, causing <u>abdominal pain</u>, <u>wind</u> and <u>diarrhoea</u>. These people are said to be <u>lactose intolerant</u>.

3) <u>Lactose-free milk</u> can be produced using <u>immobilised lactase</u>. The lactase breaks down lactose into <u>glucose</u> and <u>galactose</u>. These simple sugars can be absorbed by someone who's lactose intolerant.

4) A method called <u>continuous flow processing</u> is often used for this:

Milk

Column of immobilised lactase

Lactose free milk

• The substrate solution (milk) is run through a <u>column of immobilised lactase</u>.

• The enzymes convert the substrate (lactose) into the products (glucose and galactose), but only the <u>products</u> emerge from the column. The enzymes stay fixed in the column.

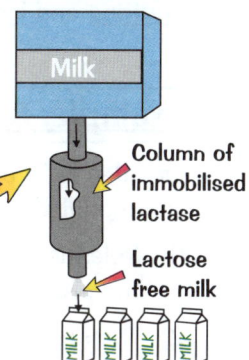

Immobilised Enzymes are Also Used in Reagent Strips

1) <u>Diabetics</u> use reagent strips to measure their <u>blood glucose concentration</u> on a <u>daily basis</u>. They're <u>quick</u> and <u>convenient</u> to use. Before reagent strips diabetics had to 'guess' when they needed to inject insulin (e.g. before meals), because there was no quick way of knowing what their glucose level was.

2) There are <u>immobilised enzymes</u> on the reagent strips.

3) A drop of blood from a finger prick is added to the strip. The enzymes in the strip cause it to <u>change different colours</u> depending on the <u>glucose concentration</u>. The colour is then compared to a <u>chart</u> to find out the level of blood sugar.

ENZYMES

Abdominal pain, wind and diarrhoea — that fudge sundae was worth it...

Lactose intolerance affects <u>millions of people</u>. There's a pretty big industry out there providing them with lactose-free milk, lactose-free ice cream, lactose-free chocolates... You get the idea. Making these things is a whole lot easier thanks to <u>immobilised enzymes</u>. There you have it — proof that science is actually useful.

Genetic Engineering

Genetic engineering may sound a bit scary, but it's not too hard to get your head round really. So fret not.

Genes Can be Transferred Between Different Organisms

1) Genetic engineering alters the genetic code of an organism. A gene giving a desirable characteristic is removed from one organism and inserted into another organism.
2) We're able to transfer genes from one organism to another because the genetic code is universal (i.e. the same four bases are used in the DNA of all organisms).
3) A genetically modified organism is called a transgenic organism.

There Are Five Main Steps to Genetic Engineering

Whatever gene you're transferring, and whatever organisms you're transferring it from or to, you need to do the same five things:

1) Identify the gene that you're after in an organism.
2) Remove the gene from the organism's DNA.
3) Cut open the DNA of the organism that you want to put the gene into.
4) Insert the gene into the DNA of the second organism — where the gene should now work.
5) The host is now a transgenic organism. You can clone it to produce more copies.

The cutting and inserting of DNA is done using enzymes.

> These steps are basically the same for any gene that you might want to transfer into another species.

Example: Bacteria Can be Engineered to Produce Human Insulin

The idea is to put the human insulin gene into bacteria so that the bacteria can make human insulin. The modified bacteria reproduce, and you end up with millions of insulin-producing bacteria.

1) Scientists identify the gene which controls the production of human insulin.

2) They remove it from the DNA of a human cell by 'cutting it out' with restriction enzymes. This leaves the DNA with so-called 'sticky ends'.

3) A loop of bacterial DNA called a plasmid (see page 28) is then prepared for the insulin gene to be inserted. Restriction enzymes are used to cut open the plasmid, leaving it with sticky ends too.

4) The insulin gene is inserted in the plasmid. The sticky ends allow another enzyme called ligase to join DNA strands together. The plasmid is then taken up by bacteria.

> The plasmid is known as a vector — something that carries a gene into another organism.

5) The bacteria are now transgenic organisms. They're checked to make sure they contain the new gene using assaying techniques and are then cultured by cloning. Millions of bacteria can be produced in this way, allowing large quantities of insulin to be harvested.

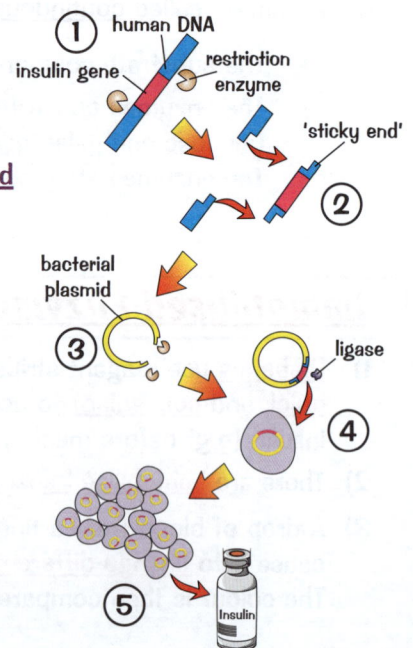

What would a genetic engine wear if it had its ears pierced?...

...A genetic engine earring, of course. More importantly though — what's a genetic engine? And why on earth would it need ears? You need to make sure you know the human insulin example inside out, but remember that this is just one example — the process is pretty much the same, whatever gene or organisms you're dealing with.

DNA Fingerprinting

Now this is more interesting — forensic science being used to catch murderers, just like on the telly.

DNA Fingerprinting Pinpoints Individuals

1) Your DNA is unique (unless you're an identical twin — then the two of you have identical DNA).

2) DNA fingerprinting (or genetic fingerprinting) is a way of comparing DNA samples to see if they come from the same person or from two different people.

3) DNA fingerprinting is used in forensic science. DNA (from hair, skin flakes, blood, semen etc.) taken from a crime scene is compared with a DNA sample taken from a suspect.

4) It can also be used in paternity tests — to check if a man is the father of a particular child.

5) Some people would like everyone's genetic fingerprints to be stored on a national genetic database. That way, DNA from a crime scene could be checked against everyone in the country to see whose it was — which would make solving some crimes much easier. But others think this is a big invasion of privacy, and they worry about how safe the data would be and what else it might be used for. There are also scientific problems — false positives can occur if errors are made in the procedure or if the data is misinterpreted.

The 'Fingerprint' is Made in a Special Gel

HOW IT WORKS

1) First you have to extract the DNA from the cells in your sample.

2) Restriction enzymes are then used to cut the DNA into fragments. They cut it at every place where they recognise a particular order of bases. Where these sections are in the DNA will be different for everyone.

3) If the DNA sample contains that little section of bases lots of times, it'll be cut into lots of little bits. If it only contains it a few times, it'll be left in bigger bits.

4) The DNA bits are separated out using a process called electrophoresis. The fragments are suspended in a gel, and an electric current is passed through the gel. DNA is negatively charged, so it moves towards the positive anode. Small bits travel faster than big bits, so they get further through the gel.

5) The DNA is "tagged" with a radioactive probe. Then it's placed onto photographic film. The film goes dark where the radioactivity is, revealing the positions of the DNA fragments.

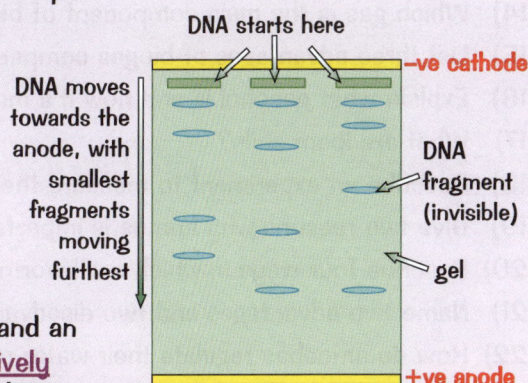

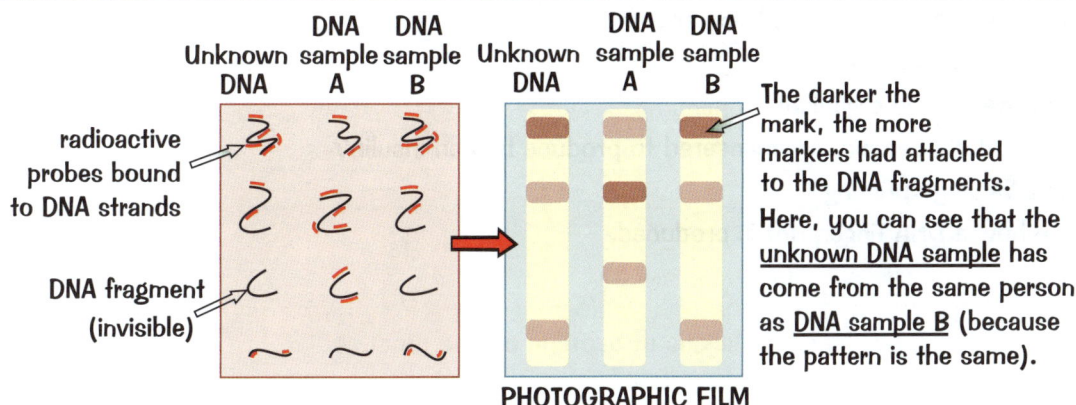

DNA starts here

DNA moves towards the anode, with smallest fragments moving furthest

−ve cathode

DNA fragment (invisible)

gel

+ve anode

radioactive probes bound to DNA strands

DNA fragment (invisible)

DNA Unknown DNA
Unknown sample sample
DNA A B

DNA DNA
Unknown sample sample
DNA A B

The darker the mark, the more markers had attached to the DNA fragments.
Here, you can see that the unknown DNA sample has come from the same person as DNA sample B (because the pattern is the same).

PHOTOGRAPHIC FILM

So the trick is — frame your twin and they'll never get you...

In the exam you might have to interpret data on DNA fingerprinting for identification. They'd probably give you a diagram similar to the one at the bottom of this page, and you'd have to say which of the known samples (if any) matched the unknown sample. Pretty easy — it's the two that look the same.

Revision Summary for Module B6

I never knew how interesting microorganisms could be, they do so many things — making yoghurt, causing disease, clearing up sugar spills, making booze, biogas and insulin. And as for those useful enzymes... they're a barrel of laughs. Anyway, just the revision summary to go and then you're done with this section. Yay :)

1) State the function of the following parts of a bacterial cell: a) flagellum, b) cell wall, c) bacterial DNA.
2) Describe the main stages in making yoghurt.
3) Describe how viruses reproduce.
4) Describe four ways in which diseases can be transmitted.
5) Describe the four stages in an infectious disease.
6) How are antiseptics and antibiotics used to control disease?
7) Explain why natural disasters often cause rapid spread of disease.
8) Describe how Alexander Fleming discovered penicillin.
9) State the word equations for anaerobic respiration and aerobic respiration in yeast.
10) How is the rate of breakdown of sugar by yeast affected by temperature?
Sketch a graph to illustrate your answer.
11) Describe the main stages in brewing beer.
12) How could you increase the alcohol concentration of a fermented product?
13) Give two ways in which energy can be transferred from biomass.
14) Which gas is the main component of biogas?
15) List three advantages of biogas compared to fossil fuels.
16) Explain what gasohol is and how it's made.
17) What are loam soils?
18) Describe an experiment to measure the air content in a soil sample.
19) Give two reasons why humus is important to soil life.
20) Describe four ways in which earthworms improve soil fertility.
21) Name two advantages and two disadvantages of living in water.
22) How do amoebas regulate their water content?
23) Explain why phytoplankton populations usually increase in summer.
24) Explain the process of eutrophication. Name two things that can cause it.
25) Why do biological washing powders need a moderate wash temperature and neutral pH?
26) Name an enzyme that breaks down sucrose. What is this enzyme used for in the food industry?
27) Give two advantages of immobilising enzymes.
28) What is lactose intolerance?
29) What is a transgenic organism?
30) How are bacteria genetically engineered to produce human insulin?
31) What is DNA fingerprinting?
32) Describe how a DNA fingerprint is produced.

Atoms, Molecules and Compounds

Here we go then... <u>atoms</u> are the building blocks that everything is made from. Atoms can <u>join up</u> with other atoms to make <u>molecules</u>. Molecules containing <u>different types</u> of atoms make up <u>compounds</u>.

Atoms *Have a* Positive Nucleus *with* Orbiting Electrons

Atoms are <u>really tiny</u>. They're <u>too small to see</u>, even with a microscope. They have a <u>nucleus</u> which is <u>positively</u> charged, and <u>electrons</u> which are <u>negatively</u> charged. The electrons <u>move around</u> the nucleus in layers known as <u>shells</u>.

Atoms can form <u>bonds</u> to make <u>molecules</u> or <u>compounds</u>. It's the <u>electrons</u> that are involved in making bonds. Sometimes an atom <u>loses</u> or <u>gains</u> one or more <u>electrons</u> and this gives it a <u>charge</u> (<u>positive</u> if it <u>loses</u> an electron, and <u>negative</u> if it <u>gains</u> one).

Charged atoms are known as <u>ions</u>. If a <u>positive ion</u> meets a <u>negative ion</u> they'll be <u>attracted</u> to one another and <u>join together</u>. This is called an <u>ionic bond</u>.

The other main type of bond is called a <u>covalent bond</u> — atoms in a covalent bond <u>share</u> a pair of electrons.

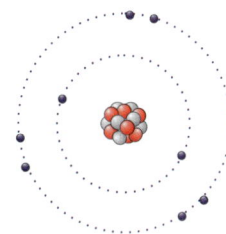

You Need to Know About *Displayed* and *Molecular Formulas*

You need to be able to say <u>how many atoms</u> of each type there are in a substance when you're given its <u>formula</u>. Here are some examples:

This is called a <u>molecular formula</u>. It shows the <u>number</u> and <u>type</u> of <u>atoms</u> in a molecule.

CH_4

H
$H-C-H$
H

<u>Methane</u> contains 1 carbon atom and 4 hydrogen atoms.

H_2O

$H_{}H$
O

<u>Water</u> contains 2 hydrogen atoms and 1 oxygen atom.

This is called a <u>displayed formula</u>. It shows the <u>atoms</u> and the <u>covalent bonds</u> in a molecule as a picture.

Don't panic if the molecular formula has <u>brackets</u> in it. They're easy too.

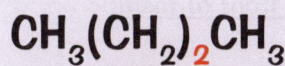

$CH_3(CH_2)_2CH_3$

The 2 after the bracket means that there are 2 lots of CH_2. So altogether there are 4 carbon atoms and 10 hydrogen atoms.

Drawing the <u>displayed formula</u> of the compound is a good way to count up the number of atoms.

Do it a bit at a time.

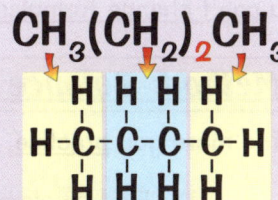

$CH_3(CH_2)_2CH_3$

$H \quad H \quad H \quad H$
$H-C-C-C-C-H$
$H \quad H \quad H \quad H$

In the exam they might give you a <u>displayed formula</u> and ask you to write down the <u>molecular formula</u>. Easy — just count up the number of each type of atom and write it as above, e.g. CH_4, H_2O, etc. Even better... you can write $CH_3(CH_2)_2CH_3$ as C_4H_{10}. It just doesn't get any easier. Not in Chemistry.

You Need to *Remember* Some Formulas

◀ One formula, two formulas, or even two formulae.

Here are some <u>formulas</u>. Learn them now. There are only twelve, and you'll have come across most of them already. You'll need to learn others later, but these'll be a good start.

1) Carbon dioxide — CO_2
2) Hydrogen — H_2
3) Water — H_2O
4) Oxygen — O_2
5) Magnesium hydroxide — $Mg(OH)_2$
6) Hydrochloric acid — HCl
7) Calcium chloride — $CaCl_2$
8) Magnesium chloride — $MgCl_2$
9) Sodium carbonate — Na_2CO_3
10) Calcium carbonate — $CaCO_3$
11) Sulfuric acid — H_2SO_4
12) Magnesium sulfate — $MgSO_4$

Some chemicals have slightly more interesting names...

With so many chemicals around, you'd think there might be some <u>interesting names</u>... And so there are. There's windowpane (C_9H_{12}). And angelic acid ($CH_3CHC(CH_3)COOH$). There's the mineral that's named after the mineralogist <u>Wilfred Welsh</u>, which goes by the name of welshite ($Ca_2SbMg_4FeBe_2Si_4O_{20}$). And if you think that diethyl azodicarboxylate is a bit much, you can just call it <u>DEAD</u>. Better than boring names like 'ethene'.

Chemical Equations

If you're going to get anywhere in chemistry you need to know about <u>chemical equations</u>...

Chemical Changes are Shown Using Chemical Equations

One way to show a chemical reaction is to write a <u>word equation</u>. It's not as <u>quick</u> as using chemical symbols and you can't tell straight away <u>what's happened</u> to each of the <u>atoms</u>, but it's <u>dead easy</u>. Here's an example — you're told that <u>methane</u> burns in <u>oxygen</u> giving <u>carbon dioxide</u> and <u>water</u>. So here's the word equation:

The molecules on the left-hand side of the equation are called the <u>reactants</u> (because they react with each other).

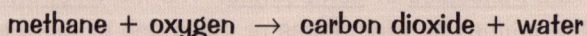

methane + oxygen → carbon dioxide + water

The molecules on the right-hand side are called the <u>products</u> (because they've been produced from the reactants).

Symbol Equations Show the Atoms on Both Sides

Chemical <u>changes</u> can be shown in a kind of <u>shorthand</u> using symbol equations. Symbol equations just show the <u>formulas</u> of the <u>reactants</u> and <u>products</u>...

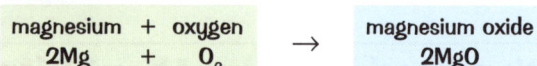

$$\text{magnesium} + \text{oxygen} \rightarrow \text{magnesium oxide}$$
$$2Mg + O_2 \rightarrow 2MgO$$

You'll have spotted that there's a '2' in front of the Mg and the MgO. The reason for this is explained below...

Symbol Equations Need to be Balanced

1) There must always be the <u>same</u> number of atoms on <u>both sides</u> — they can't just <u>disappear</u>.

2) You <u>balance</u> the equation by putting numbers <u>in front</u> of the formulas where needed. Take this equation for reacting sulfuric acid with sodium hydroxide:

$$H_2SO_4 + NaOH \rightarrow Na_2SO_4 + H_2O$$

The <u>formulas</u> are all correct but the numbers of some atoms <u>don't match up</u> on both sides. You <u>can't change formulas</u> like H_2SO_4 to H_2SO_5. You can only put numbers <u>in front of them</u>:

Method: Balance Just One Type of Atom at a Time

The more you <u>practise</u>, the <u>quicker</u> you get, but all you do is this:

1) Find an element that <u>doesn't balance</u> and <u>pencil in a number</u> to try and sort it out.

2) <u>See where it gets you</u>. It may create <u>another imbalance</u>, but if so, pencil in <u>another number</u> and see where that gets you.

3) Carry on chasing <u>unbalanced</u> elements and it'll <u>sort itself out</u> pretty quickly.

<u>I'll show you</u>: In the equation above you'll notice we're short of <u>H atoms</u> on the RHS (Right-Hand Side).

1) The only thing you can do about that is make it <u>$2H_2O$</u> instead of just H_2O:

$$H_2SO_4 + NaOH \rightarrow Na_2SO_4 + 2H_2O$$

2) But that now gives <u>too many</u> H atoms and O atoms on the RHS, so to balance that up you could try putting <u>2NaOH</u> on the LHS (Left-Hand Side):

$$H_2SO_4 + 2NaOH \rightarrow Na_2SO_4 + 2H_2O$$

3) And suddenly there it is! <u>Everything balances</u>. And you'll notice the Na just sorted itself out.

They can ask you in the exam to balance symbol equations using formulas that have bits in <u>brackets</u> — like $CH_3(CH_2)_2CH_3$ on the last page. Don't worry about that, just make sure you're clear before you start <u>how many</u> of <u>each type</u> of atom there are — in this case it's <u>4 carbons</u> and <u>10 hydrogens</u>.

It's all about getting the balance right...

Balancing equations isn't as scary as it looks — you just plug numbers in until it works itself out. Get some practice in — you'll see. You can balance equations with <u>displayed formulas</u> in exactly the same way. Just make sure there are the same number of each type of atom on both sides — dead easy.

The Mole

The mole might seem a bit confusing. I think it's the word that puts people off. It's very difficult to see the relevance of the word "mole" to anything but a small burrowing animal. BUT... It's not actually that hard...

"THE MOLE" is Simply the Name Given to a Certain Number

Just like "a million" is this many: 1 000 000; or "a billion" is this many: 1 000 000 000,
"a mole" is this many: 602 300 000 000 000 000 000 000 or 6.023×10^{23}.

Don't worry — you don't need to remember this number.

1) And that's all it is. Just a number. The burning question, of course, is why is it such a silly long one like that, and with a six at the front?

2) The answer is that when you get precisely that number of atoms or molecules, of any element or compound, then, conveniently, they weigh exactly the same number of grams as the relative atomic mass, A_r (or relative formula mass, M_r) of the element or compound. This is arranged on purpose of course, to make things easier.

> One mole of atoms or molecules of any substance will have a mass in grams equal to the relative formula mass (A_r or M_r) for that substance.

EXAMPLES:

Carbon has an A_r of 12.	So one mole of carbon weighs exactly 12 g
Nitrogen gas, N_2, has an M_r of 28 (2×14).	So one mole of N_2 weighs exactly 28 g
Carbon dioxide, CO_2, has an M_r of 44.	So one mole of CO_2 weighs exactly 44 g
Hexane, $CH_3(CH_2)_4CH_3$, has an M_r of 86 ($12+3+((12+2)\times4)+12+3$).	So one mole of pentane weighs exactly 86 g

This means that 12 g of carbon, or 28 g of N_2, or 44 g of CO_2, or 86 g of hexane all contain the same number of particles, namely one mole or 6.023×10^{23} atoms or molecules.

3) Molar mass is just another way of saying 'the mass of one mole'.
Molar mass is measured in grams per mole. For example carbon has a molar mass of 12 g/mol.

Nice Easy Formula for Finding the Number of Moles in a Given Mass:

$$\text{NUMBER OF MOLES} = \frac{\text{Mass in g} \quad \text{(of element or compound)}}{M_r \quad \text{(of element or compound)}}$$

EXAMPLE 1: How many moles are there in 66 g of carbon dioxide?
M_r of CO_2 = 12 + (16 × 2) = 44
No. of moles = Mass (g) / M_r = 66/44 = 1.5 moles   Easy peasy.

This one's a tiny bit trickier. You have to rearrange the formula above.

EXAMPLE 2: What mass of carbon is there in 4 moles of carbon dioxide?
There are 4 moles of carbon in 4 moles of CO_2.
The mass of 4 moles of carbon = number of moles × M_r = 4 × 12 = 48 g

Relative Masses are Masses of Atoms Compared to Carbon-12

Atoms and molecules are much too tiny to weigh. So their masses are compared to 1/12th the mass of an atom of carbon-12. Carbon-12 is an isotope of carbon.

Learn this definition:

> The RELATIVE ATOMIC MASS of an element is the average mass of an atom of the element compared to the mass of $\frac{1}{12}$th of an atom of CARBON-12.

What do moles do for fun? Moller skate... boom boom...

Did you know that a mole can dig a tunnel at a rate of 18 feet per hour (that's really fast) and then move through an empty tunnel at 80 feet per hour. The word 'mole' can also mean a spy who infiltrates organisations and becomes a trusted member. And a small, brown skin lesion, otherwise known as melanocytic naevi. Great.

Reacting Masses and Empirical Formulas

You Can Use Moles to Calculate Masses in Reactions

You can work out the masses in a reaction using moles.

For example: Calculate the mass of aluminium oxide formed when 135 g of aluminium is burned in air.

1) Write out the balanced equation: $4Al + 3O_2 \rightarrow 2Al_2O_3$

2) Calculate the number of moles of aluminium in 135 g:

$$\text{Moles} = \frac{\text{mass}}{M_r} = \frac{135}{27} = 5$$

3) Look at the ratio of moles in the equation:

4 moles of Al react to produce 2 moles of Al_2O_3 — half the number of moles are produced.
So 5 moles of Al will react to produce 2.5 moles of Al_2O_3

4) Calculate the mass of 2.5 moles of aluminium oxide: $\text{mass} = \text{moles} \times M_r = 2.5 \times 102 = 255 \text{ g}$

You Can Calculate the Percentage Composition by Mass of Compounds

For example, if you're told there are 42.9 g of potassium (K) in 61.6 g of potassium hydroxide (KOH) you could:

• use the experimental data to calculate the percentage composition of K in KOH: $(42.9 \div 61.6) \times 100 = \underline{69.6\%}$.

• or use the molecular formula, atomic masses and the formula below...

$$\text{percentage composition by mass} = \frac{A_r \times \text{No. of atoms (of that element)}}{M_r \text{ (of whole compound)}} \times 100 = \frac{39 \times 1}{56} \times 100 = 69.6\%$$

Empirical Formulas are the Simplest Ratio of Atoms in a Compound

The empirical formula just gives the smallest whole number ratio of atoms in a compound.

For example: Ethane: chemical formula = C_2H_6 empirical formula = CH_3.

Glucose: chemical formula = $C_6H_{12}O_6$ empirical formula = CH_2O.

You have to be able to calculate an empirical formula from the masses of each element in a compound or the percentage composition by mass of each element in a sample of the compound.

It doesn't matter if you're given masses or percentages — you use the same easy stepwise method:

1) List all the elements in the compound (there are usually only two or three).

2) Underneath them, write their experimental masses or percentages.

3) Divide each mass or percentage by the A_r for that particular element.

4) Turn the numbers you get into a simple ratio by multiplying and/or dividing them by well-chosen numbers.

5) Get the ratio in its simplest form, and that tells you the empirical formula of the compound.

EXAMPLE: Find the empirical formula of the iron oxide produced when 44.8 g of iron reacts with 19.2 g of oxygen. (A_r for iron = 56, A_r for oxygen = 16)

METHOD:

		Fe	O
1)	List the two elements:	Fe	O
2)	Write in the experimental masses:	44.8	19.2
3)	Divide by the A_r for each element:	$44.8 \div 56 = 0.8$	$19.2 \div 16 = 1.2$
4)	Multiply by 10...	8	12
	...then divide by 4	2	3
5)	So the simplest formula is 2 atoms of Fe to 3 atoms of O, i.e. $\underline{Fe_2O_3}$.		

With this empirical formula I can rule the world! — mwa ha ha ha...

Now try these: 1) What is the empirical formula of: a) C_7H_{14}, b) $C_6H_{12}O_6$, c) Al_2Cl_6?

2) Find the empirical formula when 2.4 g of carbon react with 0.8 g of hydrogen.

Concentration

Another dull and boring page. But at least there are some more calculations on it.

Concentration is a Measure of How Crowded Things Are

The concentration of a solution can be measured in moles per dm³ (i.e. moles per litre).
So 1 mole of stuff in 1 dm³ of solution has a concentration of 1 mole per dm³ (or 1 mol/dm³).

> The more solute you dissolve in a given volume, the more crowded
> the solute molecules are and the more concentrated the solution.

Concentration can also be measured in grams per dm³. So 56 grams of stuff
dissolved in 1 dm³ of solution has a concentration of 56 grams per dm³.

There's a calculation you can do to convert moles per dm³ to grams per dm³
(see below). In the exam, look out for which one the question's asking for.

1 litre		
=	1000 cm³	
=	1 dm³	

Concentration = No. of Moles ÷ Volume

Here's a nice formula triangle for you to learn:

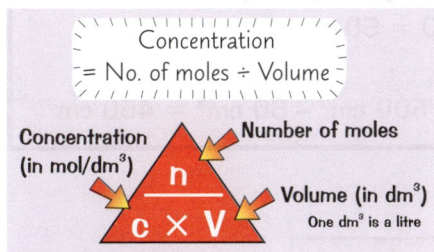

Concentration = No. of moles ÷ Volume

Concentration (in mol/dm³)
Number of moles
$$\frac{n}{c \times V}$$
Volume (in dm³)
One dm³ is a litre

Example 1: What's the concentration of a solution with 2 moles of salt in 500 cm³?

Answer: Easy — you've got the number of moles and the volume, so just stick it in the formula...

Concentration = $\frac{2}{0.5}$ = **4 moles per dm³**

Convert the volume to litres (i.e. dm³) first by dividing by 1000.

Example 2: How many moles of sodium chloride are in 250 cm³ of a 3 molar solution of sodium chloride?

Answer: Well, 3 molar just means it's got 3 moles per dm³. So using the formula...
Number of moles = concentration × volume = 3 × 0.25 = **0.75 moles**

3 molar is sometimes written '3 M'.

Converting Moles per dm³ to Grams per dm³

They might ask you to find out a concentration in grams per dm³.
If they do, don't panic — you just need another formula triangle.

Number of moles = mass ÷ relative formula mass.

$$\frac{m}{n \times M_r}$$
Mass (in grams)
Number of moles
Relative formula mass

Example 1: You have a solution of sulfuric acid of 0.04 mol/dm³.
What is the concentration in GRAMS per dm³?

Step 1: Work out the relative formula mass for the solute (you should be
given the relative atomic masses, e.g. H = 1, S = 32, O = 16):
So, H_2SO_4 = (1 × 2) + 32 + (16 × 4) = 98

Step 2: Convert the concentration in moles into concentration in grams. So, in 1 dm³:
Mass in grams = moles × relative formula mass
= 0.04 × 98 = 3.92 g
So the concentration in g/dm³ = **3.92 g/dm³**

Example 2: The concentration of a solution of sulfuric acid is 19.6 g/dm³.
What is the concentration in MOLES per dm³?

Step 1: The relative formula mass of H_2SO_4 = 98
Step 2: Moles = mass in grams ÷ relative formula mass
= 19.6 ÷ 98 = 0.2 mol   So the concentration in mol/dm³ = **0.2 mol/dm³**

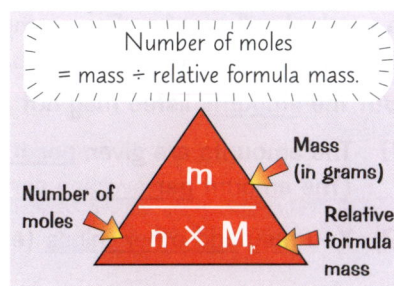

Murray wasn't great at concentration.

Numbers? — and you thought you were doing chemistry...

High concentration is like the whole of a rugby team in a mini. Or everyone in Britain living on the Isle of Wight.
Low concentration is like a guy stranded on a desert island, or a small fish in a big lake.

Concentration

Concentration is important. Are you listening... I said concentration is important.

It's Important to Get the Right Concentration

'Diluting' something usually means 'watering it down'.

You might be given a concentrated solution of something and asked to dilute it to make a weaker solution.
Don't worry, it's not that complicated:

> **Example:** Explain how you'd produce 500 cm^3 of a 0.1 mol/dm^3 solution of KOH (potassium hydroxide) if you're given a 1.0 mol/dm^3 solution of KOH and some water.
>
> **Step 1:** Work out the RATIO of the two concentrations...
> Divide the two concentrations to get a number less than 1.
> 0.1 ÷ 1.0 = 1/10 ⟵ Always divide the small number by the big one.
> It's a 1/10 ratio so you'll be doing a 1 in 10 dilution.
>
> **Step 2:** Multiply this ratio by the volume of solution you want to END UP WITH.
> (This tells you how much of your ORIGINAL ACID you need to dilute.)
> Volume to dilute = ratio × final volume = 1/10 × 500 = 50 cm^3
>
> **Step 3:** Work out the VOLUME OF WATER you'll need.
> Volume of water = total volume – volume to dilute = 500 cm^3 – 50 cm^3 = 450 cm^3

Food Packaging Gives Guideline Daily Amounts (GDAs)

On most food packaging you'll find nutritional information tables — these tell you the amounts of nutrients in the food. Guideline Daily Amounts (GDAs) are the amounts of nutrients that an average adult should eat each day in a healthy diet — food labels often tell you what percentage of various GDAs a product will supply. For example, this information was found on the side of a hot oat cereal packet.

NUTRITIONAL INFORMATION		
	/40 g serving	GDA
Thiamin (B1)	0.5 mg	34%
Riboflavin (B2)	0.5 mg	34%
Calcium	480 mg	60%
Iron	4.8 mg	34%

But the amounts listed may not always be the amount you eat, because...

1) The amounts are given per 100 g (or 100 ml) of the food — but you may eat more or less than this. (The amount per average serving is also sometimes listed — e.g. per 40 g for this cereal.)

2) You may add other things (e.g. milk to cereals — which will increase how much calcium you get).

You Can Use Sodium Content to Estimate the Mass of Salt

You need to be careful how much salt (sodium chloride) you eat. Sometimes salt is included in the nutritional information — but if not, you can estimate it from the mass of sodium...

For example, if a slice of bread contains 0.2 g sodium — how much salt does it contain?
(A$_r$ sodium = 23 and M$_r$ sodium chloride = 58.5)

1) Find the ratio of sodium chloride's M$_r$ to sodium's A$_r$:   58.5 ÷ 23 = 2.543...

2) Multiply this by the amount of sodium: 2.543... × 0.2 = 0.5086... = 0.5 g salt

But the sodium present probably won't all come from sodium chloride — there might be other sodium compounds too, e.g. sodium nitrate (often used as a preservative). So this is probably an overestimate.

This page contains your GDA of concentration calculations...

Why is it that people only read the backs of cereal packets... one of life's little mysteries. Possibly.

Titrations

Titrations are a method of analysing the concentrations of solutions. They're pretty important. Some people don't think they're the most exciting game in town. But I secretly enjoy them, now I've got the hang of them.

Titrations are Used to Find Out Concentrations

1) Titrations allow you to find out exactly how much acid is needed to neutralise a quantity of alkali (or vice versa).

2) Using a pipette and pipette filler, add some alkali (usually 25 cm³) to a conical flask, along with two or three drops of indicator. (The pipette filler stops you getting a mouthful of alkali.)

3) Fill a burette with the acid. Make sure you do this BELOW EYE LEVEL — you don't want to be looking up if some acid spills over.

4) Using the burette, add the acid to the alkali a bit at a time — giving the conical flask a regular swirl. Go especially slowly when you think the end-point (colour change) is about to be reached.

5) The indicator changes colour when all the alkali has been neutralised, e.g. phenolphthalein is pink in alkalis, but colourless in acids.

6) Record the volume of acid used to neutralise the alkali.

You can also do titrations the other way round — adding alkali to acid.

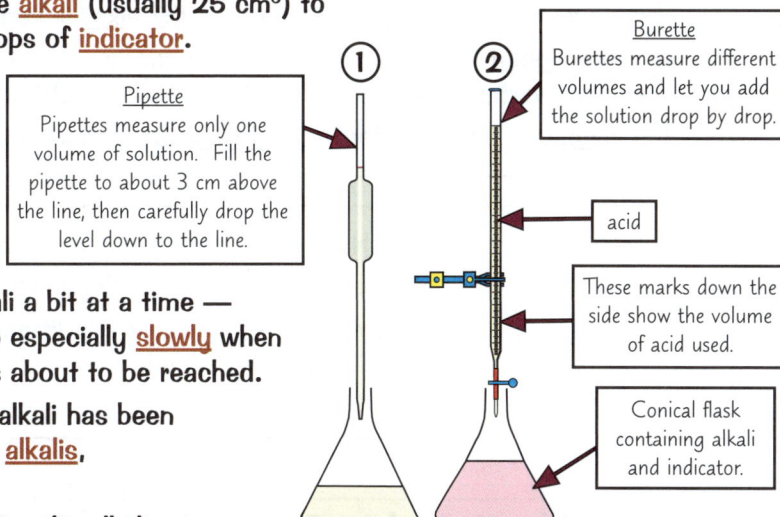

Pipette
Pipettes measure only one volume of solution. Fill the pipette to about 3 cm above the line, then carefully drop the level down to the line.

Burette
Burettes measure different volumes and let you add the solution drop by drop.

acid

These marks down the side show the volume of acid used.

Conical flask containing alkali and indicator.

You need to get several consistent readings

- To increase the accuracy of your titration and to spot any anomalous results, you need several consistent readings.

- The first titration you do should be a rough titration to get an approximate idea of where the solution changes colour (the end-point).

- You then need to repeat the whole thing a few times, making sure you get (pretty much) the same answer each time (within 0.2 cm³).

Use Single Indicators for Titrations

1) Universal indicator is used to estimate the pH of a solution because it can turn a variety of colours. Each colour indicates a narrow range of pH values.

2) It's made from a mixture of different indicators. The colour gradually changes from red in acidic solutions to violet in alkaline solutions.

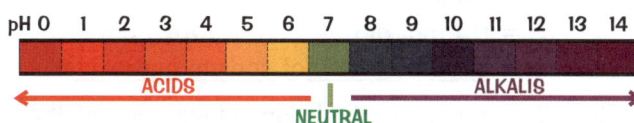

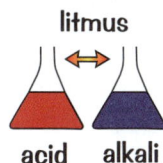

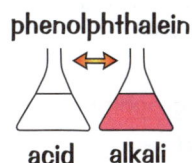

pH 0 1 2 3 4 5 6 7 8 9 10 11 12 13 14

ACIDS   NEUTRAL   ALKALIS

litmus

acid   alkali

phenolphthalein

acid   alkali

3) But during an acid-base titration you want to see a sudden colour change, at the end-point.

4) So you need to use a single indicator, such as litmus — this is blue in alkalis and red in acids.

How do you get lean molecules? Feed them titrations...

Before the end of this module, you'll be a dab hand at titrations — whether you want to be or not. They're not too tricky really — you just need to make as sure as you can that your results are accurate, which means going slowly near the end-point and then repeating the whole process.

Titrations

Yes, I know — more on titrations. Complicated stuff this.

pH Curves Show pH Against Volume of Acid or Alkali Added

When you're doing a titration, you'll get a sudden change in pH. So if you plot pH against volume of acid or alkali added, you get a funky S-shape. You need to be able to interpret these pH curves.

This pH curve shows the change in pH as an alkali is added to 25 cm³ of acid.

1) There's a very gradual increase in pH as the alkali is added.

2) At the endpoint of the titration, there's a sudden change in pH (shown by the nearly vertical line). Here, this happens when 25 cm³ has been added.

3) The volume of alkali needed to neutralise the acid in this example is 25 cm³.

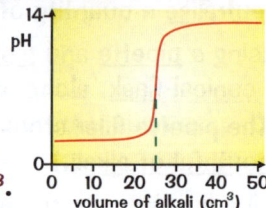

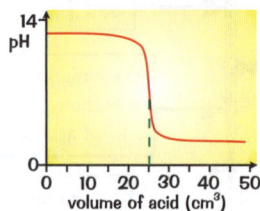

This pH curve shows the change in pH as an acid is added to 25 cm³ of alkali.

1) There's a very gradual decrease in pH as the acid is added.

2) Again, the endpoint of this titration was after 25 cm³ of acid had been added.

You Might be Asked to Calculate the Concentration

In the exam you might be given the results of a titration experiment, and asked to calculate the concentration of the acid when you know the concentration of the alkali (or vice versa).

Example: Say you start off with 25 cm³ of sodium hydroxide (NaOH) in your flask, and you know that its concentration is 0.100 moles per dm³.

You then find from your titration that it takes 49 cm³ of hydrochloric acid (whose concentration you don't know) to neutralise the sodium hydroxide.

You can work out the concentration of the acid in moles per dm³.

Step 1: Work out how many moles of the "known" substance you have:

Number of moles = concentration × volume
= 0.1 mol/dm³ × (25 ÷ 1000) dm³
= 0.0025 moles of sodium hydroxide

Step 2: Write down the balanced equation of the reaction...

$NaOH + HCl \longrightarrow NaCl + H_2O$

...and work out how many moles of the "unknown" stuff you must have had.

Using the equation, you can see that for every mole of sodium hydroxide you had...

...there was also one mole of hydrochloric acid.

So if you had 0.0025 moles of sodium hydroxide...

...you must have had 0.0025 moles of hydrochloric acid.

Step 3: Work out the concentration of the "unknown" stuff.

Concentration = number of moles ÷ volume
= 0.0025 mol ÷ (49 ÷ 1000) dm³ = 0.0510 mol/dm³

This is the same formula triangle that's on page 47.

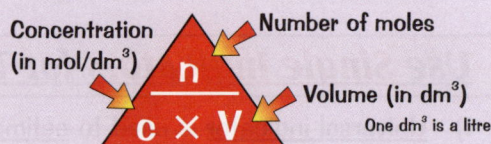

Concentration (in mol/dm³)   Number of moles

$$\frac{n}{c \times V}$$

Volume (in dm³)
One dm³ is a litre

Cover up the thing you're trying to find — then what's left is the formula you need to use.

Don't forget to put the units.

You've got to concentrate whilst doing titrations...

Answer on page 116.

Time for some practice... 25 cm³ of a 0.2 mol/dm³ solution of sulfuric acid, H_2SO_4, was used to neutralise 40 cm³ of calcium hydroxide solution, $Ca(OH)_2$. What's the concentration of calcium hydroxide?

Gas Volumes

The rate of a reaction can be measured by the amount of gas produced. But first it's got to be collected.

The Collection Method Depends on the Gas

In your experiments a conical flask is the standard apparatus to use when you're trying to collect gases produced by a reaction. But what you connect to the flask depends on what it is you're trying to collect...

① **Gas Syringe**

You can use a gas syringe to collect pretty much any gas. Gas syringes usually give volumes accurate to the nearest cm³, so they're pretty accurate. You have to be quite careful though — if the reaction is too vigorous, you can easily blow the plunger out the end of the syringe.

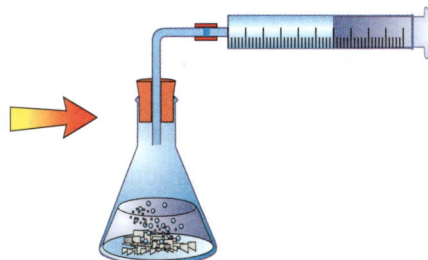

② **Upturned Measuring Cylinder or Burette**

You can use a delivery tube to bubble the gas into an upside-down measuring cylinder or gas jar filled with water.

But this method's no good for collecting things like hydrogen chloride or ammonia (because they just dissolve in the water).

You can also use an upturned burette, which is a bit more accurate — you can measure to the nearest 0.1 cm³.

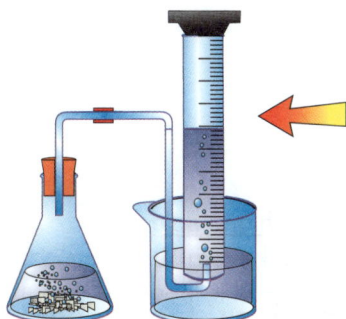

You Can Measure the Mass of Gas Produced Too

1) You can measure the mass of gas that a reaction produces by carrying out the experiment on a mass balance.

2) As the gas is released, the mass disappearing is easily measured on the balance.

3) This is the most accurate of the three methods described on this page because the mass balance is very accurate. But it has the disadvantage of releasing the gas straight into the room.

One Mole of Gas Occupies a Volume of 24 dm³

Remember dm³ is just a fancy way of writing 'litre', so 1 dm³ = 1000 cm³

Learn this fact — you're going to need it:

> One mole of any gas always occupies 24 dm³ (= 24 000 cm³) at room temperature and pressure (RTP = 25 °C and 1 atmosphere)

Example 1: What's the volume of 4.5 moles of chlorine at RTP?

Answer: 1 mole = 24 dm³, so 4.5 moles = 4.5 × 24 dm³ = 108 dm³

Volume
Moles × 24

Example 2: How many moles are there in 8280 cm³ of hydrogen gas at RTP?

Answer: Number of moles = $\frac{\text{Volume of gas}}{\text{Volume of 1 mole}}$ = $\frac{8.28}{24}$ = 0.345 moles

Don't forget to convert from cm³ to dm³.

Pity there's no laughing gas around...

Measuring the mass of gas is more accurate than measuring the volume. Some gas will always escape between starting the reaction and managing to get the bung into the conical flask. There's no way you can do it fast enough. I doubt even Superman could... well, maybe he could.

Following Reactions

If you <u>follow a reaction</u> you can work out loads of stuff — when it stopped, how fast it was, what it had for tea.

Reactions Stop When One Reactant is Used Up

When some <u>magnesium carbonate</u> ($MgCO_3$) is dropped into a beaker of <u>hydrochloric acid</u>, you can tell a <u>reaction</u> is taking place because you see lots of <u>bubbles of gas</u> being given off.

After a while, the amount of fizzing <u>slows down</u> and the reaction eventually <u>stops</u>...

1) The reaction stops when all of one of the reactants is <u>used up</u>. Any other reactants are in <u>excess</u>.

2) The reactant that's <u>used up</u> in a reaction is called the <u>limiting reactant</u>. (If the limiting reactant was the acid, you'd see unreacted $MgCO_3$ in the bottom of the flask.)

3) The amount of product formed is <u>directly proportional</u> to the amount of <u>limiting reactant</u>. For example, if you <u>halve</u> the amount of limiting reactant the volume of gas produced will also <u>halve</u>. If you <u>double</u> the amount of limiting reactant the volume of gas will <u>double</u> (as long as it is still the limiting reactant).

4) This is because if you add <u>more reactant</u> there will be <u>more reactant particles</u> to take part in the reaction, which means <u>more product particles</u>.

You've Got to be Able to Read Graphs and Tables...

In this experiment, some <u>magnesium carbonate</u> was added to a solution of <u>hydrochloric acid</u>. Any gases released were <u>collected</u> using a <u>gas syringe</u> — the <u>volume</u> was recorded every 10 s.

Time (s)	0	10	20	30	40	50	60	70	80	90
Volume of gas (cm³)	0	34	58	76	84	90	94	96	96	96

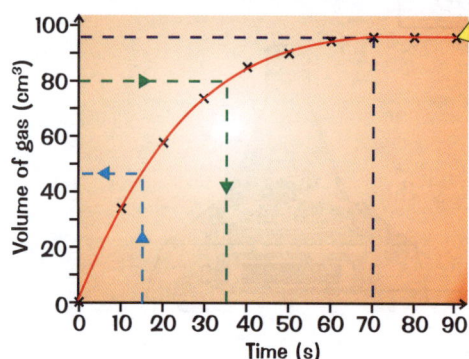

The results are on this graph.

1) The <u>total volume of gas</u> produced is 96 cm³.

2) The reaction had <u>stopped</u> after about 70 s — no more gas was produced (so the line on the graph went <u>horizontal</u>).

Examples: How much gas was produced after 15 s? **47 cm³**
How long did it take to produce 80 cm³ of gas? **35 s** Easy.

Faster Rates of Reaction are Shown by Steeper Curves

If the above reaction had been <u>quicker</u>, the graph would have been <u>steeper</u>.

You might get asked to sketch graphs like these so make sure you understand why they are different.

1) <u>Reaction 1</u> on the right represents a <u>fairly slow</u> reaction. It's not too steep.

2) <u>Reactions 1, 2 and 3</u> all produce the <u>same amount</u> of <u>product</u> (the lines go horizontal at the same height) — this shows they all have the <u>same amount</u> of <u>limiting reactant</u>. But lines 2 and 3 are <u>steeper</u>, which shows that the reactions are happening <u>more quickly</u>.

3) <u>Reaction 4</u> produces <u>more product</u> as well as going <u>faster</u>. This can <u>only</u> happen if there's <u>more</u> of the <u>limiting reactant</u>.

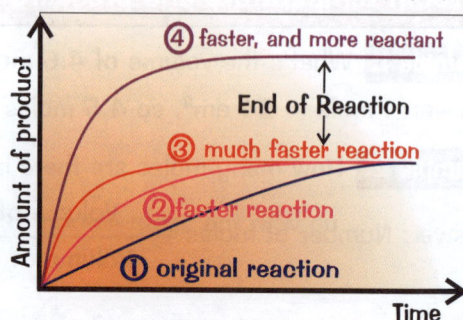

Reactions always slow down — no stamina, you see...

Reactions always go <u>fastest</u> right at the <u>beginning</u> — it's when there are the <u>highest concentrations</u> of reactants. The reactants eventually run out, or at least one of them does. Nothing ever lasts. Sigh...

Equilibrium

A <u>reversible reaction</u> is one where the <u>products</u> can react with each other and <u>convert back</u> to the original chemicals. In other words, <u>it can go both ways</u>.

> **A <u>REVERSIBLE REACTION</u> is one where the <u>PRODUCTS</u> of the reaction can <u>THEMSELVES REACT</u> to produce the <u>ORIGINAL REACTANTS</u>**
>
> A + B ⇌ C + D

The '⇌' shows the reaction goes <u>both ways</u>.

Reversible Reactions <u>Will Reach</u> Equilibrium

1) As the <u>reactants</u> (A and B) react, their concentrations <u>fall</u> — so the <u>forward reaction</u> will <u>slow down</u>. But as more and more <u>products</u> (C and D) are made and their concentrations <u>rise</u>, the <u>backward reaction</u> will <u>speed up</u>.

2) After a while the forward reaction will be going at <u>exactly the same rate</u> as the backward one — this is <u>equilibrium</u>.

3) At equilibrium <u>both</u> reactions are still <u>happening</u>, but there's <u>no overall effect</u> (it's a dynamic equilibrium). This means the <u>concentrations</u> of reactants and products have reached a balance and <u>won't change</u>.

4) Equilibrium is only reached if the reversible reaction takes place in a '<u>closed system</u>'. A <u>closed system</u> just means that none of the reactants or products can <u>escape</u>.

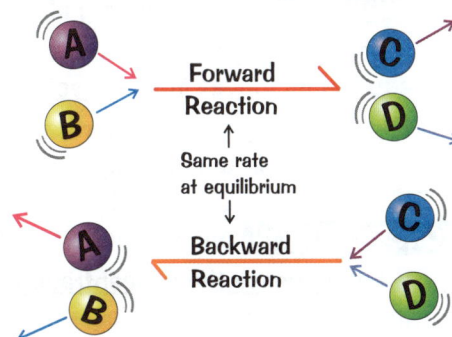

Forward Reaction

↑
Same rate at equilibrium
↓

Backward Reaction

The <u>Position of Equilibrium</u> <u>Can be on the</u> <u>Right</u> or the <u>Left</u>

When a reaction's at equilibrium it <u>doesn't</u> mean the amounts of reactants and products are <u>equal</u>.

1) Sometimes the equilibrium will <u>lie to the right</u> — this basically means "<u>lots of the products and not much of the reactants</u>" (i.e. the concentration of product is greater than the concentration of reactant).

2) Sometimes the equilibrium will <u>lie to the left</u> — this basically means "<u>lots of the reactants but not much of the products</u>" (the concentration of reactant is greater than the concentration of product).

3) The exact <u>position of equilibrium</u> depends on the <u>conditions</u> (as well as the reaction itself).

Three Things <u>Can Change the</u> <u>Position</u> of <u>Equilibrium</u>:

1) **TEMPERATURE**
2) **PRESSURE** (only affects equilibria involving gases)
3) **CONCENTRATION**

1 equilibrium, but 2 equilibria.

The next page tells you <u>why</u> these things affect the equilibrium position — for now just learn that they do. But now's a good time to make a mental note of this potential elephant trap...

> <u>Adding a CATALYST doesn't change the equilibrium position:</u>
>
> 1) Catalysts speed up <u>both</u> the <u>forward</u> and <u>backward</u> reactions by the <u>same amount</u>.
>
> 2) So, adding a catalyst means the reaction reaches equilibrium <u>quicker</u>, but you end up with the <u>same amount</u> of product as you would without the catalyst.

Dynamic equilibrium — lots of activity, but not to any great effect...*

Many important <u>industrial</u> reactions (e.g. the Haber process) are reversible. But chances are, just sticking the reactants together into a sealed box won't give a very good <u>yield</u> (i.e. not much product). So what you do is change the <u>conditions</u> — if you do it right, you get more products, and so more money. And that keeps the <u>accountants</u> happy, which, after all, is the main thing in life.

Changing Equilibrium

Now here's an interesting thing — if you change the conditions, the equilibrium will try to counteract that change. So if you decrease the temperature, the equilibrium will move to produce more heat. Sneaky.

The Equilibrium Tries to Minimise Any Changes You Make

TEMPERATURE All reactions are exothermic in one direction and endothermic in the other.

1) If you decrease the temperature, the equilibrium will move to try and increase it — the equilibrium moves in the exothermic direction to produce more heat.

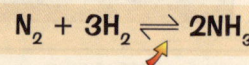

2) If you raise the temperature, the equilibrium will move to try and decrease it — the equilibrium moves in the endothermic direction.

$$N_2 + 3H_2 \rightleftharpoons 2NH_3$$

The forward reaction is exothermic — a decrease in temperature moves the equilibrium to the right (more products).

PRESSURE Changing this only affects an equilibrium involving gases.

1) If you increase the pressure, the equilibrium tries to reduce it — the equilibrium moves in the direction where there are fewer moles of gas.

2) If you decrease the pressure, the equilibrium tries to increase it — it moves in the direction where there are more moles of gas.

$$N_2 + 3H_2 \rightleftharpoons 2NH_3$$

There are 4 moles on the left, but only 2 on the right. So, if you increase the pressure, the equilibrium shifts to the right.

CONCENTRATION Same reaction again... $N_2 + 3H_2 \rightleftharpoons 2NH_3$

1) If you increase the concentration of the reactants by adding more N_2 or H_2, the equilibrium tries to decrease it by shifting to the right (making more NH_3).

2) If you increase the concentration of product by adding more NH_3, the equilibrium tries to reduce it again by shifting to the left (making more N_2 and H_2).

If you decrease the concentration of N_2, H_2 or NH_3 by removing them, the equilibrium moves to try and increase the concentration again.

Make Sure You Can Read Equilibrium Tables and Graphs

You might be asked to interpret data about equilibrium, so you'd better know what you're doing. The Haber process is a great example of all this...

$$N_2 + 3H_2 \rightleftharpoons 2NH_3$$

The forward reaction is exothermic.

First off, a table...

Pressure (atmospheres)	100	200	300	400	500
% of ammonia in reaction mixture at 450 °C	14	26	34	39	42

1) As the pressure increases, the proportion of ammonia increases (exactly what you'd expect — since increasing the pressure shifts the equilibrium to the side with fewer moles of gas — here, the right).

And now a graph...

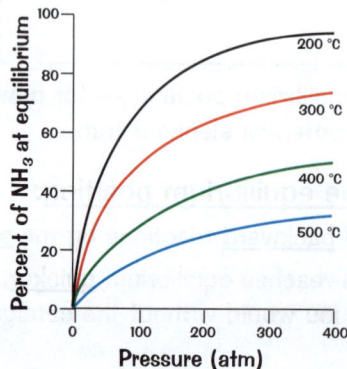

2) This time, each different line represents a different temperature.

3) As the temperature increases, the proportion of ammonia decreases (the backward reaction is endothermic, so this speeds up to try and reduce the temperature again).

4) The conditions that will give you most ammonia are high pressure and low temperature.

An equilibrium is like a particularly stubborn mule...

It's good science this stuff. You do one thing, and the reaction does the other. On the face of it, that sounds like it'd be pretty annoying, but in reality it's what gives you control of what happens. And in industry, control is what makes the whole shebang profitable. Mmmm... Money.

The Contact Process

And here's another example where getting the conditions right makes you <u>more product</u>. Whoop.

The <u>Contact Process</u> is Used to Make <u>Sulfuric Acid</u>

1) The first stage is to make <u>sulfur dioxide</u> (SO_2) — usually by burning <u>sulfur</u> in <u>air</u>.

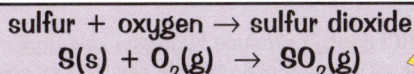

> sulfur + oxygen → sulfur dioxide
> $S(s) + O_2(g) \rightarrow SO_2(g)$

See page 58 if you don't know what the **(s)**, **(l)**, **(g)** and **(aq)** symbols mean.

This isn't the contact process I wanted to learn about...

2) The sulfur dioxide is then <u>oxidised</u> (with the help of a catalyst) to make <u>sulfur trioxide</u> (SO_3).

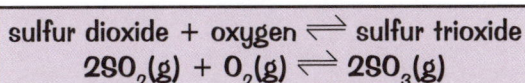

> sulfur dioxide + oxygen $\rightleftharpoons$ sulfur trioxide
> $2SO_2(g) + O_2(g) \rightleftharpoons 2SO_3(g)$

3) Next, the sulfur trioxide is used to make <u>sulfuric acid</u>.

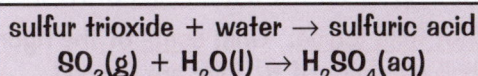

> sulfur trioxide + water → sulfuric acid
> $SO_3(g) + H_2O(l) \rightarrow H_2SO_4(aq)$

In reality, dissolving SO_3 like this doesn't work — the reaction is dangerous as a lot of heat's produced — but this is the reaction you need to <u>know</u>, so <u>learn it</u>. (In practice, you dissolve SO_3 in sulfuric acid first.)

The <u>Conditions</u> Used to Make SO₃ are <u>Carefully Chosen</u>

The reaction in step 2 is <u>reversible</u>. So, the <u>conditions</u> used can be <u>controlled</u> to get a <u>higher yield</u> (more product).

> $2SO_2 + O_2 \rightleftharpoons 2SO_3$

The forward reaction is exothermic.

TEMPERATURE

1) Oxidising sulfur dioxide to form sulfur trioxide is <u>exothermic</u> (it <u>gives out</u> heat).

2) So to get <u>more product</u> you'd think the temperature should be <u>reduced</u> (so the equilibrium will shift to the <u>right</u> to <u>replace the heat</u>).

3) Unfortunately, reducing the temperature <u>slows</u> the reaction right down — not much good.

4) So a <u>compromise</u> temperature of <u>450 °C</u> is used — to get quite a high yield quite quickly.

PRESSURE

1) There are <u>two moles</u> of <u>product</u>, compared to <u>three moles</u> of <u>reactants</u>.

2) So to get <u>more product</u>, you'd think the pressure should be <u>increased</u> (so that the equilibrium will shift to the <u>right</u> to <u>reduce the pressure</u>).

3) But increasing the pressure is <u>expensive</u>, and as the equilibrium is already on the right, it's not really <u>necessary</u>.

4) In fact, <u>atmospheric pressure</u> (1 atmosphere) is used.

CATALYST

1) To <u>increase</u> the rate of reaction a <u>vanadium pentoxide catalyst</u> (V_2O_5) is used.

2) It <u>DOESN'T</u> change the <u>position</u> of the equilibrium.

With a <u>fairly high temperature</u>, a <u>low pressure</u> and a <u>vanadium pentoxide catalyst</u>, the reaction goes <u>pretty quickly</u> and you get a <u>good yield</u> of SO_3 (about 99%).

And that's how chemistry works in real life.

The lonely hearts column — go on, start the contact process...

It's a tough one... do you <u>raise</u> the <u>temperature</u> to get a <u>faster</u> rate of reaction, or <u>reduce</u> it to get a better <u>yield</u>... In the end you <u>compromise</u> (as is so often the case in life... sigh). And that's before you even start to worry about the <u>cost</u> of raising the temperature. Decisions, decisions...

Strong and Weak Acids

Right then. Acids. Brace yourself.

Acids Produce Protons in Water

The thing about acids is that they ionise — they produce hydrogen ions, H⁺.
For example,

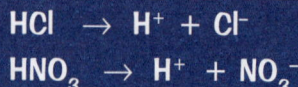

$$HCl \rightarrow H^+ + Cl^-$$
$$HNO_3 \rightarrow H^+ + NO_3^-$$

An H⁺ ion is just a proton.

But HCl doesn't produce hydrogen ions until it meets water — so hydrogen chloride gas isn't an acid.

Acids Can be Strong or Weak

1) Strong acids (e.g. sulfuric, hydrochloric and nitric) ionise completely in water. This means every hydrogen atom releases a hydrogen ion — so there are loads of H⁺ ions.

2) Weak acids (e.g. ethanoic, citric and carbonic) do not fully ionise. Only some of the hydrogen atoms in the compound release hydrogen ions — so only small numbers of H⁺ ions are formed.

   For example,

   Strong acid: $HCl \longrightarrow H^+ + Cl^-$

   Weak acid: $CH_3COOH \rightleftharpoons H^+ + CH_3COO^-$

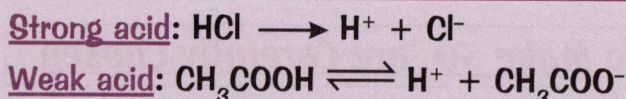

   Use a 'reversible reaction' arrow for a weak acid.

3) The ionisation of a weak acid is a reversible reaction, which sets up an equilibrium mixture. Since only a few H⁺ ions are released, the equilibrium lies well to the left.

4) The pH of an acid or alkali is a measure of the concentration of H⁺ ions in the solution. Strong acids typically have a pH of about 1 or 2, while the pH of a weak acid might be 4, 5 or 6.

5) The pH of an acid or alkali can be measured with a pH meter or with universal indicator paper (or can be estimated by seeing how fast a sample reacts with, say, magnesium).

Don't Confuse Strong Acids with Concentrated Acids

1) Acid strength (i.e. strong or weak) tells you what proportion of the acid molecules ionise in water.

2) The concentration of an acid is different. Concentration measures how many moles of acid there are in a litre (1 dm³) of water. Concentration is basically how watered down your acid is.

3) Note that concentration describes the total number of dissolved acid molecules — not the number of molecules that produce hydrogen ions.

4) The more moles of acid per dm³, the more concentrated the acid is.

5) So you can have a dilute but strong acid, or a concentrated but weak acid.

Strong Acids are Better Electrical Conductors than Weak Acids

1) Ethanoic acid has a much lower electrical conductivity than the same concentration of hydrochloric acid. It's all to do with the concentration of the ions.

2) It's the ions that carry the charge through the acid solutions as they move. So the lower concentration of ions in the weak acid means less charge can be carried. Simple.

3) Electrolysis of hydrochloric acid or ethanoic acid produces H₂ because they both produce H⁺ ions.

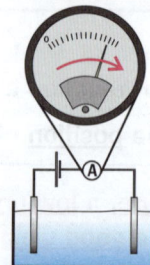

Hydrochloric acid (1 mol/dm³)   Ethanoic acid (1 mol/dm³)

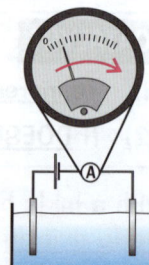

Concentration — oh so important when revising chemistry...

Acids are acidic because of H⁺ ions. And strong acids are strong because they let go of all their H⁺ ions at the drop of a hat... well, at the drop of a drop of water. This is tricky — no doubt about it, but if you can get your head round this, then you can probably cope with just about anything.

Strong and Weak Acids

Here's a nice bit of science... not the easiest thing in the book, but I like it.

Strong Acids React Faster Than Weak Acids

Strong and weak acids react with reactive metals and with carbonates in the same way.

1) Both hydrochloric acid (strong) and ethanoic acid (weak) will react with magnesium to give hydrogen.

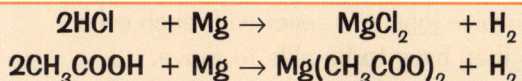

$$2HCl + Mg \rightarrow MgCl_2 + H_2$$
$$2CH_3COOH + Mg \rightarrow Mg(CH_3COO)_2 + H_2$$

And both hydrochloric acid and ethanoic acid will react with calcium carbonate to give carbon dioxide.

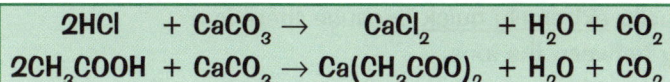

$$2HCl + CaCO_3 \rightarrow CaCl_2 + H_2O + CO_2$$
$$2CH_3COOH + CaCO_3 \rightarrow Ca(CH_3COO)_2 + H_2O + CO_2$$

2) The difference between the reactions of the two acids will be the rate of reaction. Ethanoic acid will react more slowly than hydrochloric acid of the same concentration.

3) It's all to do with the equilibrium in the weak acid reaction ($CH_3COOH \rightleftharpoons H^+ + CH_3COO^-$).

4) When you put a weak acid into water, it releases a few H^+ ions, but the concentration of H^+ ions is low compared to what you'd get with a strong acid. So when you add magnesium (or calcium carbonate), the collision frequency between the reactants is low.

5) When the H^+ ions react the concentration of H^+ ions decreases, so the equilibrium shifts to compensate — meaning a few more H^+ ions are released. These ions then react, so the equilibrium shifts... and so on. As more ions are removed, more are supplied — kind of a drip-feed arrangement.

6) This is completely different to what you get with a strong acid, where all of the acid molecules are ionised and loads of H^+ ions are just sitting there ready and waiting to go. So when you add magnesium (or calcium carbonate), the collision frequency between the reactants is really high.

The Volume of Gas Produced Depends Upon the Amount of Acid

1) Hydrochloric acid (strong) will react faster than ethanoic acid (weak), but the amount of product you get will be the same (if you start with the same amount and they're the same concentration, etc.).

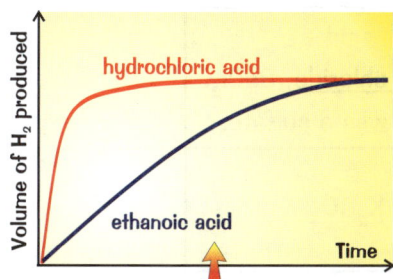

Hydrochloric acid reacts faster (steeper curve), but both reactions give the same amount of hydrogen.

2) This is because if the concentrations are the same, the number of molecules in a litre (say) of water will be the same.

3) And each of these molecules can let go of one H^+ ion.

$$HCl \longrightarrow H^+ + Cl^-, \text{ and } CH_3COOH \rightleftharpoons H^+ + CH_3COO^-$$

It's just that hydrochloric acid has let go of them all at once, whereas ethanoic acid lets them go gradually.

4) But since the total number of H^+ ions available is the same, the volume of gaseous product will be the same (it's the H^+ ions that are the important bits in acid reactions).

Jumping jack flash, HCl makes gas...

Hydrochloric acid is nasty stuff. It's corrosive and irritating, damages almost everything it touches and will burn skin. Yet we have it in our stomachs. Luckily we have a thick layer of mucus to protect our stomach walls.

Precipitation Reactions

Precipitates don't dissolve, remember...

Precipitation Reactions Make an Insoluble Substance

1) Precipitation reactions normally involve two solutions reacting together to make an insoluble substance.
2) The insoluble substance is called the precipitate, and it makes the solution turn cloudy.
3) Most precipitation reactions involve ions. To react with each other, these ions need to collide, so they have to be able to move.
4) This means the ionic substances have to be in solution or molten as the ions in solid ionic substances can't move.
5) These reactions are usually extremely quick because there is a high collision frequency between the ions.

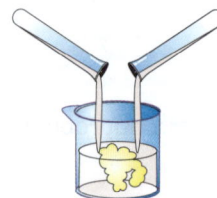

Ionic Equations Show Just the Useful Bits of Reactions

Look at this precipitation reaction...

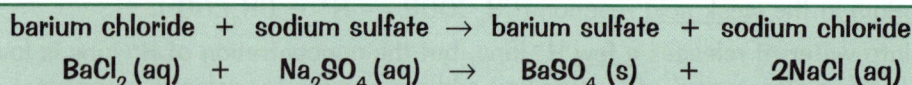

| barium chloride + sodium sulfate → barium sulfate + sodium chloride |
| $BaCl_2$ (aq) + Na_2SO_4 (aq) → $BaSO_4$ (s) + 2NaCl (aq) |

The (aq) and the (s) are state symbols — make sure you know them.
(s) = solid,
(l) = liquid,
(g) = gas,
(aq) = aqueous (dissolved in water)

1) You can tell it's a precipitation reaction because you start off with two solutions (look at the state symbols — they're both 'aq'), but you end up with a solid. This solid is the precipitate — it'll turn the water cloudy.
2) The 'interesting' bit of this reaction is the bit involving the barium and the sulfate ions — it's these that form the precipitate.
3) The sodium and chloride ions were dissolved in solution before the reaction, and they're still dissolved afterwards. They're called spectator ions because they don't change during the reaction.
4) An ionic equation concentrates on the interesting bits of a reaction, and ignores the spectator ions. So the ionic equation for this equation would be:

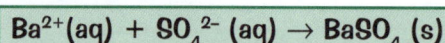

$$Ba^{2+}(aq) + SO_4^{2-} (aq) \rightarrow BaSO_4 (s)$$

Test for Sulfates (SO_4^{2-}) and Halides (Cl^-, Br^-, I^-)

You can use precipitation reactions to try and identify mystery substances. The colour of any precipitate can help you decide what ions are present.

Test for Sulfate ions, (SO_4^{2-})

1) To test for a sulfate ion, SO_4^{2-}, add dilute HCl, followed by barium chloride, $BaCl_2$.
2) A white precipitate of barium sulfate means the original compound was a sulfate.

$$Ba^{2+}(aq) + SO_4^{2-}(aq) \longrightarrow BaSO_4(s)$$

3) For example, adding HCl and barium chloride to potassium sulfate, K_2SO_4, or magnesium sulfate, $MgSO_4$, will produce a white precipitate.

Test for Chloride (Cl^-), Bromide (Br^-) or Iodide (I^-) ions

To test for chloride, bromide or iodide ions, add dilute nitric acid, HNO_3, followed by lead nitrate, $Pb(NO_3)_2$.

A chloride gives a white precipitate of lead chloride. $Pb^{2+}(aq) + 2Cl^-(aq) \longrightarrow PbCl_2(s)$

A bromide gives a cream precipitate of lead bromide. $Pb^{2+}(aq) + 2Br^-(aq) \longrightarrow PbBr_2(s)$

An iodide gives a yellow precipitate of lead iodide. $Pb^{2+}(aq) + 2I^-(aq) \longrightarrow PbI_2(s)$

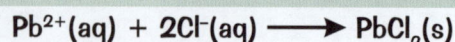

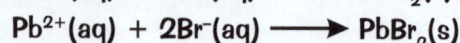

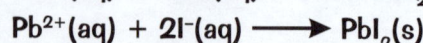

If you aren't part of the solution, you're part of the precipitate...

Think of an ionic equation as a bit like Match of the Day — just an edited highlights package.

Preparing Insoluble Salts

You can use precipitation reactions to make insoluble salts.
You just need to pick the right reactants, then mix them together.

Pick the Right Reactants...

1) To make an insoluble salt you need some ions — e.g. to make lead iodide (PbI_2), you need some lead ions and some iodide ions. And these ions need to be in solution, so they can move about.

2) Fortunately, nitrates are soluble — so if you use a solution of lead nitrate ($Pb(NO_3)_2$), you have your supply of lead ions. You can get your iodide ions from, say, potassium iodide (KI).

3) Mix your ingredients together, and voilà — you have yourself an insoluble salt. Here's the reaction.

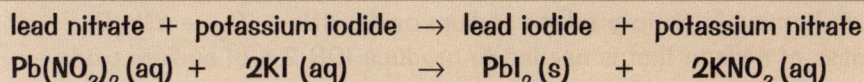

lead nitrate + potassium iodide → lead iodide + potassium nitrate

$$Pb(NO_3)_2\,(aq) + 2KI\,(aq) \rightarrow PbI_2\,(s) + 2KNO_3\,(aq)$$

Or even...

$$Pb^{2+}\,(aq) + 2I^-\,(aq) \rightarrow PbI_2\,(s)$$

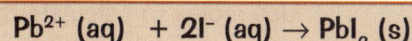

4) If this is all you do, your salt will be wet, and mixed in with other stuff. The method below will help you avoid that...

...Then Precipitate, Filter and Dry

Stage 1

1) Add 1 spatula of lead nitrate to a test tube, and fill it with distilled water. Shake it thoroughly to ensure that all the lead nitrate has dissolved. Then do the same with 1 spatula of potassium iodide. (Use distilled water to make sure there are no other ions about.)

2) Tip the two solutions into a small beaker, and give it a good stir to make sure it's all mixed together. The salt should precipitate out.

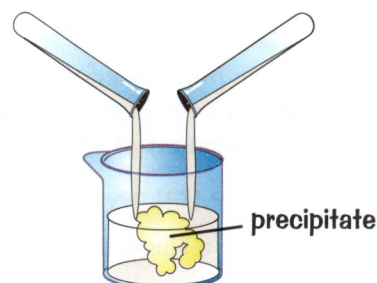

precipitate

Stage 2

filter paper

filter funnel

1) Put a folded piece of filter paper into a filter funnel, and stick the funnel into a conical flask.

2) Pour the contents of the beaker into the middle of the filter paper. (Make sure that the solution doesn't go above the filter paper — otherwise some of the solid could dribble down the side.)

3) Swill out the beaker with more distilled water, and tip this into the filter paper — to make sure you get all the product from the beaker.

Stage 3

1) Rinse the contents of the filter paper with distilled water to make sure that all the soluble salts have been washed away.

2) Then just scrape the lead iodide on to some fresh filter paper and leave it to dry.

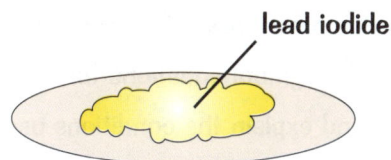

lead iodide

Get two solutions, mix 'em together — job's a good 'un...

Well, wouldn't you know — precipitation reactions can be used for all sorts of things. Testing for ions in solutions, making insoluble salts, and urmm... demonstrating the absolute wonderness of ionic equations. Ah-hem. Never mind. You've gotta learn about them anyway...

Revision Summary for Module C5

Ah, revision summaries... my favourite part of the section. And yours no doubt, since they're always at the end. There are lots of calculations in this section, but that's good (honest), because you can expect a fair few in the exam as well. And as a wise man once said... it's best to practise before the exam, because once you're in there, it's a bit late really. So get your calculator fired up, and away you go...

1) What is the formula relating moles, mass and M_r?

2)* How many moles are there in 284 g of sodium sulfate, Na_2SO_4?

3)* What mass of chlorine is there in 2 moles of magnesium chloride, $MgCl_2$?

4) Give the definition of the relative atomic mass of an element.

5)* Here's the equation for sodium burning in air to produce sodium oxide: $4Na + O_2 \rightarrow 2Na_2O$. Use moles to calculate the mass of sodium that is needed to produce 108.2 g of sodium oxide.

6)* What is an empirical formula? Find the empirical formula of the compound formed when 21.9 g of magnesium, 29.3 g of sulfur and 58.3 g of oxygen react.

7)* Calculate the concentration of the solution in g/dm^3 formed when 7.5 g of calcium hydroxide, $Ca(OH)_2$, is dissolved in: a) 1 dm^3 of water, b) 2 dm^3 of water.

8)* How many moles of barium chloride are in 500 cm^3 of a 0.2 molar solution of barium chloride?

9)* How would you produce 250 cm^3 of a 0.2 mol/dm^3 solution of sulfuric acid if you were given a 1.0 mol/dm^3 solution of sulfuric acid, and water?

10) This nutritional information table was found on an orange juice carton: Angela says that one glass will give her 42% of the guideline daily amount of vitamin C. Why might she be wrong?

NUTRITIONAL INFORMATION	
Typical values for 100 ml	
Energy	197 kJ
	46 kcal
Carbohydrate	10.4 g
Vitamin C	25 mg (42% GDA)

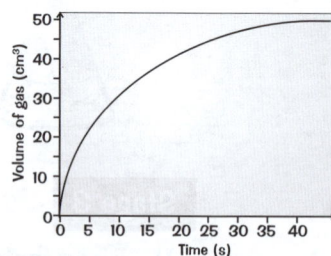

11) Why do you need to get several consistent readings in titrations?

12) Why is a single indicator like phenolphthalein used in titrations?

13) Sketch a pH curve for the titration where hydrochloric acid is added to sodium hydroxide.

14)* In a titration, 22.5 cm^3 of nitric acid was required to neutralise 25 cm^3 of potassium hydroxide with a concentration of 0.15 moles per dm^3. Calculate the concentration of the nitric acid in: a) mol/dm^3, b) g/dm^3.

15) Name 3 methods used for measuring the amount of gas produced in a reaction. Give their advantages.

16) What volume does one mole of gas take up at room temperature and pressure?

17) What is the limiting reactant in a reaction?

18)* The graph shows the volume of hydrogen produced when magnesium metal was placed into a hydrochloric acid solution.
a) How much hydrogen had evolved at the end of the reaction?
b) How long did it take to produce 35 cm^3 of hydrogen?

19) What is a reversible reaction? Explain why it could reach an equilibrium.

20) Describe how three different factors affect the position of equilibrium.

21) Write the symbol equations for the three reactions in the Contact Process.

22) State and explain the conditions used in the Contact Process.

23) What is the difference between the strength of an acid and its concentration?

24) Explain why weak acids react slower than strong acids.

25) What is the ionic equation for the reaction between lead nitrate and sodium bromide?

26) How would you test for: a) a sulfate, b) a halide?

27) Describe how you would obtain a dry sample of lead chloride from lead nitrate and calcium chloride.

* Answers on page 116.

Redox Reactions

In chemistry, things get oxidised and reduced all the time. And you need to learn about it.

If Electrons are Transferred, It's a Redox Reaction

1) Oxidation can mean the addition of oxygen (or a reaction with it), and reduction can be the removal of oxygen, but on this page we're looking at oxidation and reduction in terms of electrons.

2) A loss of electrons is called oxidation. A gain of electrons is called reduction.

3) REDuction and OXidation happen at the same time — hence the term "REDOX".

4) An oxidising agent accepts electrons and gets reduced.

5) A reducing agent donates electrons and gets oxidised.

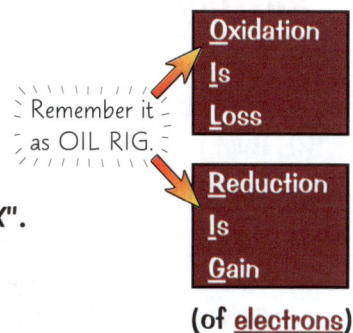

Remember it as OIL RIG.

Oxidation Is Loss

Reduction Is Gain

(of electrons)

Some Examples of Redox Reactions:

1) Chlorine gas is passed into a solution of an iron(II) salt. The solution turns from green to yellow as the iron(II) ion is oxidised to iron(III). The Fe^{2+} ion loses an electron to form Fe^{3+}.

$$Fe^{2+} - e^- \rightarrow Fe^{3+}$$

2) The chlorine causes this to happen — it's the oxidising agent.

$$\tfrac{1}{2}Cl_2 + e^- \rightarrow Cl^-$$

3) The chlorine must've gained the electron that the Fe^{2+} lost. The chlorine's been reduced. The iron(II) ion must be the reducing agent.

1) Iron atoms are oxidised to iron(II) ions when they react with dilute acid.

$$Fe - 2e^- \rightarrow Fe^{2+}$$

2) The iron atoms lose electrons. They're oxidised by the hydrogen ions.

3) The hydrogen ions gain electrons. They're reduced by the iron atoms.

$$2H^+ + 2e^- \rightarrow H_2$$

Displacement Reactions are Redox Reactions

1) Displacement reactions involve one metal kicking another one out of a compound. Learn this rule:

A MORE REACTIVE metal will displace a LESS REACTIVE metal from its compound.

2) If you put a reactive metal into the solution of a dissolved metal compound, the reactive metal will replace the less reactive metal in the compound.

Example: Put iron in a solution of tin(II) sulfate and the more reactive iron will "kick out" the less reactive tin from the solution. You end up with iron(II) sulfate solution and tin metal.

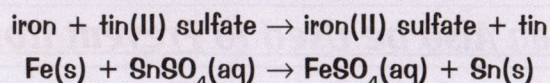

		reactivity ↑
MAGNESIUM	Mg	
ZINC	Zn	
IRON	Fe	
TIN	Sn	

iron + tin(II) sulfate → iron(II) sulfate + tin

$$Fe(s) + SnSO_4(aq) \rightarrow FeSO_4(aq) + Sn(s)$$

In this reaction the iron loses 2 electrons to become a 2+ ion — it's oxidised.

The tin ion gains these 2 electrons to become a tin atom — it's reduced.

$$Fe + SO_4{}^{2-} \rightarrow FeSO_4 + 2e^-$$

$$Sn^{2+} + 2e^- \rightarrow Sn$$

3) In displacement reactions it's always the metal ion that gains electrons and is reduced. The metal atom always loses electrons and is oxidised.

4) In the exam you could be asked to write word or symbol equations to show displacement reactions. You could also be asked to predict whether or not a displacement reaction will happen. All you have to remember is that more reactive metals displace less reactive ones and you'll be fine and dandy.

REDOX — great for bubble baths. Oh no, wait...

Try writing some displacement reaction equations now — write the equation for the reaction between zinc and iron chloride ($FeCl_2$). What's being oxidised? What's being reduced? You need to practise till you can do it in your sleep.

Rusting of Iron

Rusting is a <u>favourite topic</u> of examiners everywhere...

Rusting of Iron is a Redox Reaction

1) Iron and some steels will <u>rust</u> if they come into contact with air and water.
Rusting only happens when the iron's in contact with <u>both oxygen</u> (from the air) and <u>water</u>.

2) Rust is a form of <u>hydrated iron(III) oxide</u>.

3) Learn the <u>equation for rust</u>: ⟹ iron + oxygen + water → hydrated iron(III) oxide

4) Rusting of iron is a <u>redox reaction</u>.

5) This is why. <u>Iron loses electrons</u> when it reacts with oxygen.
Each Fe atom <u>loses three electrons</u> to become Fe^{3+}. Iron's <u>oxidised</u>.

6) <u>Oxygen gains electrons</u> when it reacts with iron.
Each O atom <u>gains two electrons</u> to become O^{2-}. Oxygen's <u>reduced</u>.

Remember <u>OIL RIG</u>.

Metals are Combined with Other Things to Prevent Rust

1) Iron can be prevented from rusting by mixing it with <u>other metals</u> to make alloys.

2) <u>Steels</u> are alloys of iron with <u>carbon</u> and small quantities of other metals.

3) One of the most common steels is <u>stainless steel</u> — a rustproof alloy of iron, carbon and <u>chromium</u>.

Oil, Grease and Paint Prevent Rusting

You can <u>prevent rusting</u> by coating the iron with a <u>barrier</u>. This <u>keeps out the water</u>, <u>oxygen</u> or <u>both</u>.

1) <u>Painting</u> is ideal for large and small structures. It can also be nice and <u>colourful</u>.

2) <u>Oiling</u> or <u>greasing</u> has to be used when <u>moving parts</u> are involved, like on <u>bike chains</u>.

A Coat of Tin Can Protect Steel from Rust

1) <u>Tin plating</u> is where a coat of tin is applied to the object, e.g. food cans.

2) The tin acts as a <u>barrier</u>, stopping water and oxygen in the air from reaching the <u>surface</u> of the iron.

3) This only works as long as the <u>tin remains intact</u>. If the tin is <u>scratched</u> to reveal some iron, the <u>iron will lose electrons</u> in <u>preference</u> to the tin and the iron will rust even faster than if it was on its own.

4) That's why it's <u>not</u> always a good idea to buy the <u>reduced bashed tins</u> of food at the supermarket. They could be starting to <u>rust</u>.

More Reactive Metals Can Also be Used to Prevent Iron Rusting

You can also prevent rusting using the <u>sacrificial</u> method. You place a <u>more reactive metal</u> with the iron. The water and oxygen then react with this "sacrificial" metal instead of with the iron.

1) <u>Galvanising</u> is where a coat of <u>zinc</u> is put onto the object. The zinc acts as sacrificial protection — it's <u>more reactive</u> than iron so it'll <u>lose electrons in preference</u> to iron. The zinc also acts as a barrier. Steel <u>buckets</u> and <u>corrugated iron roofing</u> are often galvanised.

2) Blocks of metal, e.g. <u>magnesium</u>, can be bolted to the iron. Magnesium will <u>lose electrons in preference to iron</u>. It's used on the hulls of <u>ships</u>, or on <u>underground iron pipes</u>.

Galvanising protects the metal underneath even when the zinc gets scratched.

<u>Don't get confused</u> about sacrificial protection — it's <u>not a displacement reaction</u>. There isn't a metal reacting with a metal salt — oxygen's reacting with a more reactive metal instead of a less reactive one.

Alloy there Jim Lad...

<u>Rust</u> is one of those really annoying things. It eats your bike, your car, your ship... but then doesn't touch that lovely woolly cardigan that your gran gave you. On the plus side though, you can use it to dye your clothes, just place a rusty object on the fabric, add a splash of vinegar, and voilà — a beautiful orange stain. Marvellous.

Electrolysis

It's time for some underlined electrolysis now. You've got to be able to predict the products of electrolysis using aqueous electrolytes. Well, what are you waiting for — crack on...

Electrolysis Means "Splitting Up with Electricity"

1) Electrolysis is the breaking down of a substance using electricity.
2) An electric current is passed through a molten or dissolved ionic compound, causing it to decompose.
3) This creates a flow of charge through the electrolyte.
4) The positive ions in the solution will move towards the cathode (-ve electrode) and gain electrons.
5) The negative ions in the solution will move towards the anode (+ve electrode) and lose electrons.
6) As ions gain or lose electrons they become atoms or molecules and are discharged from the solution at the electrodes.

It May be Easier to Discharge Ions from Water than the Solute

1) In aqueous solutions, as well as the ions from the solute (the ionic compound), there are hydrogen ions (H^+) and hydroxide ions (OH^-) from the water.
2) Sometimes, it's easier to discharge the ions from the water instead of the ones from the solute.
3) This means hydrogen could be produced at the cathode, and oxygen at the anode.

A solution of aqueous sulfuric acid (H_2SO_4) contains three different ions: SO_4^{2-}, H^+ and OH^-.

- Hydrogen ions (from the water or sulfuric acid) can accept the electrons (from the cathode). So at the cathode, hydrogen gas is produced.

$$2H^+ + 2e^- \rightarrow H_2$$

- Hydroxide ions (from water) can lose electrons more easily than sulfate ions. So at the anode oxygen is produced.

$$4OH^- - 4e^- \rightarrow O_2 + 2H_2O$$

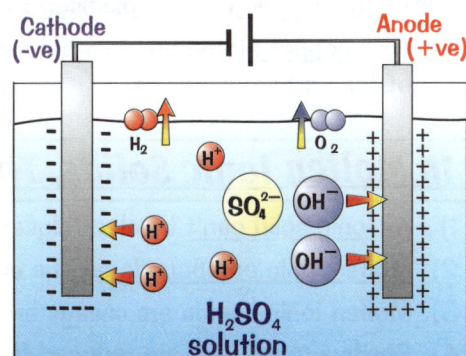

A solution of aqueous sodium hydroxide (NaOH) contains three different ions: Na^+, OH^- and H^+.

- Hydrogen ions (from the water) can accept the electrons (from the cathode) more easily than the sodium ions. So at the cathode, hydrogen gas is produced.

$$2H^+ + 2e^- \rightarrow H_2$$

- Hydroxide ions (from water or sodium hydroxide) can lose electrons (to the anode). So at the anode oxygen is produced.

$$4OH^- - 4e^- \rightarrow O_2 + 2H_2O$$

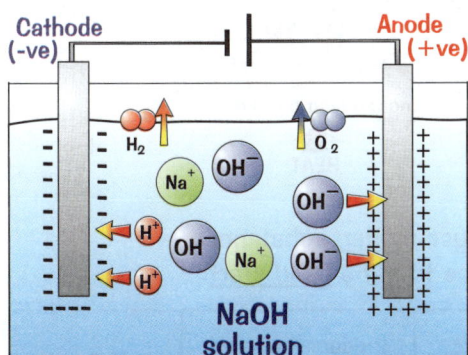

4) The electrolysis of H_2SO_4 and NaOH are both redox reactions — reduction takes place at the cathode and oxidation takes place at the anode.

Everyone needs good electrons...

The hardest bit's over now. Remember that with aqueous solutions, there are ions from the dissolved substance and from the water. With H_2SO_4 and NaOH, you get hydrogen and oxygen because it's easier to use the ions from the water than the ones from the solute — just remember that and you'll be fine.

Electrolysis

Just one more example of an aqueous electrolyte then we'll move swiftly on to molten electrolytes. Oh goody.

Copper(II) Sulfate Can be Electrolysed to Form Copper and Oxygen

Here's what happens during the electrolysis of copper(II) sulfate solution when you use carbon electrodes.

The cathode (-ve electrode) starts as a piece of carbon and gets coated with a layer of copper.

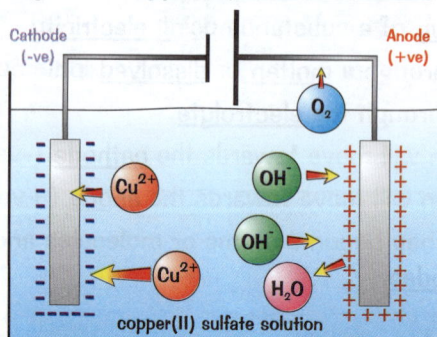

Cathode (-ve)   Anode (+ve)

O_2

Cu^{2+} OH$^-$

Cu^{2+} OH$^-$

H_2O

copper(II) sulfate solution

The hydroxide ions are discharged from the solution and converted to oxygen and water at the anode (+ve electrode).

The reaction at the cathode is:
$Cu^{2+} + 2e^- \rightarrow Cu$

The reaction at the anode is:
$4OH^- - 4e^- \rightarrow O_2 + 2H_2O$

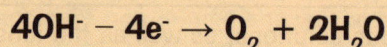

1) The copper ions (Cu^{2+}) are easier to discharge from the solution than the H$^+$ ions.

2) So they are attracted to the negative cathode and are reduced to copper atoms (instead of H$^+$ ions being reduced to H_2).

3) The hydroxide ions are oxidised to oxygen and water at the anode.

4) Pure copper atoms bond to the cathode and form a thin layer of copper over the surface of the carbon electrode.

In Molten Ionic Solids, There's Only One Source of Ions

1) An ionic solid can't be electrolysed because the ions are in fixed positions and can't move.

2) Molten ionic compounds can be electrolysed because the ions can move freely and conduct electricity.

3) Molten ionic liquids are always broken up into their elements.

4) Positive metal ions are reduced (i.e. they gain electrons) to atoms at the cathode:

$$Pb^{2+} + 2e^- \rightarrow Pb$$

5) Negative ions are oxidised (i.e. they lose electrons) to atoms at the anode:

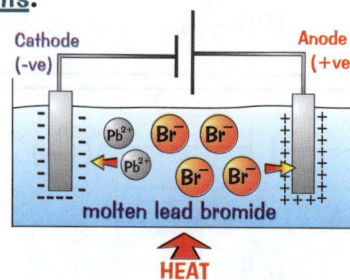

$$2Br^- \rightarrow Br_2 + 2e^-$$

Cathode (-ve)   Anode (+ve)

Pb^{2+} Br$^-$ Br$^-$

Pb^{2+} Br$^-$ Br$^-$

molten lead bromide

HEAT

You can melt lead bromide using a Bunsen burner.

6) It's easy to predict what products you get when you electrolyse molten substances — it's getting the half-equations right that's difficult. Learn these to get a head start:

Molten Electrolyte	Product Produced at Cathode	Half-Equation at Cathode	Product Produced at Anode	Half-Equation at Anode
lead iodide, PbI_2	lead	$Pb^{2+} + 2e^- \rightarrow Pb$	iodine	$2I^- \rightarrow I_2 + 2e^-$
potassium chloride, KCl	potassium	$K^+ + e^- \rightarrow K$	chlorine	$2Cl^- \rightarrow Cl_2 + 2e^-$
aluminium oxide, Al_2O_3	aluminium	$Al^{3+} + 3e^- \rightarrow Al$	oxygen	$2O^{2-} \rightarrow O_2 + 4e^-$

Which element does a robber fear most? Copper...

There's an awful lot on this page and the best way to learn it is to cover, scribble, check. You know it works.

Electrolysis

Here come the calculations. Run... while you still can...

Number of Electrons Transferred Increases with Time and Current

1) The amount of product made during electrolysis depends on the number of electrons that are transferred.

2) If you increase the number of electrons, you increase the amount of substance produced.

> This can be achieved by: • electrolysing for a longer time.
> • increasing the current.

Amount of Product is Proportional to Time and Current

1) Current is a flow of charge, and it's charge that determines how much product is formed during electrolysis. More charge means more product.

2) Generally, the amount of charge (Q, measured in coulombs) flowing through a circuit is equal to the current (I) multiplied by the time in seconds (t): $Q = It$

3) This means that the charge and therefore the amount of product created during electrolysis are directly proportional to the time taken and the current used.

You Can Use Q = It to Work Out the Amount of Product Formed

Example 1: In an electrolysis experiment, a current of 2.0 A is passed through the electrolyte for 40 seconds. Calculate the amount of charge flowing through the circuit.

Method: This one's simple, you just have to use the equation $Q = It$.

$Q = I \times t = 2.0\,A \times 40$ seconds = __80.0 coulombs__. Simple. Now lets try a more tricky one...

Example 2: Dorothy is conducting an electrolysis experiment using aqueous tin(II) chloride ($SnCl_2$). She collects the chlorine from the reaction in a test tube held above the anode and measures the time taken to fill the test tube. She runs three different experiments changing the current used each time. Her results are shown below.

Experiment	Current in amps	Time taken to fill test tube in seconds
A	0.5	100
B	1	50
C	2	?

Use the information in the table to work out the time taken
for the test tube to fill up with chlorine in experiment C.

Method: First, work out the charge using $Q = It$ and the data from experiment A.

$Q = It = 0.5 \times 100 = 50$ coulombs.

Then use this value to work out the time taken in experiment C.
You just have to rearrange the equation so you can find t.

$t = Q \div I = 50 \div 2 = \underline{25\ seconds}$.

> You'll get the same answer if you use the data from experiment B.

If you can remember that the time is inversely proportional to the current you can skip a few steps of the calculation. From experiment A to experiment C the current has increased by a factor of 4. If they're inversely proportional this means that the time will have to decrease by a factor of 4. $100 \div 4 = \underline{25\ seconds}$. Job done.

The more time you spend on this page, the more you'll learn...

This stuff isn't easy — in fact it's devilishly complicated. So take your time over it. Read it through once. If you don't get it, read it through again. If you still don't get it, have a cup of tea before reading it again. That should help.

Fuel Cells

Fuel cells are great — they use hydrogen and oxygen to make electricity.

Hydrogen and Oxygen Give Out Energy When They React

1) <u>Hydrogen and oxygen react</u> to produce <u>water</u>.

2) The reaction between hydrogen and oxygen is <u>exothermic</u> — it <u>releases energy</u>.

3) You can show this on an <u>energy level diagram</u>.

4) The higher a line is on the diagram the <u>more energy</u> the substances have. For example the H_2 and O_2 molecules have a higher energy than the H_2O molecules.

5) When the new bonds are formed the <u>excess energy</u> is given out in the form of heat.

6) You could be asked to interpret energy level diagrams for <u>other reactions</u> too. For example:

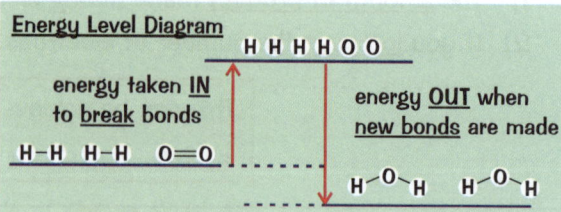

<u>Question</u>: Explain what happens to the <u>temperature</u> of the reaction mixture during the reaction shown by the diagram on the right.

<u>Answer</u>: The energy level of the products is higher than the reactants, so the reaction is <u>endothermic</u> and it'll get <u>colder</u>.

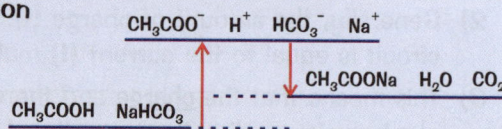

Energy Level Diagram

H H H H O O

energy taken <u>IN</u> to <u>break</u> bonds

H—H H—H O=O

energy <u>OUT</u> when <u>new bonds</u> are made

H—O—H   H—O—H

CH_3COO^- H^+ HCO_3^- Na^+

CH_3COONa H_2O CO_2

CH_3COOH $NaHCO_3$

Fuel Cells Use Fuel and Oxygen to Produce Electrical Energy

1) A <u>fuel cell</u> is an electrical cell that's supplied with a <u>fuel</u> and <u>oxygen</u> and uses <u>energy</u> from the reaction between them to produce electrical energy <u>efficiently</u>.

2) There are a few <u>different types</u> of fuel cells, using different fuels and different electrolytes. The one they want you to know about is the <u>hydrogen-oxygen fuel cell</u>.

3) This fuel cell combines hydrogen and oxygen to produce heat <u>energy</u> and nice clean <u>water</u>. That means there are no nasty pollutants to worry about.

Hydrogen-Oxygen Fuel Cells Involve a Redox Reaction

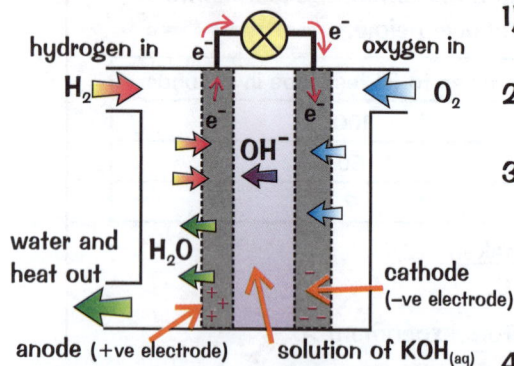

hydrogen in e^- e^- oxygen in

H_2 OH$^-$ O_2

e^- e^-

water and heat out H_2O

anode (+ve electrode)   cathode (−ve electrode)

solution of KOH$_{(aq)}$

1) The electrolyte is often a solution of <u>potassium hydroxide</u>. The electrodes are often porous carbon with a catalyst.

2) <u>Hydrogen</u> goes into the <u>anode compartment</u> and <u>oxygen</u> goes into the <u>cathode compartment</u>.

3) At the −ve <u>cathode</u>, oxygen gains electrons (from the cathode) and reacts with <u>water</u> (from the electrolyte) to make OH$^-$ ions.

$$O_2 + 4e^- + 2H_2O \rightarrow 4OH^-$$

The oxygen gas is <u>gaining electrons</u> — this is <u>reduction</u>.

4) <u>OH$^-$</u> ions in the electrolyte move to the <u>anode</u> (+ve).

5) At the +ve <u>anode</u>, hydrogen combines with the hydroxide ions to produce <u>water</u> and <u>electrons</u>. The hydrogen gas <u>loses electrons</u>. This is <u>oxidation</u>.

$$2H_2 + 4OH^- \rightarrow 4H_2O + 4e^-$$

6) The electrons <u>flow</u> through an external circuit from the <u>anode</u> to the <u>cathode</u> — this is the electric <u>current</u>.

7) The overall reaction is <u>hydrogen plus oxygen</u>, which gives <u>water</u>.

hydrogen + oxygen → water
$$2H_2 + O_2 \rightarrow 2H_2O$$

There's <u>reduction</u> at the cathode and <u>oxidation</u> at the anode, so the whole thing is a <u>REDOX</u> reaction.

They can ask you for this equation in the exam — luckily it's a nice simple one.

Fuel cells — they're simply electrifying...

This page is <u>tough stuff</u>. I'm afraid you'll have to <u>learn it</u> — yes, <u>even</u> the nasty fuel cell diagram and equations.

Fuel Cells

They can ask you about the <u>real-world applications</u> of fuel cells. <u>Spacecraft</u> and (one day soon maybe) <u>cars</u> are the main ones. You'll probably need to describe a few <u>advantages</u> and <u>disadvantages</u> of fuel cells too.

Hydrogen-Oxygen Fuel Cells Have Lots of Advantages...

1) Hydrogen fuel cells are <u>great</u> — they're <u>much more efficient</u> than <u>power stations</u> or <u>batteries</u> at producing electricity. If you use the heat produced as well, their efficiency can be greater than <u>80%</u>.

2) In a <u>fuel cell</u>, the electricity is generated <u>directly</u> from the <u>reaction</u> — it has a direct energy transfer (so no turbines, generators, etc.).

3) Because there aren't a lot of <u>stages</u> to the process of generating electricity there are <u>fewer places</u> for energy to be <u>lost as heat</u>.

4) Unlike a car engine or a fossil fuel burning power station, there are <u>no moving parts</u>, so energy isn't lost through friction.

5) With <u>hydrogen</u> as the fuel, the only product is <u>water</u>. There's <u>no pollution</u>.

...But also Lots of Disadvantages

1) Hydrogen fuel cells may sound fantastic but it's not all sunshine and lollipops...

2) Producing the <u>hydrogen</u> needed to power the fuel cell requires a lot of <u>energy</u>. This energy may have come from burning non-renewable <u>fossil fuels</u> — which causes <u>pollution</u>.

3) Hydrogen fuel cells often contain <u>poisonous catalysts</u> which eventually have to be disposed of. Getting rid of the catalysts takes a lot of <u>time</u> and <u>money</u> and may cause <u>environmental problems</u>.

Hydrogen-Oxygen Fuel Cells are Used in Spacecraft

1) <u>Hydrogen fuel cells</u> are used to provide electrical power in <u>spacecraft</u>.

2) Hydrogen and oxygen are <u>readily available</u> from the spacecraft <u>rocket fuel tanks</u> (the reaction between hydrogen and oxygen is used to fuel the spacecraft's rockets).

3) The fuel cells are <u>lightweight</u> and <u>compact</u> so they don't take up valuable room.

4) They also don't have any <u>moving parts</u> that could go wrong.

5) Some of the product of the reaction (water) is used as <u>drinking water</u> — which saves the astronauts having to take gallons of drinking water with them.

6) There are <u>no other waste products</u> or pollutants to get rid of.

The Car Industry is Developing Fuel Cells

1) The car industry is developing <u>fuel cells</u> to replace conventional petrol/diesel engines.

2) Fuel cell vehicles don't produce any conventional pollutants — no <u>carbon dioxide</u>, no <u>nitrogen oxides</u>, no <u>sulfur dioxide</u>, no <u>carbon monoxide</u>. The only by-products are <u>water</u> and <u>heat</u>. This would be a major advantage in <u>cities</u>, where air pollution from traffic is a big problem.

3) As hydrogen can be obtained by <u>decomposing water</u> (see page 65) there is a <u>large amount available</u> for use as a fuel. This is a big advantage over using <u>non-renewable</u> fossil fuels like <u>petrol</u>.

Could we all be filling up our cars with hydrogen one day...

These fuel cells sound great — but you have to <u>think</u>. Once you've got the hydrogen, yeah, fuel cells are <u>ace</u>. But producing that hydrogen takes a lot of either fossil fuels or energy. That doesn't mean fuel cells won't be more important in the future, only that you need to look at the <u>whole picture</u> and weigh up the pros and cons.

CFCs and the Ozone Layer

Scientists changed their minds about CFCs as they found out more evidence about them.

At First Scientists Thought CFCs were Great...

1) Chlorofluorocarbons (CFCs for short) are organic molecules containing carbon, chlorine and fluorine, e.g. dichlorodifluoromethane CCl_2F_2 — this is like methane but with two chlorine and two fluorine atoms (and an extremely long name) instead of the four hydrogen atoms.

2) CFCs are non-toxic, non-flammable and chemically inert (unreactive). They're insoluble in water and have low boiling points. Scientists were very happy that they'd found some non-toxic and inert chemicals which were ideal for many uses.

3) Chlorofluorocarbons were used as coolants in refrigerators and air-conditioning systems.

4) CFCs were also used as propellants in aerosol spray cans.

This is called the "hole in the ozone layer".

...But Then They Discovered the Shocking Truth

1) In 1974 scientists found that chlorine could help to destroy ozone (see equations on p71).

2) In 1985 scientists found evidence of decreasing ozone levels in the atmosphere over Antarctica.

3) Measurements in the upper atmosphere show high levels of compounds produced by the breakdown of CFCs. This supports the hypothesis that CFCs break down and destroy ozone.

4) Scientists are now sure that CFCs are linked to the depletion (thinning) of the ozone layer.

- Ozone is a form of oxygen with the formula O_3 — it has three oxygen atoms per molecule, unlike ordinary oxygen which has two atoms per molecule.

- It hangs about in the ozone layer, way up in the stratosphere (part of the upper atmosphere), doing the very important job of absorbing ultraviolet (UV) light from the Sun. Ozone absorbs UV light and breaks down into an oxygen molecule and an oxygen atom: $O_3 + UV \text{ light} \rightarrow O + O_2$ The oxygen molecule and oxygen atom join together to make ozone again: $O + O_2 \rightarrow O_3$

- Reducing the amount of ozone in the stratosphere results in more UV light passing through the atmosphere. Increased levels of UV light hitting the surface of the Earth can cause medical problems like increased risk of sunburn and skin cancer.

Some Countries Have Banned the Use of CFCs

1) Scientists' view that CFCs could damage the ozone layer caused a lot of concern.

2) But it took a while for society to do something about the mounting scientific evidence. Governments waited until the research had been thoroughly peer reviewed and evaluated before making a decision.

3) In 1978 the USA, Canada, Sweden and Norway banned CFCs as aerosol propellants.

4) After the ozone hole was discovered many countries (including the UK) got together and decided to reduce CFC production and eventually ban CFCs completely.

That's "chlorofluorocarbon" not "Chelsea Football Club"...

The ozone in the stratosphere is amazing stuff — it absorbs UV light and stops us from having to bear the full force of the Sun's UV output. Too much UV causes sunburn and skin cancer, so anything that damages the ozone and lets more UV through is a bad thing in the long run. So no more CFCs in fridges and spray cans.

CFCs and the Ozone Layer

CFCs damage ozone by forming <u>free radicals</u>. Learn what they are first, then how they attack ozone.

Free Radicals are Made by Breaking Covalent Bonds

1) A <u>covalent bond</u>, remember, is one where <u>two atoms share electrons</u> between them, like in H_2.

2) A covalent bond can <u>break unevenly</u> to form <u>two ions</u>, e.g. $H-H \rightarrow H^+ + H^-$.
The H^- has <u>both</u> of the shared electrons, and the poor old H^+ has <u>neither</u> of them.

3) But a covalent bond can also break <u>evenly</u> — and then <u>each atom</u> gets <u>one</u> of the shared electrons, e.g. $H-H \rightarrow H\cdot + H\cdot$ — the $H\cdot$ is called a <u>free radical</u>. (The unpaired electron is shown by a <u>dot</u>.)

4) The unpaired electron makes the free radical <u>very, very reactive</u>.

Chlorine Free Radicals from CFCs Damage the Ozone Layer

Learn these equations.

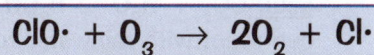

1) <u>Ultraviolet light</u> makes the carbon-chlorine bonds in CFCs break to form <u>free radicals</u>:

$$CCl_2F_2 \rightarrow CClF_2\cdot + Cl\cdot$$

2) This happens <u>high up in the atmosphere</u> (in the <u>stratosphere</u>), where the <u>ultraviolet light</u> from the Sun is <u>stronger</u>.

3) <u>Chlorine free radicals</u> from this reaction react with <u>ozone</u> (O_3), turning it into ordinary oxygen molecules (O_2) and chlorine oxide ($ClO\cdot$):

$$O_3 + Cl\cdot \rightarrow ClO\cdot + O_2$$

4) The chlorine oxide molecule is <u>very reactive</u>, and reacts with ozone to make two <u>oxygen molecules</u> and <u>another Cl· free radical</u>:

$$ClO\cdot + O_3 \rightarrow 2O_2 + Cl\cdot$$

5) This Cl· free radical now goes and reacts with <u>another ozone molecule</u>. This is a <u>chain reaction</u>, so just <u>one chlorine free radical</u> from one CFC molecule can go around breaking up <u>a lot of ozone molecules</u>.

> CFCs <u>don't attack ozone directly</u>. They break up and form chlorine atoms (chlorine free radicals) which attack ozone. The chlorine atoms <u>aren't used up</u>, so they can carry on breaking down ozone.

CFCs Stay in the Stratosphere for Ages

1) CFCs are <u>not very reactive</u> and will only react with one or two chemicals that are present in the atmosphere. And they'll only break up to form <u>chlorine atoms</u> in the stratosphere, where there's plenty of high-energy ultraviolet light around. They won't do it in the lower atmosphere.

2) This means that the CFCs in the stratosphere now will take a <u>long time</u> to be removed.

3) Remember, each CFC molecule produces one chlorine atom which can react with an <u>awful lot</u> of ozone molecules. <u>Thousands</u> of them, in fact.

4) So the millions of CFC molecules that are present in the stratosphere will continue to destroy ozone for a long time — even <u>after all CFCs have been banned</u>. Each molecule will <u>stay around</u> for a long time, and each molecule will <u>destroy a lot of ozone</u> molecules.

Alkanes and HFCs are Safe Alternatives to CFCs

1) Alkanes <u>don't react</u> with ozone, so they can provide a safe alternative to CFCs.

2) <u>Hydrofluorocarbons</u> (<u>HFCs</u>) are compounds very similar to CFCs — but they contain <u>no chlorine</u>. It's the chlorine in CFCs that attacks ozone, remember.

3) Scientists have investigated the compounds that could be produced by breakdown of HFCs in the upper atmosphere, and <u>none of them</u> seem to be able to <u>attack ozone</u>. <u>Evidence suggests</u> HFCs are <u>safe</u>.

Oooh, here comes the tricky science bit...

Here's the deal — <u>yes</u>, you do need to know what a free radical is, and <u>yes</u> you do need to learn the equations for the reaction between chlorine atoms and ozone. You can't just glide your eyes over the equations and hope for the best. <u>Cover the page and scribble them down</u>, then check what you wrote. It'll be worth it in the end.

Hardness of Water

Water where you live might be <u>hard</u> or <u>soft</u>. It depends on the <u>rocks</u> your water meets on its way to you.

Hard Water Makes Scum and Scale

1) <u>Hard water</u> won't easily form a <u>lather</u> with soap. It makes a <u>nasty scum</u> instead. So to get a decent lather you need to use <u>more soap</u> or <u>softer water</u>.

2) Hard water also forms <u>limescale</u> (calcium carbonate) on the insides of pipes, boilers and kettles. <u>Limescale</u> is a <u>thermal insulator</u>. This means that a <u>kettle</u> with <u>limescale on the heating element</u> takes <u>longer to boil</u> than a <u>clean</u> non-scaled-up kettle. Scale can even <u>eventually block pipes</u>.

Hardness is Caused by Ca^{2+} and Mg^{2+} Ions

Hard water contains <u>calcium ions</u> (Ca^{2+}), <u>magnesium ions</u> (Mg^{2+}), or both. As water flows over rocks and through soils containing calcium and magnesium compounds, these ions dissolve in it.

1) <u>Magnesium sulfate</u> ($MgSO_4$) dissolves in water — and so does calcium sulfate ($CaSO_4$) (though only a little bit).

2) <u>Calcium carbonate</u> commonly exists as chalk, limestone or marble. It doesn't dissolve in water, but it will react with <u>acids</u>. And since <u>CO_2</u> from the air <u>dissolves in rainwater</u> (forming <u>carbonic acid</u>, $CO_2 + H_2O \rightarrow H_2CO_3$), rainwater is slightly <u>acidic</u>. This means that calcium carbonate can react with rainwater to form <u>calcium hydrogencarbonate</u> ($H_2CO_3 + CaCO_3 \rightarrow Ca(HCO_3)_2$), which is <u>soluble</u>.

Overall the <u>equation</u> for the reaction is:

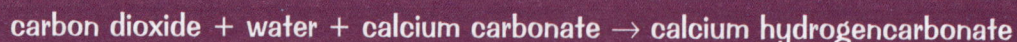

> carbon dioxide + water + calcium carbonate $\rightarrow$ calcium hydrogencarbonate

Temporary Hardness Can be Removed by Boiling

There are two kinds of hardness — <u>temporary</u> and <u>permanent</u>.
Temporary hardness is caused by the <u>hydrogencarbonate</u> ion, <u>HCO_3^-</u>, in $Ca(HCO_3)_2$.
Hardness caused by dissolved <u>calcium sulfate</u> (among other things) is <u>permanent hardness</u>.

1) <u>Temporary hardness</u> is removed by <u>boiling</u>. The calcium hydrogencarbonate <u>decomposes</u> to form insoluble $CaCO_3$. This <u>won't work</u> for permanent hardness, though. Heating a <u>sulfate</u> ion does <u>nowt</u>. (This calcium carbonate precipitate is the 'limescale' on your kettle — it's <u>insoluble</u>.)

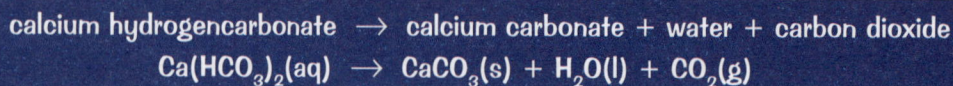

> calcium hydrogencarbonate $\rightarrow$ calcium carbonate + water + carbon dioxide
> $Ca(HCO_3)_2(aq) \rightarrow CaCO_3(s) + H_2O(l) + CO_2(g)$

2) <u>Both types of hardness</u> are removed by adding washing soda — <u>sodium carbonate</u>, Na_2CO_3. The carbonate ions join onto the calcium ions and make an <u>insoluble precipitate</u> of calcium carbonate. This works whether the hardness is due to calcium sulfate or calcium hydrogencarbonate.

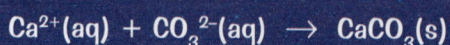

> $Ca^{2+}(aq) + CO_3^{2-}(aq) \rightarrow CaCO_3(s)$

3) <u>Both types of hardness</u> can also be removed by '<u>ion exchange resin</u>'. This clever bit of chemistry has lots of <u>sodium ions</u> (or <u>hydrogen ions</u>) and 'exchanges' them for calcium or magnesium ions.

Ice is fairly hard, come to think of it...

One thing that I've never understood is that they sell water softeners in areas that <u>already</u> have soft water. Hmm... For the exam, you're supposed to know how the calcium and magnesium salts that cause hard water <u>get into</u> the water in the first place, and how they can be <u>removed</u>. So make sure you know it.

Hardness of Water

In hard water areas, you need much more soap to get a nice lather as you wash your hands. At some point in the past, someone noticed this — and decided to design a test to show exactly how hard or soft your water is.

An Experiment to Compare the Hardness of Water Samples

METHOD:

1) Add 100 cm³ of water to a conical flask.

2) Add 1 cm³ soap solution to the water. Put a bung in and shake.

3) Repeat this until a good lasting lather is formed. (A lasting lather is one where the bubbles cover the surface for at least 30 seconds.)

4) Record how much soap was needed.

Add soap 1 cm³ at a time

shake   shake   shake

Good lather

This method was carried out on 3 different samples of water —
distilled water, local tap water and imported tap water.
Fresh samples of each type of water were then boiled, and the experiment was repeated.

Here's the TABLE OF RESULTS:

Sample	Volume of soap solution needed to give a good lather	
	using unboiled water in cm³	using boiled water in cm³
Distilled	1	1
Local water	7	1
Imported water	14	8

The results tell you the following things about the water:

1) Distilled water contains little or no hardness — only the minimum amount of soap was needed.

2) The imported water contains more hardness than local water — more soap was needed to produce a lather.

3) The local water contains only temporary hardness — all the hardness is removed by boiling. You can tell because the same amount of soap was needed for boiled local water as for distilled water.

4) The imported water contains both temporary and permanent hardness. 8 cm³ of soap is still needed to produce a lather after boiling.

5) If your brain's really switched on, you'll see that the local water and the imported water contain the same amount of temporary hardness. In both cases, the amount of soap needed in the boiled sample is 6 cm³ less than in the unboiled sample.

My dad's water is harder than your dad's water...

Sigh. Anyhow, the usual message here. There is an exam coming up, and any of this hard water stuff could be on it, including interpreting results. Read through experimental data carefully — don't drop any easy marks.

Alcohols

There's a whole group of compounds called <u>alcohols</u>, and they're rather useful to industrial chemists.

Alcohols *Have an '-OH' Functional Group and End in '-ol'*

1) The <u>general formula</u> of an alcohol is $C_nH_{2n+1}OH$.
2) So if an alcohol has <u>2 carbons</u> (n = 2), its formula will be $C_2H_{(2\times2)+1}OH$, which is <u>C_2H_5OH</u>.
3) The basic <u>naming</u> system is the same as for alkanes — but replace the final '<u>-e</u>' with '<u>-ol</u>'.

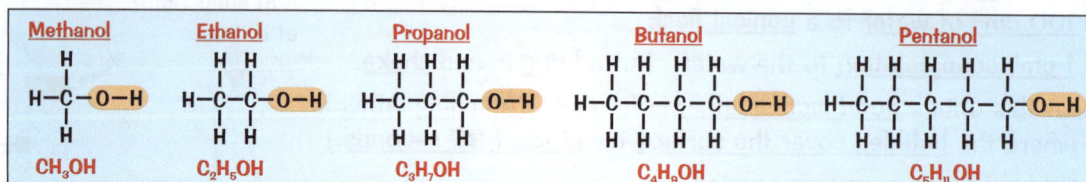

Methanol — CH_3OH Ethanol — C_2H_5OH Propanol — C_3H_7OH Butanol — C_4H_9OH Pentanol — $C_5H_{11}OH$

Fermentation *Produces* Ethanol

1) Fermentation is used to convert <u>sugars</u> (usually a glucose solution) into <u>ethanol</u>.

glucose → ethanol + carbon dioxide
$$C_6H_{12}O_6 \rightarrow 2C_2H_5OH + 2CO_2$$

2) The reaction is brought about by <u>enzymes</u> (biological catalysts) found in <u>yeasts</u>.
3) The <u>temperature</u> needs to be <u>carefully controlled</u>. If it's <u>too cold</u> the yeast is inactive, so the reaction's really <u>slow</u> — but if it's <u>too hot</u> the enzymes in the yeast are <u>denatured</u> (destroyed). The reaction's carried out at an optimum (ideal) temperature between 25 °C and 50 °C.
4) It's also important to prevent <u>oxygen</u> getting at the alcohol. This is because oxygen converts <u>ethanol</u> to <u>ethanoic acid</u> (which is what you get in <u>vinegar</u>).
5) Once the reaction stops the mixture can be distilled using <u>fractional distillation</u> to give pure ethanol.

Ethanol *Can Also be Made by* Hydrating Ethene

1) This is how ethanol is usually made <u>industrially</u>.
2) <u>Ethene</u> (C_2H_4) will react with <u>steam</u> (H_2O) to make <u>ethanol</u>.
3) The reaction needs a <u>temperature</u> of 300 °C and a <u>pressure</u> of 70 atmospheres. To speed up the reaction the ethene and steam are passed over a heated <u>phosphoric acid catalyst</u>.

ethene + water (steam) → ethanol
$$C_2H_4 + H_2O \rightarrow C_2H_5OH$$

Fermentation *vs* Hydration

In the exam you may be asked to <u>compare</u> the two methods of producing ethanol.

Manufacture: Fermentation is usually a <u>batch</u> process which is slow and inefficient. Ethene hydration uses a <u>continuous</u> process so the ethanol is made more quickly. Hydration requires much harsher reaction <u>conditions</u> so is a more <u>expensive</u> process to run.

Sustainability: The ethanol made by fermentation is a <u>renewable fuel</u>. It's made from renewable resources (e.g. sugar cane or sugar beets), so we <u>won't run out</u>. The ethene produced in the hydration reaction is a <u>non-renewable fuel</u>. It's produced from <u>crude oil</u>, which will one day <u>run out</u>.

Purity: The ethanol made by fermentation <u>isn't very pure</u> and has to be purified by distillation before it's used. The ethanol made by hydration is of a much <u>higher purity</u>.

Atom Economy: Fermentation has a <u>lower atom economy</u> than hydration as not all of the atoms in the reactants are used to make the ethanol.

Percentage yield: The yield of a hydration reaction is very low but by <u>recycling</u> any unused reactants you can achieve yields of up to 95%. The yields achieved by using fermentation are <u>much lower</u>.

300 °C, 70 atm, acid — why don't home brewers hydrate ethene...

Learn the equations for the <u>hydration of ethene</u> and the <u>fermentation of ethanol</u>. They're both very important reactions.

Fats and Oils

Lard, glorious lard! Hot butter and blubber...

Fats and Oils Come from Animals or Plants

1) Animal fats and oils include lard (pork fat), blubber (whale fat), ghee (butter oil) and cod liver oil.
2) Plant fats and oils include walnut oil, coconut oil, olive oil and soya oil.
3) Fats are solid and oils are liquid at room temperature. For example, lard is solid at room temperature, olive oil is liquid at room temperature.
4) Fats and oils are esters. An ester is what you get when you react an acid with an alcohol. Fats and oils are produced when an alcohol called glycerol reacts with some acids called fatty acids.
5) These natural fats and oils are important raw materials for the chemical industry — e.g. in paints, machine lubricants, detergents and cosmetics. They can be used as alternatives to chemicals made from crude oil.

Emulsions Can be Made from Oil and Water

1) Oils don't mix in water — they're immiscible.
2) However, you can mix immiscible liquids like oil and water to make an emulsion. You have to shake the two liquids vigorously. This'll break up the oil into very small droplets which disperse through the water.

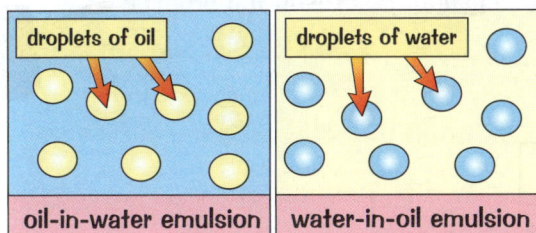

droplets of oil

droplets of water

oil-in-water emulsion

water-in-oil emulsion

3) Milk is an oil-in-water emulsion (oil droplets suspended in water). There's less oil than water.
4) Butter is a water-in-oil emulsion (water droplets suspended in oil). There's more oil than water.

Vegetable Oils Can be Used to Produce Biodiesel

1) Vegetable oils such as rapeseed oil and soybean oil can be processed and turned into fuels.
2) Vegetable oil provides a lot of energy — that's why it's suitable for use as a fuel.
3) A particularly useful fuel made from vegetable oils is called biodiesel. Biodiesel has similar properties to ordinary diesel fuel — it burns in the same way, so you can use it as an alternative to diesel fuel.

Fats and Oils are Used to Make Soaps

1) Vegetable oils react with alkali to make soap.
2) Natural fats and oils are boiled up with sodium hydroxide. The hot sodium hydroxide splits up the fats and oils to produce a soap and glycerol.
3) This process is called saponification. Yes, yet another long chemistry word.
4) The chemical reaction first breaks up the fat or oil to release glycerol and fatty acids. This is called hydrolysis (it means "breaking apart with water"). Then the fatty acids react with the sodium hydroxide to make soap.

Learn the word equation: fat + sodium hydroxide → soap + glycerol

A pint of milk fell on my head — I was overcome with emulsion...

Hundreds of years ago they used to make soap mainly from animal fat. Today vegetable fats and oils are used as well — e.g. palm oil and olive oil, as in Palmolive®. I'm pretty sure the animals are dead chuffed.

Module C6 — Chemistry Out There

Using Plant Oils

Oils are quite runny at room temperature. That's fine for salad dressing, say, but not so good for spreading in your sandwiches. For that, you could hydrogenate the oil to make margarine...

Unsaturated Oils Contain C=C Double Bonds

1) Oils and fats contain long-chain molecules with lots of carbon atoms.

2) They can be either saturated or unsaturated.

3) Saturated oils and fats only have single C-C bonds.

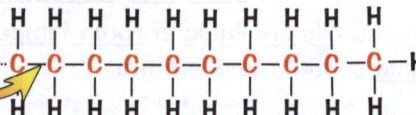

4) Unsaturated oils and fats contain at least one C=C double bond in their carbon chains.

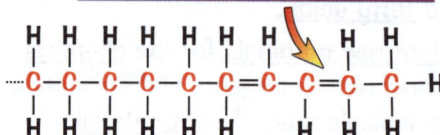

5) Monounsaturated fats contain one C=C double bond somewhere in their carbon chains. Polyunsaturated fats contain more than one C=C double bond.

6) C=C double bonds can be detected by reacting with bromine water.

   • An unsaturated oil or fat will decolourise bromine water or bromine. An addition reaction takes place at the double bond and a colourless dibromo compound is formed.

   • Saturated oils and fats don't have any double bonds so cannot react with the bromine — the bromine water stays orange.

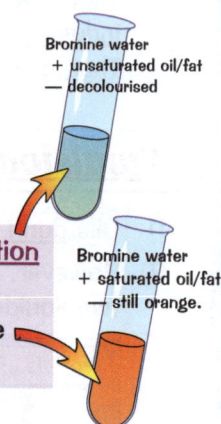

Bromine water + unsaturated oil/fat — decolourised

Bromine water + saturated oil/fat — still orange.

Unsaturated Oils Can be Hydrogenated

1) Unsaturated vegetable oils are liquid at room temperature.

2) They can be hardened by reacting them with hydrogen in the presence of a nickel catalyst at about 60 °C. This is called hydrogenation. The hydrogen reacts with the double-bonded carbons and opens out the double bonds.

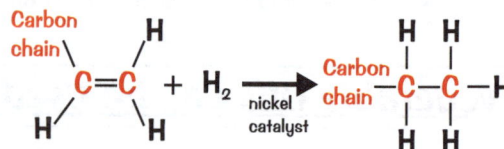

$$Carbon\ chain \diagdown C=C \diagdown H \quad + \quad H_2 \quad \xrightarrow[\text{catalyst}]{\text{nickel}} \quad Carbon\ chain - C - C - H$$

3) Margarine is usually made from partially hydrogenated vegetable oil — turning all the double bonds in vegetable oil to single bonds would make the margarine too hard and difficult to spread. Hydrogenating most of them gives margarine a nice, buttery, spreadable consistency.

Vegetable Oils in Foods Can Affect Health

1) Vegetable fats and oils tend to be unsaturated, while animal fats and oils tend to be saturated.

2) In general, saturated fats are less healthy than unsaturated fats (as saturated fats increase the amount of cholesterol in the blood, which can block up the arteries and increase the risk of heart disease).

3) Natural unsaturated oils such as olive oil and sunflower oil reduce the amount of blood cholesterol.

4) Partially hydrogenated vegetable oil increases the amount of "bad" cholesterol in the blood, and decreases the amount of "good" cholesterol, which is particularly bad news. Eating foods made with partially hydrogenated vegetable oils can increase the risk of heart disease.

Double bonds — licensed to saturate...

This is tricky stuff. In a nutshell... there are saturated and unsaturated fats and you can test for them using bromine. By reacting unsaturated fats with hydrogen you give them more single bonds — this makes 'em more spreadable. And finally, unsaturated fats tend to be better for you because they're less likely to cause clotting in your arteries. Phew.

Detergents

Here's a splendid example of better, cleaner living through Chemistry.

Detergents have a Hydrophilic Head and a Hydrophobic Tail

1) Detergents and soaps have a hydrophobic part and a hydrophilic part.

2) Hydrophobic means it doesn't like water. This part of the molecule is normally a long hydrocarbon chain or 'tail'.

3) Hydrophilic means that something loves water. This part of the molecule is normally small and ionic — the 'head'.

4) The hydrophilic end of the molecule forms strong intermolecular forces with water molecules.

5) The hydrophobic part forms strong intermolecular forces with molecules of oil and fat.

6) This means that when detergents come into contact with fat or oil a droplet of oil/fat forms, surrounded by a coating of detergent. This helps lift oily dirt out of fabric — see the diagram.

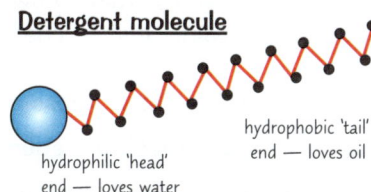

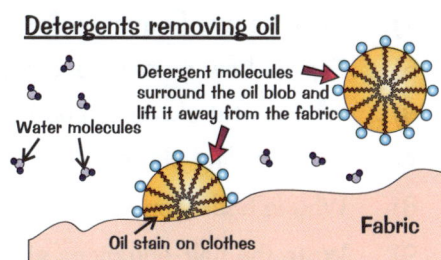

Detergent molecule

hydrophilic 'head' end — loves water

hydrophobic 'tail' end — loves oil

Detergents removing oil

Water molecules

Detergent molecules surround the oil blob and lift it away from the fabric

Oil stain on clothes

Fabric

Dry Cleaning Uses Solvents to Remove Stains

1) Dry cleaning can be any cleaning process that doesn't use water — other solvents are used instead.

2) These solvents are much better than detergents at removing oil and grease and will clean stains that won't dissolve in water.

3) This is because the solvent can completely dissolve the oil and grease, removing the stains. Here's how it works:

- There are weak intermolecular forces between the solvent molecules. There are also weak intermolecular forces between the molecules of grease.

- When the solvent is applied to the clothes, intermolecular forces are formed between the solvent and grease molecules, so the grease molecules are surrounded by molecules of solvent.

- When the solvent is removed, the grease is removed with it and the clothes are left squeaky clean.

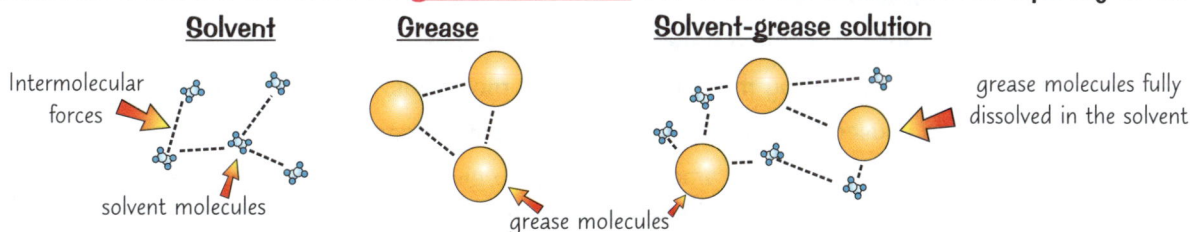

Solvent

Intermolecular forces

solvent molecules

Grease

grease molecules

Solvent-grease solution

grease molecules fully dissolved in the solvent

Washing Clothes at a Lower Temperature Saves Energy

1) Biological detergents contain enzymes which are biological catalysts. They help break down some large insoluble molecules into smaller soluble molecules which can be easily removed.

2) Most enzymes work best at lower temperatures so biological detergents mean you can do your washing at lower temperatures. Turning your washing machine down from a 40 °C to a 30 °C wash uses about 40% less energy. And that means it saves you money on your bills... Hooray.

3) At higher temperatures, the enzymes found in biological detergents are denatured (destroyed). This means that biological detergents don't work as well at temperatures above about 40 °C.

4) Washing at a cooler temperature also means you can wash more delicate clothes in the washing machine.

Detergents and solvents — what a washout...

Pretty neat don't cha think... Well, maybe not but you've still got to learn it. There's quite a lot to get your head around on this page, so make sure you know how detergents work and also how dry cleaning solvents work. And remember that washing your clothes at a lower temperature can save energy and money.

Revision Summary for Module C6

Time to test yourself. If you can't answer these now, you won't be able to answer them in the exam.
When you've done these you can just sit back and wait for your exam. Well, you could... but that would
be silly. You need to keep your brain in the chemistry mood all the way through to the exam — don't let
any of that hard-earned knowledge just dribble away. A few days before the exam, come and try all these
questions again. Just to check you've still got what it takes.

1) Fill in the gaps: A loss of electrons is _____. A gain of electrons is _____.

2) Give a symbol half-equation for the oxidation of Fe^{2+} to Fe^{3+}.

3) What is a displacement reaction?

4) Give the word equation for the rusting of iron.

5) Explain how greasing and painting protect against rust.

6) Why isn't it always a good plan to buy dented cans of beans?

7) An oil drilling platform uses sacrificial protection. What's "sacrificial protection"?

8) Why is hydrogen released during the electrolysis of $H_2SO_4(aq)$?

9) Write the half-equations at each electrode for the electrolysis of $PbI_2(l)$.

10) Describe two ways in which you could increase the amount of product made during electrolysis.

11)* If 2 amps of current flows for 3 seconds, how much charge is that, in coulombs?

12) Sketch an energy level diagram for the reaction between hydrogen and oxygen.

13) Give the definition of a fuel cell.

14) Write down the overall reaction in an hydrogen-oxygen fuel cell.

15) Give two advantages of hydrogen fuel cells over conventional ways of generating electricity

16) Give an advantage of hydrogen fuel cells as a power source in a spacecraft.

17) Why is the car industry researching fuel cells?

18) Why were CFCs initially popular?

19) What's the name for the part of the upper atmosphere that contains the ozone layer?

20) How are free radicals formed?

21) Write an equation for the reaction between ozone and chlorine atoms.

22) One CFC molecule can destroy thousands of ozone molecules. Why is this?

23) Is water hardness caused by calcium sulfate permanent or temporary?

24)* A sample of water requires a large amount of soap to give a good lather both when it is unboiled
and after it is boiled. What type of hardness does it have — none, temporary or permanent?

25) What's the general formula for alcohols?

26) What's the optimum temperature range for fermentation?

27) Compare the sustainability of ethene hydration and fermentation of sugars.

28) Are fats and oils: a) alkanes, b) alcohols, c) esters?

29) Write down a word equation for saponification.

30) How would you test margarine to see if it's saturated or unsaturated?

31) Which are healthier, saturated or unsaturated fats?

32) What does hydrophilic mean? What does hydrophobic mean?

33) Describe how solvents remove stains.

* Answers on page 116.

Speed and Velocity

When you're talking about the motion of a car, it's not enough just to talk about its speed. Sure, I'm driving at 30 mph, but which way am I going? Am I heading towards that tree over there or not? And that lorry over there is also going at 30 mph — but is it heading towards me? And am I getting paranoid? Yes.

Speed *is Just a* Number, *but* Velocity *Has* Direction *Too*

1) To measure the speed of an object, you only need to measure how fast
   it's going — the direction is not important.
   E.g. speed = 30 mph.

2) Velocity is a more useful measure of motion, because it describes both the speed and direction.
   E.g. velocity = 30 mph due north.

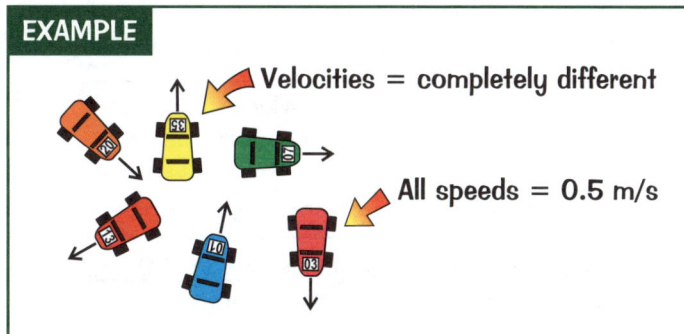

EXAMPLE

Velocities = completely different

All speeds = 0.5 m/s

3) A quantity like speed, that has only
   a number, is called a scalar quantity.

   Scalar quantities:
   speed, mass,
   temperature, time,
   length, etc.

4) A quantity like velocity, that has a
   direction as well, is a vector quantity.

   Vector quantities:
   velocity, force, displacement,
   acceleration, momentum, etc.

Relative *Speed* Compares *the* Speeds *of Two Different Objects*

1) When you look out of a car window, a car that's overtaking you looks like it's not moving very fast.

2) Whereas a car on the opposite side of the motorway seems to whizz past at 100 miles an hour.

3) It's all to do with relative speed — how fast something's going relative to something else.

4) The easiest way to think of it is to imagine yourself in a moving car,
   watching another vehicle from the window.

A car going the same way as you will only
have a small speed relative to your car...

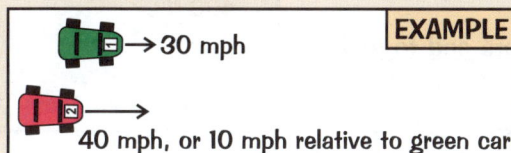

EXAMPLE

→30 mph

40 mph, or 10 mph relative to green car

...whereas a car going the opposite way will
have a much bigger speed relative to you.

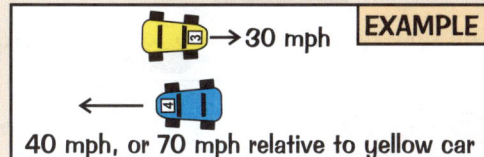

EXAMPLE

→30 mph

40 mph, or 70 mph relative to yellow car

My speed relative to Lewis Hamilton is — well, slower...

You could do an experiment in the lab to find relative speeds. Put a ticker tape machine on a trolley, and attach the ticker tape to a toy car. Depending on whether the car and trolley are moving in the same or opposite directions, you'd get different results. Experiments — good excuse to put the books down for a bit, anyway.

Combining Velocities and Forces

If a parrot has the <u>wind behind it</u>, it flies a bit <u>faster</u>. Likewise, if it's flying <u>into the wind</u>, it'll be slower. To work out the velocity as seen by a "<u>stationary observer</u>" (someone <u>standing still</u>), you have to <u>combine</u> the <u>velocity of the parrot</u> with the <u>velocity of the wind</u>. Get ready for a bit of <u>maths</u> — this is vector stuff...

To Combine Two Vectors, You Add Them End to End

1) With or Against the Current — EASY

It's <u>easy</u> when the plane (or whatever) is flying <u>directly into the wind</u> (or whatever), or with the <u>wind behind it</u>. On the vector diagrams you just need arrows going back and forwards, like this:

EXAMPLE: A light plane is flying east. Its airspeed indicator shows 120 km/h.

It is flying into a wind of 20 km/h — i.e. within a stream of air that's moving west at 20 km/h. What is its resultant velocity?

Plane Velocity
Wind Velocity

Draw the vectors <u>end to end</u>:

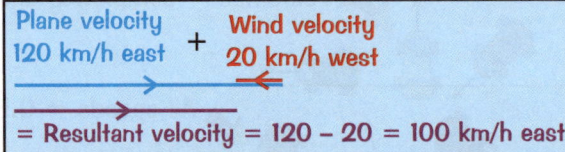

Plane velocity 120 km/h east **+** Wind velocity 20 km/h west

= Resultant velocity = 120 – 20 = 100 km/h east

Sometimes these are called vector sums.

So an observer on the ground would see the plane going <u>east at 100 km/h</u>. (If the plane and the wind were in the <u>same direction</u> you'd <u>add</u> the velocities together to get the resultant velocity.)

2) Across the Current — A Bit More Maths

If the <u>plane</u> (or whatever) is flying <u>across the wind</u> (or whatever), it's a bit <u>more tricky</u>.

EXAMPLE: A boat is going west at 14 m/s (according to the speed indicator) in a river with a current running north at 8 m/s. What is its resultant velocity?

Draw the vectors <u>end to end</u>. It makes a <u>triangle</u> (because the vectors are at right-angles):

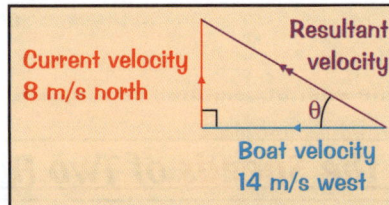

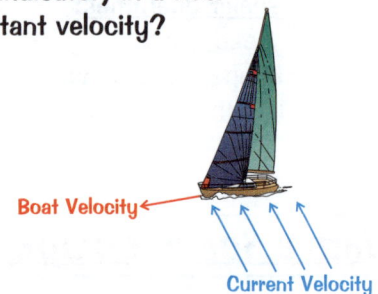

Current velocity 8 m/s north
Resultant velocity
θ
Boat velocity 14 m/s west

Boat Velocity
Current Velocity

To work out the resultant velocity, you need both speed and direction. It's a right-angled triangle, so:

For <u>speed</u> you need <u>Pythagoras</u>' theorem: speed = $\sqrt{(8^2 + 14^2)}$ = <u>16.1 m/s</u>

And for <u>direction</u>, it's good old <u>trigonometry</u>: tan θ = 8/14, so θ = tan^{-1} (8/14) = <u>29.7°</u>

It's the Same with Forces and ANY Vectors at Right Angles

EXAMPLE: Two big <u>beasties</u> are pulling a boat along a canal, with forces at <u>right angles</u> to each other. Find the resultant force.

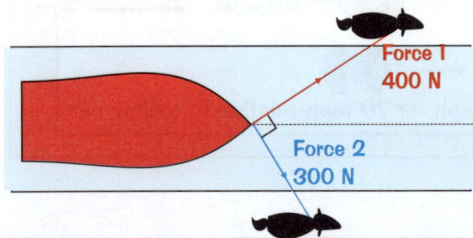

Force 1 400 N
Force 2 300 N
θ
Resultant Force

Force 1 400 N
Force 2 300 N

Draw the vectors <u>end to end</u>, to make a right-angled triangle:
And it's Pythagoras again:

Size of Force = $\sqrt{(300^2 + 400^2)}$ = <u>500 N</u>

Direction = angle of θ to Force 1, which you find by trig:
tan θ = 300/400, so θ = tan^{-1} (3/4) = <u>36.9°</u>

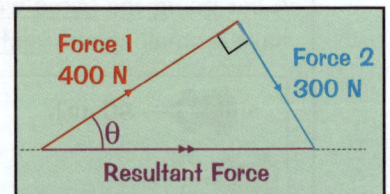

I've got a brand new combine velocity...

You use the same trick to combine <u>any vectors</u> — momentum, displacement, acceleration, anything.
Just draw the vectors end to end and, with a bit of maths, you can find the overall (resultant) vector.

Equations of Motion

These equations of motion are dead handy for working out velocity, acceleration and other goodies...

You Need to Know These Four Equations of Motion

Which of these equations you need to use depends on what you know, and what you need to find out. They're easier to use if you know them like the back of your hand.

Altogether, there are 5 things involved in these equations:

u = initial velocity (or speed),

v = final velocity (or speed),

s = displacement (or distance),

t = time,

a = acceleration.

$$s = \frac{(u + v)}{2}t \qquad v = u + at$$

$$s = ut + \frac{1}{2}at^2 \qquad v^2 = u^2 + 2as$$

You need to be able to rearrange these equations too — otherwise you're not going to be able to do the exam questions correctly, and that would be sad.

Make Sure You Use the Right Equation

If you know three things, you can find out either of the other two — if you use the right equation, that is. And if you use this method twice, you can find out both things you don't know.

HOW TO CHOOSE YOUR EQUATION:

1) Write down which three things you already know.

2) Write down which of the other things you want to find out.

3) Choose the equation that involves all the things you've written down.

4) Stick in your numbers, and do the maths.

REMEMBER:
Direction's important for velocity, acceleration & displacement — always choose which direction's positive, and stick with it.

EXAMPLE: A car going at 10 m/s due east accelerates east at 2 m/s² for 8 s. How far does the car go while accelerating?

Now, first things first... I'll say that the "positive" direction is east ("to the right").

1) You know u (= 10 m/s), a (= 2 m/s²) and t (= 8 s).

2) You want to find out the displacement, s.

3) So you need the equation with all these in: u, a, t and s — the third equation: $s = ut + \frac{1}{2}at^2$.

4) Put the numbers in: s = (10 × 8) + ½(2 × 8²) = 80 + 64 = **144 m** due east.

u = 10 m/s   a = 2 m/s²
t = 8 s
s = ?

EXAMPLE: A car going at 25 m/s decelerates at 1.5 m/s² as it heads towards a built-up area 145 m away. What will its speed be when it reaches the built-up area?

1) You know u (= 25 m/s), a (= –1.5 m/s²) and s (= 145 m).

2) You want to find out the final speed, v.

3) So you need the equation with all these in: u, a, s and v — the fourth equation: $v^2 = u^2 + 2as$.

4) Put the numbers in: v² = 25² + 2(–1.5)(145) = 190 so v = $\sqrt{190}$ = **13.8 m/s**

u = 25 m/s   a = –1.5 m/s²
s = 145 m
v = ?

a is –ve, because it's deceleration.

Motion problems — eat more figs or follow the method above...

1) LEARN THE EQUATIONS IN THE RED BOXES. It's better to learn them, there's no way round that.

2) LEARN THE METHOD IN THE BLUE BOX. Motion questions can look tricky at first, but that method works for all of them. Practise the examples again — cover up my working and do them yourself.

Projectile Motion

Is it a bird? Is it a plane? No, it's a projectile. Hmm... exciting stuff, this — things flying through the air, where the only force on them is due to gravity.

The Path of a Projectile is Always a Parabola

1) A projectile is something that is projected, or dropped, and from then on only has Earth's gravitational field (gravity) acting on it (ignoring air resistance).

2) So things like missiles, golf balls and footballs are all projectiles.

3) The path a projectile takes through the air (called its trajectory) is always parabolic, which is this shape:

4) How far a ball (or other projectile) travels depends on the angle it's launched at. It will travel furthest if it's launched at 45°.

5) If the angle's less than 45°, then the projectile won't travel as far.

6) An angle greater than 45° means the projectile will take longer to hit the ground but won't travel as far.

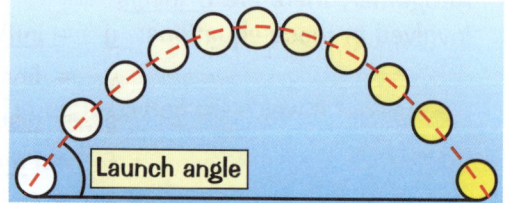

Launch angle

Deal with Horizontal and Vertical Motion Separately

1) Motion can be split into two separate bits — the horizontal bit and the vertical bit.

2) These bits are totally separate — one doesn't affect the other.

3) So gravity (which only acts downwards) doesn't affect horizontal motion at all.

4) An object projected horizontally accelerates vertically due to gravity, but has no acceleration horizontally (i.e. its velocity stays the same).

Something that starts off horizontally has constant horizontal velocity (ignoring friction/air resistance), since there are no horizontal forces and it's unaffected by gravity.

Its initial vertical velocity = 0.
Its vertical velocity increases steadily, as gravity accelerates it downwards.

5) An object can also be projected at an angle, and the motion can be split into horizontal and vertical parts. You can apply this to real-life situations, e.g. how far a ball travels depends on the angle it's struck at.

6) Both bits of the motion — the horizontal velocity and the vertical velocity — are vectors. The overall (resultant) velocity of the ball at any point is the vector sum of the separate bits (see p. 80).

Projectile Calculations Use the Equations of Motion

g = acceleration due to gravity

Example: A football is kicked horizontally from a 20 m high wall. How long is it before it lands?
Take g = 10 m/s², and ignore air resistance.

It lands when it's travelled 20 m vertically (height of the wall).
Using $s = ut + \frac{1}{2}at^2$, where u = 0, a = 10 m/s², s = 20 m:
$20 = (0 \times t) + \frac{1}{2}at^2 = \frac{10t^2}{2}$, i.e. $t = 2$ s when it lands.

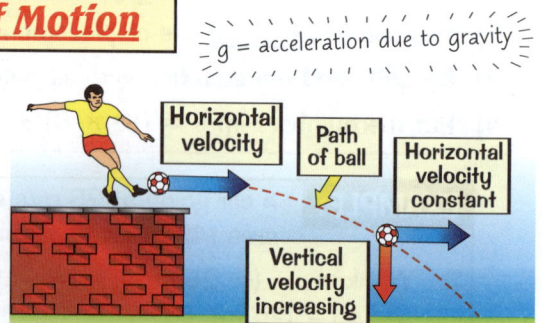

Horizontal velocity | Path of ball | Horizontal velocity constant

Vertical velocity increasing

Not to scale (otherwise he'd be a very tall man).

If its horizontal velocity is 5 m/s, how far does it travel before it lands?

Using "distance = speed × time", where v = 5 m/s and t = 2 s: $s = 5 \times 2 = 10$ m.

From above.

See previous page for more equations of motion.

What do mathematicians do if they have motion problems...?

Get a pencil and, er, draw a diagram. Always start projectile questions with a diagram. If it doesn't look like you've much info... DON'T PANIC. Remember — if it starts from rest, you know that initial velocity = 0. You also know that if it's moving under gravity, the acceleration is 10 m/s² downwards. And take it from there.

Forces and Newton's Third Law

Typical — you wait ages for a force and then two come along at once. Well, that's physics for you.

Forces Occur When Two Objects Interact

When an object exerts a force on another object it always experiences a force in return.
These two forces are sometimes called an 'interaction pair'.

1) That means if you push against a wall, the wall will push back against you in the opposite direction with exactly the same force and as soon as you stop pushing, so does the wall.

2) If you think about it, there must be an opposing force when you push (or lean) against a wall — otherwise you (and the wall) would fall over.

3) This is an example of Newton's third law of motion — if object A exerts a force on object B, then object B exerts an equal and opposite force on object A.

4) The same is true in a collision — colliding objects exert equal and opposite forces on each other.

Objects Exert a Downward Force Due to Gravity

1) If you put a book on a table, the book pushes down on the table with a force equal to its weight — and the table exerts an equal and opposite force upwards on the book.

2) This upward force is called a reaction force — because it's the table's 'response' to the force exerted by the book. If the book weighs 10 N then the table's reaction force will be 10 N.

Things Move because Forces are Applied to Different Objects

If the forces are always equal, how does anything ever go anywhere?
Well, the two forces are acting on different objects.

RECOIL

1) When a gun is fired, the bullet exerts a force on the gun equal and opposite to the force exerted by the gun on the bullet.

2) So, the bullet travels out of the barrel and the gun recoils in the opposite direction.

3) The bullet travels much faster forwards than the gun does backwards because the bullet is much lighter.

ROCKETS

1) When gas particles collide with things they exert a force on them (see p. 85).

2) In a rocket engine particles of hot gas collide with the walls, exerting a force on the walls, and the wall exerts an equal but opposite force on them.

3) The force from the wall pushes the gas particles out of the exhaust.

4) The force from the gas on the wall pushes the rocket forwards.

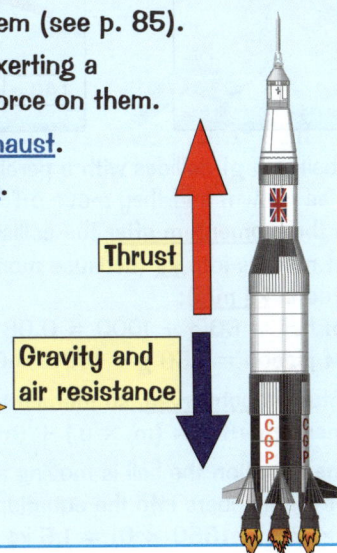

Exhaust

Force on the rocket

Thrust

Gravity and air resistance

5) The force pushing the rocket upwards must be larger than the force of gravity and air resistance, or it won't take off.

6) So, for large rockets, used to lift satellites into orbit above the Earth, you need a large number of particles moving at high speed to produce enough force to lift the rocket.

I have a reaction to forces — they bring me out in a rash...

Funnily enough, Newton's fourth law is "more revision equals better exam results". Newton was a smart guy.

Conservation of Momentum

You know that when two objects <u>collide</u> they exert <u>equal</u> but <u>opposite</u> forces on each other.
Well now you also get to learn that <u>momentum</u> is <u>conserved</u> (but not in the same way as tigers).

Momentum = Mass × Velocity

The <u>greater</u> the <u>mass</u> of an object and the <u>greater</u> its <u>velocity</u>, the <u>more momentum</u> the object has.

Momentum (kg m/s) = Mass (kg) × Velocity (m/s)

Momentum Before = Momentum After

1) In a collision when no other (external) forces act, <u>momentum is conserved</u> — i.e. the total momentum <u>after</u> is the <u>same</u> as it was <u>before</u>.

2) This explains the <u>recoil</u> action of guns too — <u>before</u> a shot is fired the gun and bullet have <u>no velocity</u>, so they have <u>no momentum</u> either. When a shot's <u>fired</u>, the bullet travels <u>forward</u> (with positive momentum) and the gun recoils <u>backward</u> (with negative momentum). The <u>combined</u> momentum of the bullet and the gun will be <u>zero</u> (because they each have the same <u>amount</u> of momentum, but in <u>opposite directions</u>).

3) Conservation of momentum also explains <u>rocket propulsion</u> and <u>explosions</u>:

<u>Rockets</u> work in much the same way as guns — they chuck a load of <u>exhaust gases</u> out <u>backwards</u>, and since momentum is conserved, the rocket moves <u>forwards</u>.

<u>Before</u> an explosion, <u>total momentum</u> = 0. When something explodes, particles are thrown out at <u>different speeds</u> and in <u>all directions</u>, so they have different <u>momentums</u> that all <u>add up to 0</u>.

Momentum of bullet = momentum of gun.

4) If two objects collide and <u>coalesce</u> (<u>join together</u>), then the total momentum of <u>both</u> objects <u>before</u> the collision = momentum of the <u>combined</u> objects <u>after</u> the collision:

$$(m_1 \times u_1) + (m_2 \times u_2) = (m_1 + m_2) \times v$$

Where:
m_1 = mass of first object
u_1 = velocity of first object
m_2 = mass of second object
u_2 = velocity of second object
v = velocity of combined objects

Example 1:

25 m/s   0 m/s

Before

After

A tennis ball (60 g) collides with a perching pigeon (350 g), as shown, and they move off together. Calculate the <u>momentum after</u> the collision.

1) Convert masses into <u>kg</u> (because momentum is measured in <u>kg m/s</u>):
mass of ball = 60 g ÷ 1000 = 0.06 kg
mass of pigeon = 350 g ÷ 1000 = 0.35 kg

2) Momentum is <u>conserved</u>, so momentum before = momentum after = $(m_1 \times u_1) + (m_2 \times u_2)$

3) Treat the direction the ball is moving as positive, and put the numbers into the equation:
(0.06 × 25) + (350 × 0) = <u>1.5 kg m/s</u>

Example 2:

2 m/s   1.5 m/s   Velocity (v) = ?

Ed   Sue

80 kg   60 kg   (80+60) kg

Before   After

Two skaters approach each other, collide and move off together as shown. At what <u>velocity</u> do they move after the collision?

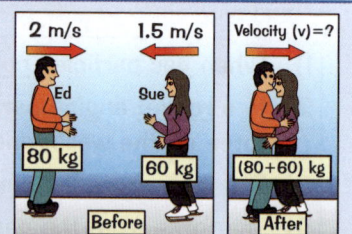

1) Choose which direction is <u>positive</u>. I'll say "<u>positive</u>" means "<u>to the right</u>".

2) Ed and Sue <u>collide</u> and <u>join</u> together, so:
$(m_{Ed} \times u_{Ed}) + (m_{Sue} \times u_{Sue}) = (m_{Ed} + m_{Sue}) \times v$

3) Put in the numbers:
(80 × 2) + (60 × (−1.5)) = (80 + 60) × v
so 70 = 140v

4) Find the velocity:
v = 70 ÷ 140
v = <u>0.5 m/s to the right</u>

Because it's <u>positive</u>.

Crash test dummies know all too well about momentum...

There are loads of great things that are <u>conserved</u> — momentum, pandas, fruit, energy... I could go on.

Pressure

Gases fly around, bump into things and exert a force on them. This is happening to you right now — the air around you is exerting pressure on you (unless you're somehow reading this in space).

Kinetic Theory Says Gases are Randomly Moving Particles

1) Kinetic theory says that gases consist of very small particles. Which they do — oxygen consists of oxygen molecules, neon consists of neon atoms, etc.

2) These particles are constantly moving in completely random directions.

3) They constantly collide with each other and with the walls of their container. When they collide, they bounce off each other, or off the walls.

4) The particles hardly take up any space. Most of the gas is empty space.

Kinetic theory is a particle model — so if you get asked to explain something using a particle model, don't panic, it's the same thing.

A Decrease in Volume Gives an Increase in Pressure

1) As gas particles move about, they bang into each other and whatever else happens to get in the way.

2) Gas particles have some mass, so when they collide with something, they exert a force on it.

3) In a sealed container, gas particles smash against the container's walls — creating an outward pressure.

4) If you put the same amount of gas in a bigger container (increased volume), the pressure will decrease, cos there'll be fewer collisions between the gas particles and the container's walls.

5) When the volume's reduced, the particles get more squashed up and so they hit the walls more often, hence the pressure increases.

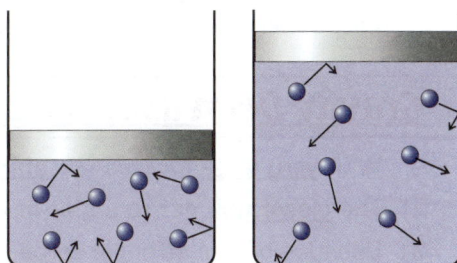

Increasing the Temperature Increases the Pressure

1) The pressure of a gas depends on how fast the particles are moving and how often they hit the walls of the container they're in.

2) If you heat a gas, the particles move faster and have more kinetic energy. This increase in kinetic energy means the particles hit the container walls harder and more often, creating more pressure.

3) If a gas is cooled, the particles have less kinetic energy. The particles hit the walls with less force and less often, so the pressure is reduced.

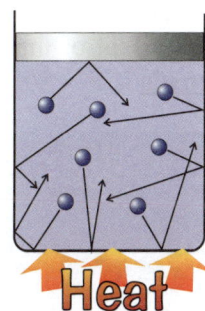

Heat

Colliding Particles Change Their Momentum

1) Gas particles are moving and have mass, so they also have momentum — $M = m \times v$.

2) When gas particles collide with the walls of a container their velocity changes.

3) A change in velocity (Δv) also means a change in momentum — $\Delta M = m \times \Delta v$.

4) You know from P3 that force = change in momentum ÷ time taken — $F = \Delta M \div t$.

5) So as particles collide with a container, they experience a change of momentum and exert a force on the walls of the container. This creates pressure.

6) Hotter particles collide more often too, so there are more particles exerting a force on the container and the pressure increases.

Less space, more collisions, more pressure — just like London...

Don't get the volume of a gas confused with the volume of your TV — same word, different thing. Nightmare.

Gravity and Orbits

In case you've forgotten... gravity is the universal force of attraction between masses. It's not really noticeable with normal masses though, only with huge ones like planets, stars and massive biscuits.

Gravity Provides the Centripetal Force That Causes Orbits

1) If an object is travelling in a circle it is constantly changing direction, which means there must be a force acting on it.

2) An orbit is a balance between the forward motion of the object and a force pulling it inwards. This is called a centripetal force (pronounced sen-tree-pee-tal) — it's directed towards the centre of the circle.

3) The planets move around the Sun in almost circular orbits. The centripetal forces that make this happen are provided by the gravitational force (gravity) between each planet and the Sun.

4) Similarly, the Moon orbits the Earth because of the centripetal force produced by the gravitational force between the Earth and the Moon.

5) Artificial satellites (see next page) orbit the Earth. The centripetal force is provided by the Earth's gravity.

6) They keep accelerating towards the Earth but their tangential motion (at a right angle to the acceleration), keeps them in an almost circular orbit.

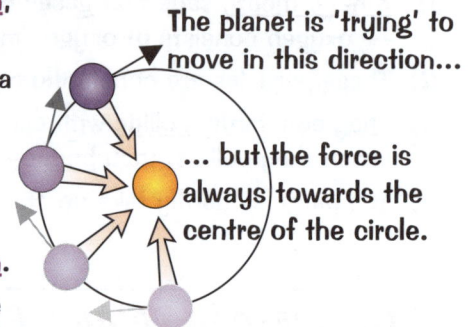

The planet is 'trying' to move in this direction...

... but the force is always towards the centre of the circle.

Gravity Decreases Quickly as You Get Further Away

1) With very large masses like stars and planets, the gravitational force is very big and acts a long way out.

2) The closer you get to a star or a planet, the stronger the force of attraction.

3) Because of this stronger force, planets nearer the Sun move faster and cover their orbit quicker.

4) Moons, artificial satellites and space stations are also held in orbit by gravity. The further out from Earth they orbit, the slower they move (see next page for more on satellites).

5) The size of the gravitational force follows the fairly famous "inverse square" relationship. The main effect of that is that the force decreases very quickly with increasing distance. The formula is $F \propto 1/d^2$, but I reckon it's easier just to remember the basic idea in words:

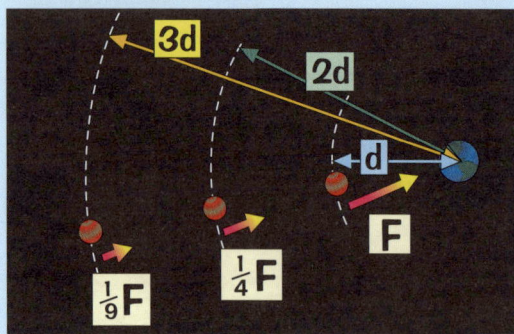

3d
2d
d
F
$\frac{1}{4}F$
$\frac{1}{9}F$

a) If you double the distance from a planet, the size of the gravitational force will decrease by a factor of four (2^2).

b) If you treble the distance, the gravitational force will decrease by a factor of nine (3^2), and so on.

c) On the other hand, if you get twice as close the gravity becomes four times stronger.

Comets Change Speed Because of Gravity

1) Periodic comets orbit the Sun, but have highly elliptical (elongated) orbits.

2) The Sun isn't at the centre of the orbit but near one end, so their orbits take them out a long way from the Sun, then back in close again.

3) The closer the comet is to the Sun the greater the gravitational force of attraction.

4) So, the comet travels much faster when it's nearer the Sun than it does in the more distant parts of its orbit.

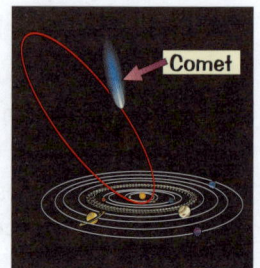

Comet

The gravity of the situation increases as you get closer to the exam...

There are also non-periodic comets, which pass through the Solar System, but don't actually orbit the Sun.

Satellites

A satellite is any object that orbits around a larger object in space. There are natural satellites, like moons, but this page just looks at the artificial ones that we put there ourselves, like for satellite phones and stuff.

Communications Satellites Stay Over the Same Point on Earth

1) Communications satellites are put in quite a high orbit over the equator and orbit once every 24 hours.

2) This means that they stay above the same point on the Earth's surface because the Earth rotates with them.

3) So they're called geostationary artificial satellites (geo(Earth)-stationary) or geosynchronous satellites.

4) They're ideal for telephone, TV and radio because they stay at the same point above the Earth and can transfer signals from one side of the Earth to another in a fraction of a second.

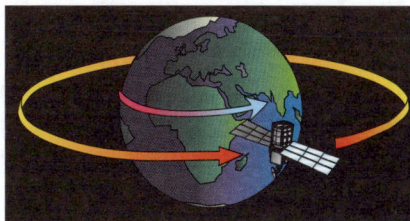

Weather and Spying Satellites Need to be in a Low Orbit

1) Geostationary satellites are too high and too stationary to take good weather or spying photos — you need low polar orbits, which pass over both poles and are nice and low.

2) In a low polar orbit, the satellite sweeps over both poles whilst the Earth rotates beneath it.

3) They're much closer to the Earth than geostationary satellites, so the pull of gravity is stronger and they move much faster.

4) So they orbit really quickly, often with a period of less than 2 hours.

5) Each time the satellite comes round it can scan the next bit of the globe. This allows the whole surface of the planet to be monitored each day.

Microwaves are Used for Satellite Communication

1) Communication to and from satellites (including satellite TV signals and satellite phones) uses microwaves.

2) For satellite TV and phones, the signal from a transmitter is transmitted into space...

3) ... where it's picked up by the satellite's receiver dish orbiting thousands of kilometres above the Earth. The satellite transmits the signal back to Earth in a different direction...

4) ... where it's received by a satellite dish on the ground.

5) Or... satellites receiving the signal then retransmit it to other satellites, and eventually back down to Earth.

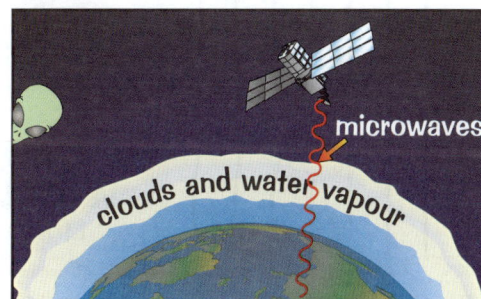

microwaves

clouds and water vapour

Microwaves Have Higher Frequencies than Radio Waves

1) Microwaves have a very high frequency — over 3000 MHz (3 GHz). Radio waves have lower frequencies than this — see next page.

2) Microwaves pass easily through the atmosphere to satellites orbiting the Earth, enabling the signal to reach distant parts of the planet.

There's more on EM waves and communication on the next page.

3) Satellites in low orbit (closer to the Earth) use lower frequencies than satellites in higher, geostationary orbit (always above the same point on Earth).

4) Satellite signals weaken because they travel long distances (losing intensity and picking up interference).

5) So digital signals are used because they're high quality — they don't suffer as much from interference.

So you can thank satellites next time you ring home from Everest...

GPS satellites transmit their position and the time, so you can find out where you are. Pretty clever stuff.

Radio Waves and Microwaves

Microwaves are used for satellite communication and their longer-wavelength cousins, radio waves, are used for (yep, you guessed it) radio communication. I don't communicate with my cousins ☹.

Different Frequency Waves Travel By Different Routes

Electromagnetic (EM) waves with different frequencies are used to transmit different types of communication signal, because they behave differently in the atmosphere:

1) Below 30 MHz — radio waves are reflected off a layer of the atmosphere called the ionosphere. This allows the wave to travel longer distances and deals with the curvature of the Earth.

2) Between 30 MHz and 30 GHz — radio waves and microwaves pass straight through the atmosphere, so transmissions must be by line of sight (because they can't reflect off the atmosphere).

3) Above 30 GHz — rain and dust in the atmosphere absorb and scatter microwaves. This reduces the strength of the signal, so the highest frequency that can be used for satellite transmissions is about 30 GHz.

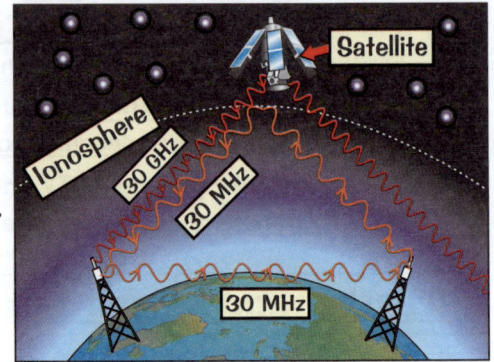

Long Wavelength Radio Waves Diffract

1) All waves tend to spread out (diffract) when they pass through a narrow gap or past an object.

2) A "narrow" gap is one which is about the same size as the wavelength.

3) Obviously then, the question of whether a gap is "narrow" or not depends on the wave in question. What may be a narrow gap for a long wavelength radio wave will be a huge gap for a microwave.

4) It should be obvious then that the longer the wavelength of a wave, the more it will diffract. You get maximum diffraction when the size of the gap is equal to the wavelength of the wave.

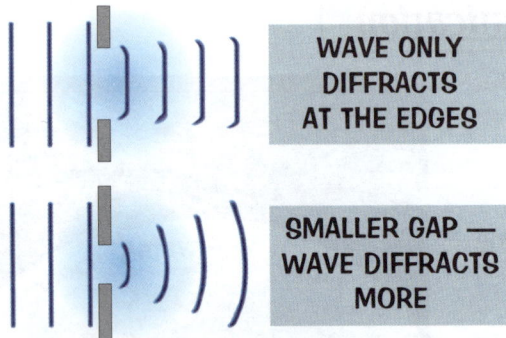

WAVE ONLY DIFFRACTS AT THE EDGES

SMALLER GAP — WAVE DIFFRACTS MORE

Long Wavelength Radio Waves Diffract Easily over Hills and into Buildings:

Shorter wavelength TV and FM radio do not diffract very much

Long wavelength radio waves diffract

These houses will get reception of long wave radio, but not TV or FM radio

5) So because long wavelength radio waves have a really large wavelength they also have a really long range. They spread out in all directions so are great for broadcasting, and can diffract over hills and through tunnels, and even over the horizon.

Dishes are Used to Receive Microwave Signals

1) Regular (terrestrial) TV and radio signals transmitted using radio waves are received using an aerial.

2) But the wavelength of microwaves is too short for aerials to be effective at receiving them.

3) So satellite TV and radio signals are received and transmitted using a dish.

4) The dishes are many times larger than the wavelength of the microwaves, so the microwaves don't diffract much — this produces a narrow beam that doesn't spread out.

5) This means the transmitting and receiving dishes need to be carefully aligned so the signal is picked up.

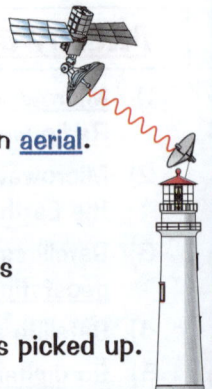

Diffraction — it can drive you round the bend...

The first person to transmit and receive radio waves was Heinrich Hertz in 1888. The unit we use for frequency (Hertz, Hz) is named after him. 10 years later, Nikola Tesla managed to build a radio controlled boat. Nifty.

Interference of Waves

Waves can <u>interfere</u> with each other, you know. Uh-huh. They can <u>add</u> to each other or <u>cancel out</u>.

When <u>Waves Meet</u> They Cause a <u>Disturbance</u> (just like teenagers)

1) All waves cause some kind of <u>disturbance</u> in a medium — water waves disturb water particles, sound waves disturb air particles, electromagnetic waves disturb electric and magnetic fields.

2) When <u>two waves meet</u> at a point they both try to cause their own disturbance.

3) Waves either disturb in the <u>same direction</u> and <u>reinforce</u> each other (<u>constructive</u> interference), or in <u>opposite directions</u> and <u>cancel</u> each other out (<u>destructive</u> interference).

4) Think of a '<u>pulse</u>' travelling down a slinky spring meeting a pulse travelling in the opposite direction. These diagrams show the <u>possible outcomes</u>:

5) The <u>total amplitude</u> of the waves at a point is the <u>sum</u> of the <u>displacements</u> (you have to take direction into account) of the waves at that point.

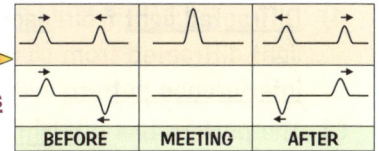

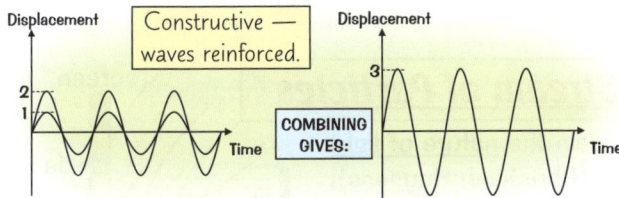

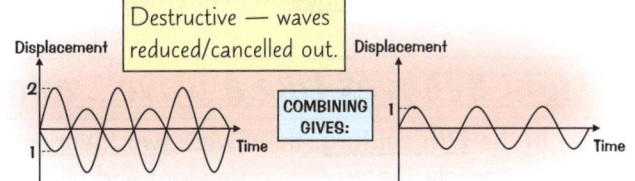

Constructive — waves reinforced.

Destructive — waves reduced/cancelled out.

COMBINING GIVES:

You Get <u>Patterns</u> of '<u>Loud</u>' and '<u>Quiet</u>' Bits with <u>Sound</u>

1) Two speakers both play the same note, at <u>exactly</u> the <u>same time</u>.

2) Depending on <u>where</u> you stand in front of them, you'll either hear a <u>loud sound</u> or <u>almost nothing</u>.

3) At certain points, the sound waves will be <u>in phase</u> — here you get <u>constructive interference</u>. The <u>amplitude</u> of the waves will be <u>doubled</u>, so you'll hear a <u>loud sound</u>.

4) These points occur where the <u>distance travelled</u> by the waves from both speakers is either the <u>same</u> or different by a <u>whole number of wavelengths</u>.

5) At certain other points the sound waves will be <u>exactly</u> <u>out of phase</u> — here you get <u>destructive interference</u> and the waves will <u>cancel out</u>. This means you'll hear almost <u>no sound</u>.

6) These out of phase points occur where the difference in the <u>distance travelled</u> by the waves (the "<u>path difference</u>") is ½ wavelength, 1½ wavelengths, 2½ wavelengths, etc.

7) This pattern of loud and quiet (constructive and destructive interference) is called an <u>interference pattern</u> — you get them for all types of <u>waves</u> (e.g. sound, light, water, microwaves).

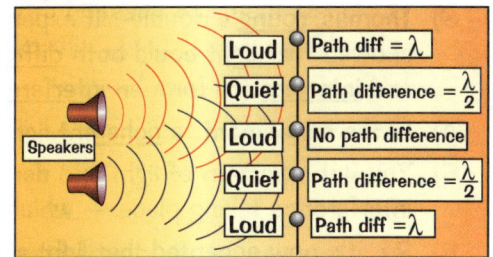

Loud	Path diff = λ
Quiet	Path difference = $\frac{\lambda}{2}$
Loud	No path difference
Quiet	Path difference = $\frac{\lambda}{2}$
Loud	Path diff = λ

Speakers

Interference Patterns <u>Need Coherent</u> Wave Sources

To get a <u>stable</u> interference pattern you need to use <u>coherent</u> wave sources. This means sources where:

1) The <u>waves</u> are at the <u>same frequency</u> (and so <u>wavelength</u>).

2) The waves are <u>in phase</u> — the <u>troughs</u> and <u>crests</u> of the waves <u>line up</u>.

3) The waves have the <u>same amplitude</u>.

For <u>light</u>, the coherent sources are <u>monochromatic</u> light (this is the type of light needed to make an <u>interference pattern</u>).

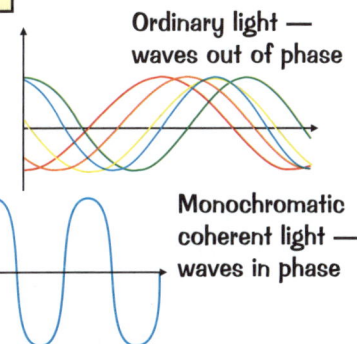

Ordinary light — waves out of phase

Monochromatic coherent light — waves in phase

Destructive interference — too many cooks spoil the wave...

It's weird, isn't it... I mean, <u>constructive</u> interference makes perfect <u>sense</u> — two waves, bigger sound... it's just <u>destructive</u> interference that gets me. I know WHY it happens... but I still find it <u>weird</u>.

Diffraction Patterns and Polarisation

When light diffracts (spreads out through a gap) it makes an interference pattern.

When Light Diffracts You Get Patterns of Light and Dark

1) You get interference patterns when waves of equal frequency or wavelength overlap.

2) When a wavefront passes through a gap, light from each point along the gap diffracts.
   It's as if every point along the wavefront is a light source in its own right. Strange but true.

3) The gap must be about the same size as the wavelength of the light, otherwise the light won't be diffracted very much.

4) Diffracted light from each of these points interferes with light diffracted from all the other points. So you get an interference pattern even from just one slit.

5) The pattern has a bright central fringe with alternating dark and bright fringes on either side of it.

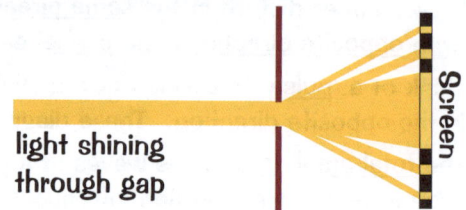

light shining through gap

Screen

Light Behaves Like a Wave... and a Stream of Particles

1) In the 17th century, there were two theories to explain the nature of light — particle theory (Isaac Newton) and wave theory (Christiaan Huygens).

2) The particle theory of light could explain reflection and refraction, but diffraction and interference are both unique to waves.

3) Thomas Young's double-slit experiment (over 100 years later) showed that light could both diffract (through two narrow slits) and interfere (to form an interference pattern on a screen).

4) In the experiment, a coherent light source (e.g. a laser) is shone through two slits.

5) You get a pattern of light and dark fringes, showing constructive and destructive interference taking place — which shows light also behaves as a wave.

6) So, it's now accepted that light shows properties of a wave (diffraction, interference and polarisation).

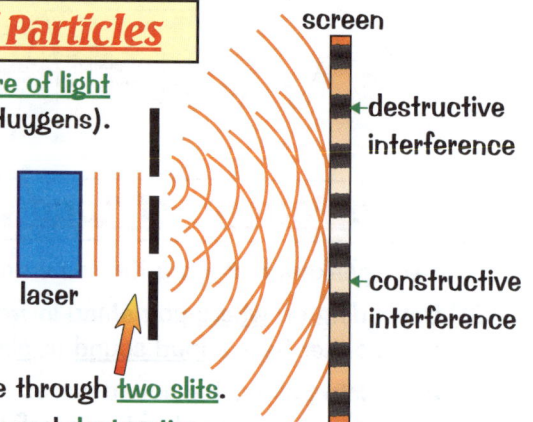

screen

destructive interference

laser

constructive interference

Transverse Waves Can be Plane Polarised

1) Electromagnetic waves are transverse waves — the vibrations are at 90° to the direction of travel of the wave.

Vibrations from side to side | Wave travelling this way

2) You can make a transverse wave by shaking a rope up and down, or side to side, or in a mixture of directions. Whichever plane you're shaking it in, it's still a transverse wave.

3) Now imagine trying to pass a rope that's waving about in all different directions through the slats of a wooden fence.

4) The only vibrations that'll get through the fence are the vertical ones. The fence filters out vibrations in all the other directions. This is called plane polarisation of the wave.

direction of waves

rope

fence

5) Ordinary light waves are a mixture of vibrations in different directions.

6) Passing the light through a polarising filter is like passing the rope through the fence — the filter only transmits (lets through) vibrations in one particular direction.

7) So plane polarised light is made up of vibrations in one direction only.

8) When light is reflected from some surfaces (like water) it is partly plane polarised.

9) Polaroid sunglasses act as polarising filters — they can filter out reflected glare from the sea or the snow.

Plane polarised — a tinted windscreen in your cockpit...

Light can be circularly polarised instead of plane polarised, but this is much more confusing so we'll ignore it.

Refraction

1) Refraction is when waves change direction as they enter a different medium.
2) This is caused entirely by the change in speed of the waves.
3) The speed change also causes the wavelength to change, but remember — the frequency doesn't change.

Refraction — Changing the Speed of a Wave Can Change its Direction

1) Waves (such as light) travel at different speeds in substances which have different densities.
2) When a wave crosses a boundary between two substances (e.g. from glass to air) it changes speed.
3) When the wave speed decreases the wave bends towards the normal.
4) When the speed increases the wave bends away from the normal.
5) E.g. when light passes from air into the glass of a window (a denser medium), it slows down — causing the light to refract towards the normal. When the light reaches the 'glass to air' boundary on the other side of the window, it speeds up and refracts away from the normal.

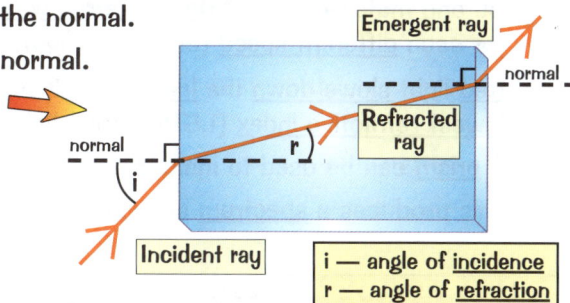

Emergent ray
normal
Refracted ray
normal
i
Incident ray
i — angle of incidence
r — angle of refraction

The Greater the Change in Speed the More Waves Bend

1) When light enters glass it slows down to about 2/3 of its normal speed (in air), i.e. its speed is about 2×10^8 m/s rather than 3×10^8 m/s.
2) The ratio of the speed of light in a vacuum to the speed of light in a medium is called the refractive index of the medium (3/2 for glass).
3) The refractive index is basically a measure of the amount of bending — the higher the refractive index, the more the light bends when it enters or leaves the medium.
4) When waves hit a boundary along the normal, i.e. at exactly 90°, then there will be no change in direction. There'll still be a change in speed and wavelength, though.
5) Some light is also reflected when it hits a different medium, such as glass (see next page).

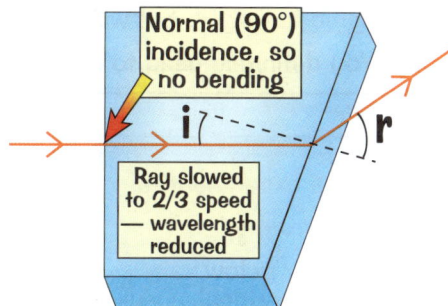

Normal (90°) incidence, so no bending
i
r
Ray slowed to 2/3 speed — wavelength reduced

Every Transparent Material Has a Refractive Index

1) The absolute refractive index of a material is defined as:

$$\text{refractive index, } n = \frac{\text{speed of light in a vacuum, c}}{\text{speed of light in the medium, v}}$$

$$n = \frac{c}{v} \quad (c = 3 \times 10^8 \text{ m/s})$$

2) Light slows down a lot in glass, so the refractive index of glass is high (around 1.5). The refractive index of water is lower (around 1.33) — so light slows down less in water than in glass.
3) The speed of light in air is about the same as in a vacuum, so the refractive index of air is 1.
4) You might have to predict the direction of refraction when given information on speed or refractive index.

Example How fast would light travel through a crystal of titanium dioxide (refractive index of 2.5)? If light passed from air into titanium dioxide at an angle, would it bend towards or away from the normal?
refractive index = speed of light in a vacuum ÷ speed of light in the medium, so speed of light in titanium dioxide = 3×10^8 m/s ÷ 2.5 = 1.2×10^8 m/s. The light slows down, so it would bend towards the normal.

Bending light's alright, but I prefer bendy straws myself...

Answer on p. 116.

Put your refractive index knowledge to the test: Light travels through a sapphire at a speed of 1.7×10^8 m/s. What is the refractive index of sapphire? In what direction would light bend as it passed from a sapphire into air?

Refraction: Two Special Cases

Refractive Index Explains Dispersion

1) <u>Different colours of light</u> are <u>refracted</u> by <u>different amounts</u>.

2) This is because they travel at <u>slightly</u> <u>different speeds</u> in any given <u>medium</u> (but the same speed in a <u>vacuum</u>).

3) The <u>refractive index</u> of a medium is the <u>ratio</u> of speed of light in a vacuum to speed of light in that medium.

4) So any material has a <u>different refractive index</u> for each <u>different speed</u> (colour) of light.

5) <u>Red</u> light <u>slows down</u> the <u>least</u> when it travels from air into glass, so it is refracted the <u>least</u> and has the <u>lowest refractive index</u> (1.514). <u>Blue light</u> has a <u>higher refractive index</u> (1.523) so is refracted <u>more</u>.

6) A <u>prism</u> can be used to make the different colours of white light emerge at <u>different angles</u>.

7) This produces a <u>spectrum</u> showing all the colours of the <u>rainbow</u>. This effect is called <u>DISPERSION</u>.

Total Internal Reflection and the Critical Angle

1) <u>Total internal reflection</u> (<u>TIR</u>) <u>only happens</u> when <u>light</u> travels from a more dense medium with a <u>higher refractive index</u> to a less dense medium with a <u>lower</u> refractive index (e.g. <u>from glass</u> to <u>water</u>).

2) If the <u>angle</u> of incidence is <u>large enough</u> (greater than the <u>critical angle</u>) the ray of light <u>won't come out at all</u>, but will <u>reflect</u> back into the glass (or whatever). This is <u>total internal reflection</u>.

3) You definitely need to learn this set of <u>three diagrams</u> which show the three conditions:

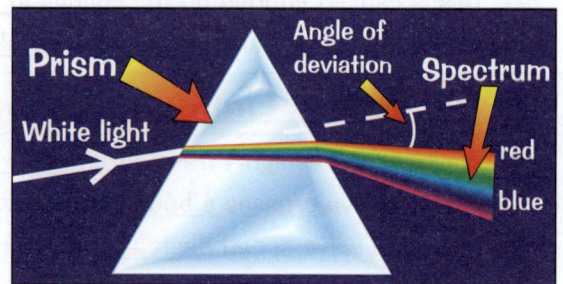

<u>Angle of Incidence LESS than the Critical Angle</u>. Most of the light <u>passes through</u> into the air but a <u>little</u> bit of it is <u>internally reflected</u>.

<u>Angle of Incidence EQUAL to the Critical Angle</u>. The emerging ray travels <u>along the surface</u>. There's quite a bit of <u>internal reflection</u>.

<u>Angle of Incidence GREATER than the Critical Angle</u>. <u>No light comes out</u>. It's <u>all</u> internally reflected, i.e. <u>total internal reflection</u>.

4) <u>Different media</u> have <u>different critical angles</u> — the <u>higher</u> the refractive index of the medium, the <u>lower</u> the critical angle will be.

5) The <u>critical angle</u> for <u>glass</u> is about <u>42°</u>. This is <u>handy</u> because it means <u>45° angles</u> can be used to get <u>TIR</u>, as in <u>optical fibres</u>, <u>prisms</u> in binoculars, <u>reflectors</u>, <u>road signs</u> and <u>cat's eyes on roads</u>.

6) You need to learn the <u>path</u> that light takes through devices that use total internal reflection:

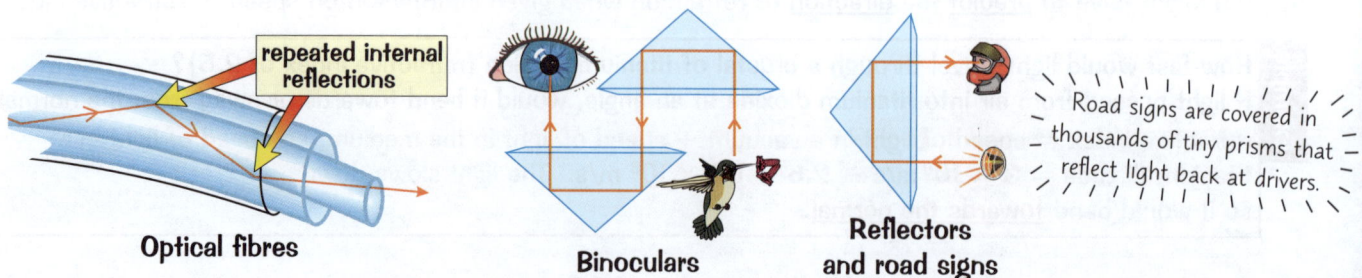

Optical fibres

Binoculars

Reflectors and road signs

Road signs are covered in thousands of tiny prisms that reflect light back at drivers.

Yay — rainbows and unicorns (okay, there aren't really any unicorns)...

You're expected to know <u>why dispersion happens</u>, and to remember that <u>red</u> light is refracted <u>less</u> than <u>blue</u> light.

Images and Converging Lenses

Lenses are usually made of glass or plastic. All lenses change the direction of rays of light by refraction.

A Real Image is Actually There — A Virtual Image is Not

1) A real image is where the light from an object comes together to form an image on a 'screen' — like the image formed on an eye's retina (the 'screen' at the back of an eye).

2) So, real images can be projected onto screens.

3) A virtual image is when the rays are diverging, so the light from the object appears to be coming from a completely different place.

4) Virtual images can't be projected onto screens.

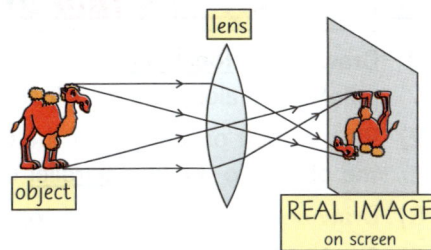

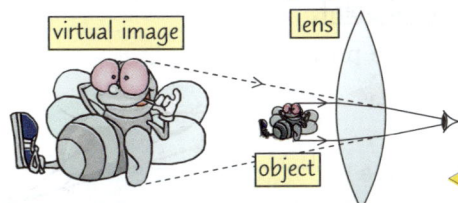

5) When you look in a mirror you see a virtual image of your face — the object (your face) appears to be behind the mirror.

6) You can get a virtual image when looking at an object through a magnifying lens — the virtual image looks bigger and further away than the object actually is.

7) To describe an image properly, you need to say 4 things:
   a) How big it is compared to the object.
   b) Whether it's upright or inverted (upside down).
   c) Whether it's real or virtual.
   d) Where it is (in relation to the lens and the focal points).

Converging (Convex) Lenses Focus Light

1) A converging lens is convex — it bulges outwards.

2) It causes rays of light to converge (move together) to a focus.

3) If the rays entering the lens are parallel to each other and to the principal axis, it focuses them at a point called the focal point.

4) The distance between the centre of the lens and the focal point is called the focal length of the lens.

5) You might have to explain the refraction of certain types of light ray:

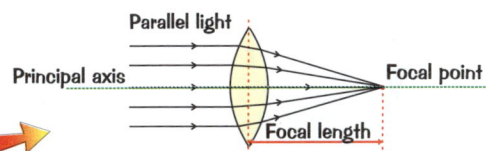

The blue ray is parallel to the principal axis.

a) A ray travelling parallel to the principal axis slows down as it enters and bends towards the normal.

b) When it hits the 'glass to air' boundary on the other side it speeds up and bends away from the normal.

c) The curvature of the lens means all the parallel rays hitting different parts of the lens are bent towards the same focal point, where an image is formed.

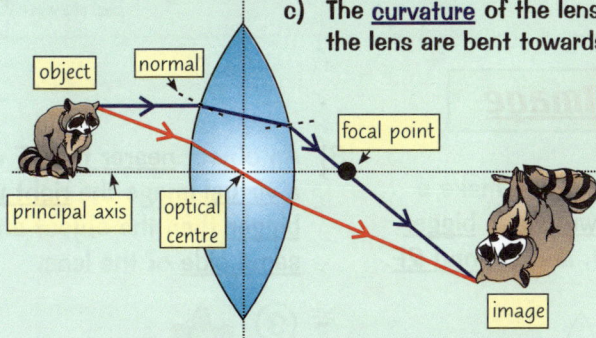

The red ray passes through the optical centre.

a) A ray passing through the optical centre of the lens appears to pass straight through.

b) It exits the lens at the same angle it entered at, but on the opposite side of the principal axis, so it's bent the same amount but in the opposite direction upon entering and exiting the lens.

6) Convex lenses work the other way round too — they can turn diverging light rays into parallel light.

7) Convex lenses can make real or virtual images, depending on how close the object is to the lens.

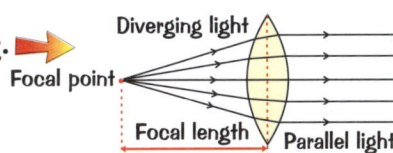

Rays travelling through the focal point: The light bends away from the normal, then towards it, producing parallel rays the other side of the lens.

Important stuff this — come on, focus focus...

So you get an exam question: "Bob looks through a magnifying glass at a beetle one focal length away from the lens. Describe the image he sees." How many things do you need to say about the image in your answer... is it one? Nope. Two? Wrong again. Three? Um, no. Four? Yep, got it. Now you're ready four the exam. Fantastic.

Ray Diagrams

Ray diagrams are those fiddly pictures you draw to work out what the image through a lens looks like. And guess what... you'll probably have to draw one in the exam.

Draw a Ray Diagram to Show the Image From a Convex Lens

1) Draw in the focal point — e.g. if the focal length is 5 cm, draw the focal point 5 cm along the principal axis from the optical centre of the lens.

2) Pick a point on the top of the object. Draw a ray going from the object to the lens parallel to the principal axis of the lens.

3) Draw another ray from the top of the object going right through the centre of the lens.

4) The incident ray that's parallel to the axis is refracted through the focal point (see previous page). Draw a refracted ray passing through the focal point.

5) A ray passing through the optical centre of the lens doesn't bend (see previous page). In a simple lens this is the in the middle (red dot in the diagram).

6) Mark where the rays meet. That's the top of the image.

7) Repeat the process for a point on the bottom of the object. When the bottom of the object is on the axis, the bottom of the image is also on the axis.

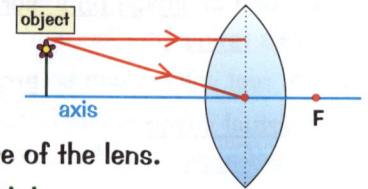

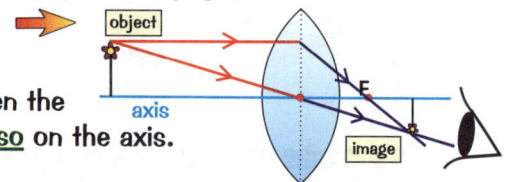

EXAMPLE:

1) and 2) — draw in focal point and incident rays from top of object:

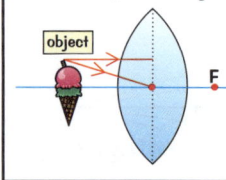

3), 4), 5) — draw refracted rays to find top of image:

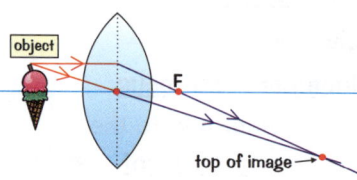

6) — Repeat for bottom of object:

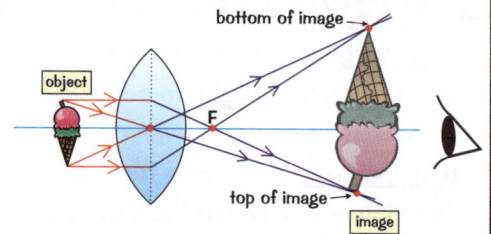

If you really want to be sure, you can draw a third incident ray.
Draw a line from the top of the object, passing through the focal point in front of the lens.
Refract it so that it leaves the lens parallel to the axis.
In the exam you can get away with just two rays, so you only need bother with the third if you want to double-check.

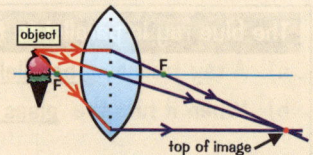

Distance from the Lens Affects the Image

1) An object at 2F will produce a real, upside down image the same size as the object, and at 2F.

2) Between F and 2F it'll make a real, upside down image bigger than the object, and beyond 2F.

3) An object nearer than F will make a virtual image the right way up, bigger than the object and on the same side of the lens.

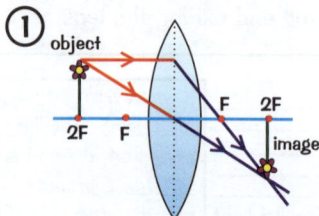

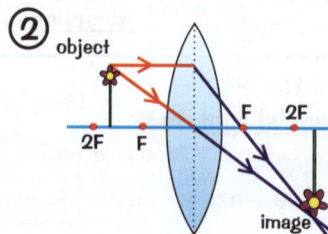

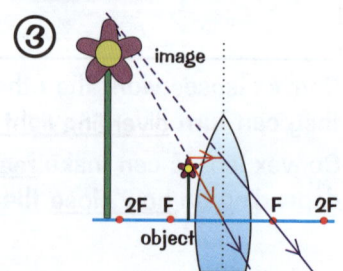

Ray...

Ray diagrams. Hmm, not the easiest things in the world. But to be frank, the method's pretty simple — it's just drawing them accurately that people fall down on — one little mistake can ruin the whole thing. No excuses.

Magnification, Cameras and Projectors

Convex lenses are used in magnifying glasses, cameras and projectors.

Convex Lenses Create Magnified Images

1) Magnifying glasses use convex lenses to create magnified images.
2) The object being magnified must be closer to the lens than the focal length.
3) The image produced is a virtual image.

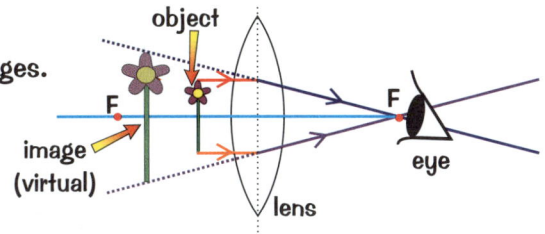

Cameras Make the Image Smaller than the Object

When you take a photograph of a flower, light from the object (flower) travels to the camera and is refracted by the lens, forming an image on the light sensor (or film in old cameras).

1) The image on the sensor is a real image because light rays actually meet there.
2) The image is smaller than the object, because the object's a lot further away than the focal length of the lens.
3) The image is inverted — upside down.

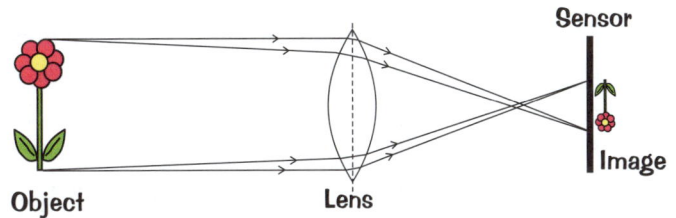

Projectors Make the Image Larger than the Object

Projectors work in a similar way to cameras, but the object is a lot closer than the focal length of the lens, so the image is larger.

1) When you project an image, the object needs to be placed upside down and very close to the lens.
2) The light from the object is refracted by the lens and produces a real, inverted and magnified image on a screen.

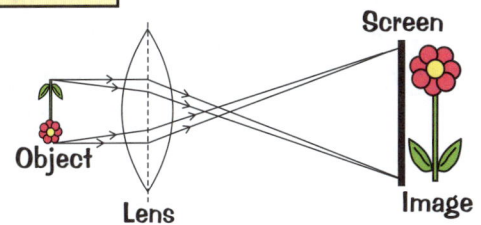

Images are Focused by Moving the Lens

1) An image will be in focus when the light that forms the image converges on the screen or the sensor.
2) In cameras and projectors the image is focused by moving the lens closer to, or further from, the object.
3) The closer to the object the lens is, the further from the lens the image will be formed (and vice versa).

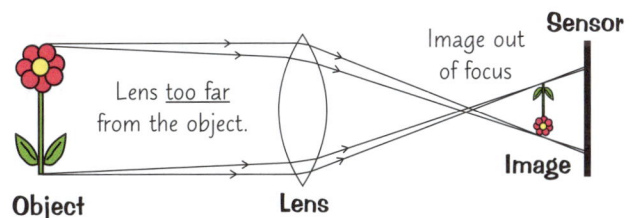

Learn the Magnification Formula

You can use the magnification formula to work out the magnification produced by a lens:

$$\text{Magnification} = \frac{\text{image size}}{\text{object size}}$$

Example: A coin with diameter 14 mm is placed a certain distance behind a magnifying lens. The virtual image produced has a diameter of 35 mm. What is the magnification of the lens at this distance?

magnification = 35 ÷ 14 = 2.5

In the exam you might have to draw a ray diagram to show where an image would be, then measure the image and work out the magnification of the lens. Another reason to draw those ray diagrams carefully...

Picture this — you've revised it, and it turns up on the exam...

Well done, you've almost made it to the end of this module. Celebrate by taking a picture of yourself.

Revision Summary for Module P5

Phew. Bit of a mixed bag, that section. If you reckon you know your stuff, then do these questions and prove it to yourself. If you can't do these questions now, you won't be able to do them in the exam.

1)   What's the difference between speed and velocity? Give an example of each.

2)* A boat is sailing due south with a velocity of 0.5 m/s relative to the water. The river is flowing at 0.2 m/s due north. Draw a vector diagram to help find the boat's resultant velocity.

3)* A bird is facing due north and flying at 12 mph relative to the air. There is a 5 mph wind blowing due west. Draw a vector diagram to help find the resultant velocity of the bird.   (Assume constant acceleration.)

4)* Find the distance travelled by a soggy pea as it is flicked from rest to a speed of 14 m/s in 0.4 s.

5)* A firework is launched upwards with an initial velocity of 13.4 m/s. Gravity causes it to accelerate downward at 10 m/s². It explodes when it's travelled 7 m. Find it's velocity at the moment before it explodes.

6)   What shape is the trajectory (path) of a projectile?

7)* A sandwich is thrown horizontally off a skyscraper at 1.5 m/s. It hits the ground 10 s later.
a) How high is the skyscraper? Take g = 10 m/s² and ignore air resistance.
b) How far will the sandwich have travelled horizontally before it hits the ground?

8)   Briefly describe Newton's third law and use it to explain recoil.

9)* If the total momentum of a system before a collision is zero, what is the total momentum of the system after the collision?

10) What happens to the pressure of a gas if:
a) the volume of the gas increases,   b) the temperature of the gas increases?

11)* What happens to the size of the gravitational force if the distance between two masses decreases by a factor of three?

12) State three differences between a low polar orbit and a geostationary orbit.

13) Briefly explain why waves with a frequency higher than 30 GHz can't be used to carry satellite signals.

14) Briefly explain why satellite transmitting and receiving dishes need careful alignment.

15) Draw simple wave diagrams to show the difference between constructive and destructive interference.

16) Use a diagram to describe the diffraction of a beam of light through a single slit.

17) What effect does a polarising filter have on the light passing through it?

18) Draw a diagram to show the path of a ray of light as it passes from:
air → rectangular block of glass → air, meeting the block of glass at an angle.

19)* The refractive index of the mineral 'jet' is 1.66.
a)   How fast will a ray of light travel through a piece of jet?
b)   Will a ray of light be travelling towards or away from the normal when it exits a piece of jet into air?

20) For which colour light does glass have the highest refractive index — blue or red?

21) What will happen to a ray of light that enters a block of glass:
a) at the critical angle,   b) at an angle greater than the critical angle?

22) What is a real image? How is it different from a virtual image?

23) Copy and complete this ray diagram to show the image formed:

object

F   F

(Draw it scaled-up so it's a bit bigger.)

24)* Peter measures the length of a seed to be 1.5 cm. When he looks at the seed through a converging lens at a certain distance, the seed appears to have a length of 4.5 cm. What is the magnification of this lens at this distance?

Circuits and Resistors

Isn't electricity <u>great</u> — hair straighteners, computers, life-support machines... Mind you, it's pretty <u>bad news</u> if the technical <u>terms</u> don't mean anything to you. So let's have a quick recap to start...

1) <u>Current</u> is the <u>flow</u> of <u>charge</u> (electrons) round the circuit. Current will <u>only flow</u> through a component if there is a <u>voltage</u> across that component. Current is <u>measured</u> in <u>amps</u>, A.

2) <u>Voltage</u> is the <u>driving force</u> that pushes the current round. Voltage is <u>measured</u> in <u>volts</u>, V.

3) <u>Resistance</u> is anything in the circuit that <u>reduces</u> the <u>current</u>. Resistance is <u>measured</u> in <u>ohms</u>, Ω.

4) <u>There's a balance</u> — the <u>relative sizes</u> of the voltage and resistance decide <u>how big</u> the current will be. If you <u>increase</u> the <u>voltage</u> then <u>more current</u> will flow. If you increase the <u>resistance</u> then <u>less</u> current will flow (or more voltage will be needed to keep the same current flowing).

Learn These Circuit Symbols

<u>Circuit diagrams</u> are a lot <u>less scary</u> if you know your symbols.

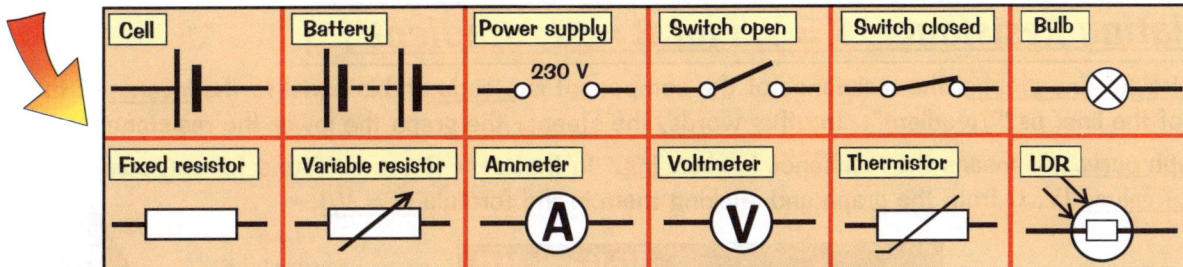

Cell	Battery	Power supply 230 V	Switch open	Switch closed	Bulb
Fixed resistor	Variable resistor	Ammeter Ⓐ	Voltmeter Ⓥ	Thermistor	LDR

Resistance is Caused by Collisions in a Conductor

1) In a <u>metal</u> conductor, the electric <u>charge</u> is carried by <u>electrons</u>.

2) When electrons <u>flow through</u> a conductor they <u>collide</u> with <u>atoms</u> in the metal — this causes <u>resistance</u>.

3) <u>Collisions</u> between electrons and atoms cause the atoms to <u>vibrate</u>.

4) The <u>more</u> atoms vibrate, the more they <u>get in the way</u> of the electrons, so the more collisions there are.

5) So an <u>increase</u> in <u>collisions</u> causes an increase in the <u>resistance</u> of the conductor.

6) The increased <u>vibration</u> of the <u>atoms</u> also increases the <u>temperature</u> of the conductor.

Variable Resistors

1) A <u>variable resistor</u> (or <u>rheostat</u>) is a resistor whose resistance can be <u>changed</u> by twiddling a knob or something.

2) They're great for <u>controlling the current</u> flowing through a circuit. Turn the resistance <u>up</u>, the current <u>drops</u>. Turn the resistance <u>down</u>, the current goes <u>up</u>.

3) The old-fashioned ones are <u>huge coils of wire</u> with a <u>slider</u> on them.

4) As you move the slider, the <u>length of wire</u> that has <u>current</u> flowing through it <u>changes</u>.

5) <u>Longer</u> wires have <u>more resistance</u>, so <u>less current</u> flowing through them. This is because the <u>longer</u> the wire, the <u>more atoms</u> the electrons will <u>collide</u> with, increasing the resistance.

6) Variable resistors are used for controlling the <u>speed of motors</u> and the <u>brightness of bulbs</u>. Turning the resistance <u>down</u> <u>increases</u> the <u>speed</u> of the motor or the <u>brightness</u> of a bulb.

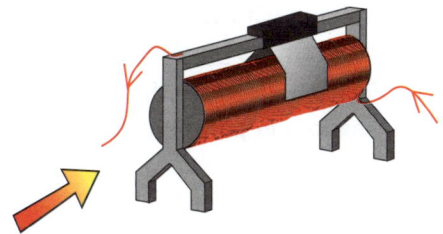

Currently I'm trying to think of a joke about resistance...

The circuit symbols here are pretty <u>simple</u> ones that you should be familiar with. There's still a <u>few more</u> to come in this module, make sure you can <u>recognise</u> and <u>draw</u> them all before the exam. I like the one for a <u>transistor</u>.

Voltage-Current Graphs and Resistance

The resistance of a component can be measured using a standard test circuit.

The Slope of a Voltage-Current Graph Shows Resistance

Voltage-current (V-I) graphs show how the current in a circuit varies as you change the voltage:

Different Resistors

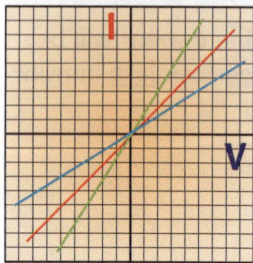

The current through a resistor (at constant temperature) is proportional to voltage. Different resistors have different resistances, hence the different slopes. Straight line graphs like this are for 'ohmic' resistors, which have a constant resistance.

A Filament Lamp

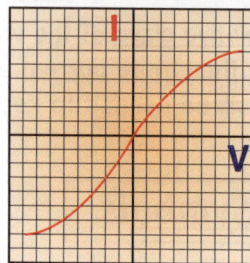

As the current increases, the temperature of the filament increases and so the resistance increases (hence the curve). Components whose resistance changes are known as 'non-ohmic' resistors.

Calculating Resistance: R = V/I (or R = "1/gradient")

For the straight-line graphs, the resistance of the component is steady and is equal to the inverse of the gradient of the line, or "1/gradient". In other words, the steeper the graph the lower the resistance.

If the graph curves, it means the resistance is changing. In that case R can be found for any point by taking the pair of values (V, I) from the graph and sticking them in the formula R = V/I.

$$\text{Resistance } (\Omega) = \frac{\text{Voltage (V)}}{\text{Current (A)}}$$

Remember: I is the symbol for electrical current.

$$\frac{V}{I \times R}$$

Resistors in Parallel Reduce the Resistance in a Circuit

Sometimes a single resistor isn't enough — combining resistors changes the resistance of a circuit. Putting resistors together in series increases the resistance, connecting them in parallel decreases it.

1) In series circuits, the total resistance is just the sum of the individual resistances:

$$R_T = R_1 + R_2 + R_3$$

2) But resistors connected in parallel provide more paths for the current to travel down.

3) So the total resistance of a parallel circuit is always less than that of the branch with the smallest resistance.

Total resistance = 6 + 3 + 7 = 16 Ω

4) A circuit with two resistors in parallel will have a lower resistance than a circuit with either of the resistors by themselves — which means the parallel circuit will have a higher current.

5) You can calculate the total resistance of resistors in parallel using this equation:

$$\frac{1}{R_T} = \frac{1}{R_1} + \frac{1}{R_2} + \frac{1}{R_3}$$

$$\frac{1}{\text{Total R}} = \frac{1}{R_1} + \frac{1}{R_2}$$

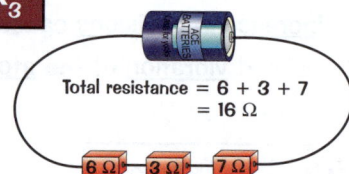

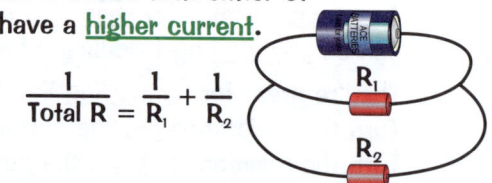

EXAMPLE:
Calculate the total resistance of the circuit shown in the diagram.

ANSWER:
Resistors connected in parallel, so use the equation $\frac{1}{R_T} = \frac{1}{R_1} + \frac{1}{R_2} + \frac{1}{R_3}$.

$\frac{1}{R_T} = \frac{1}{1} + \frac{1}{7} + \frac{1}{10} = 1 + 0.14 + 0.1 = 1.24$, so $R_T = 1 \div 1.24 = 0.8 \, \Omega$.

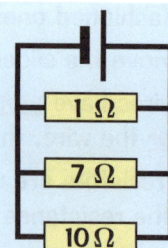

1 Ω
7 Ω
10 Ω

Voltage-current graphs — more fun than gravel...

You have to be able to interpret voltage-current graphs for your exam. Remember — the steeper the slope, the lower the resistance. And you need to know the equations inside out, back to front, upside down and in Swahili.

Potential Dividers

Potential dividers consist of a pair of resistors. They divide the potential in a circuit
so you can get outputs of different voltages.

The Higher the Resistance, the Greater the Voltage Drop

A voltage across a pair of resistors is 'shared out' according to their relative resistances. The rule is:

The larger the share of the total resistance, the larger the share of the total voltage.

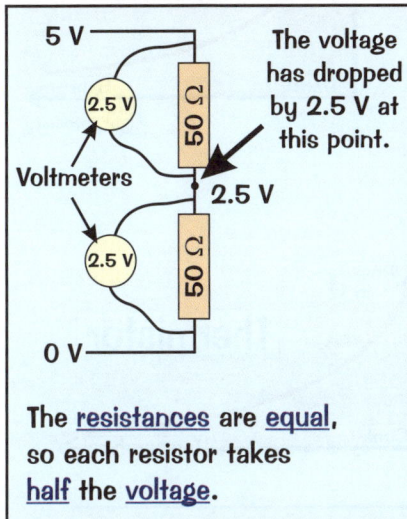

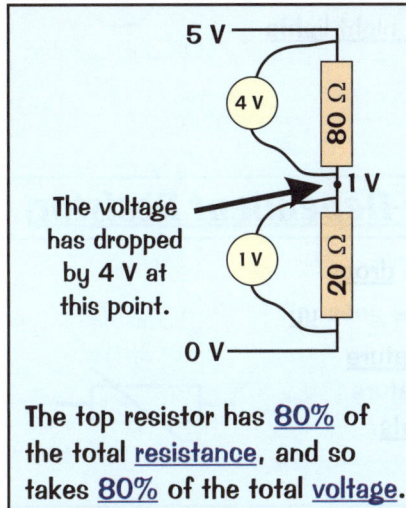

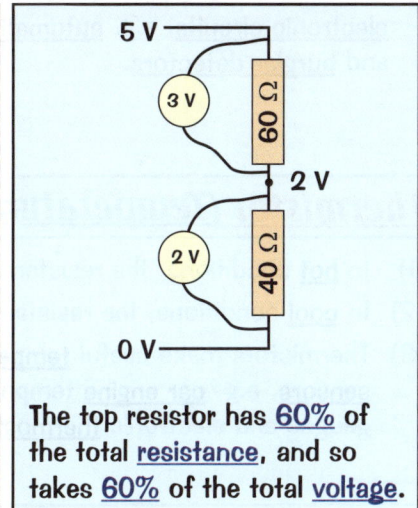

5 V — 2.5 V — 50 Ω / 2.5 V — 50 Ω — 0 V Voltmeters The voltage has dropped by 2.5 V at this point. 2.5 V	5 V — 4 V — 80 Ω / 1 V — 20 Ω — 0 V The voltage has dropped by 4 V at this point. 1 V	5 V — 3 V — 60 Ω / 2 V — 40 Ω — 0 V 2 V
The resistances are equal, so each resistor takes half the voltage.	The top resistor has 80% of the total resistance, and so takes 80% of the total voltage.	The top resistor has 60% of the total resistance, and so takes 60% of the total voltage.

The point between the two resistors is the 'output' of the potential divider.
This 'output' voltage can be varied by swapping one or both of the resistors for a variable resistor.

Potential Dividers are Quite Useful

Potential dividers are not only spectacularly interesting — they're useful as well.
They allow you to run a device that requires a certain voltage from a battery of a different voltage.
This is the formula you need to use:

$$V_{out} = V_{in} \times \left(\frac{R_2}{R_1 + R_2}\right)$$

The output voltage (V_{out}) depends on the relative values of R_1 and R_2. From the formula, you should see that
if R_2 is very big compared to R_1, the bit in the brackets cancels down to about 1, so V_{out} is approximately V_{in}.
But if R_2 is a lot smaller than R_1, the bit in brackets becomes so small that V_{out} is approximately 0.

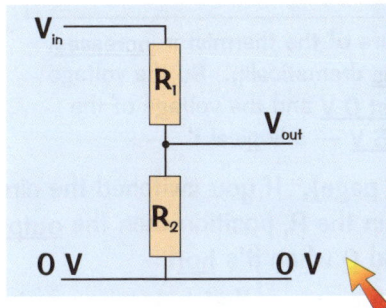

V_{in} — R_1 — V_{out} — R_2 — 0 V — 0 V

EXAMPLE:

In the diagram, the input voltage for the potential divider is 9 V.
R_1 is 20 Ω and R_2 is 40 Ω. What is the output voltage across R_2?

ANSWER:

$$V_{out} = 9\text{ V} \times \left(\frac{40}{20 + 40}\right) = \frac{9\text{ V} \times 40}{60} = 6\text{ V}$$

A potential divider like this could be used to run a 6 V device from a 9 V battery. You could replace
one of the resistors by a variable resistor, so that you could change V_{out} to any value between 0 and 9
volts. If you had two variable resistors you could have much finer control of an output voltage with an
adjustable threshold — useful for controlling heat and light sensors (see next page).

My boyfriend's mother is a potential divider...

You won't believe this, but potential dividers get even more exciting on the next page. I know you're worried that
you won't be able to cope with the adrenaline rush but it's just something you have to get used to with Physics...

LDRs and Thermistors

Some resistors <u>change</u> their resistance depending on the <u>conditions</u>.
You need to know about two of them — <u>light-dependent resistors</u> and <u>thermistors</u>.

Light-Dependent Resistor (or "LDR" to Thee and Me)

1) In <u>bright light</u>, the resistance <u>falls</u>.
2) In <u>darkness</u>, the resistance is <u>highest</u>.
3) This makes it a useful device for various <u>electronic circuits</u>, e.g. <u>automatic night lights</u> and <u>burglar detectors</u>.

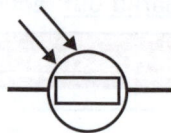

LDR circuit symbol.

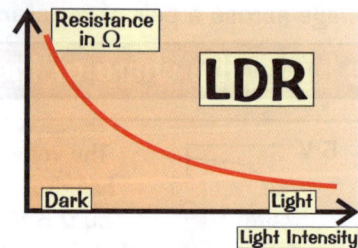

Thermistor (Temperature-Dependent Resistor)

1) In <u>hot</u> conditions, the resistance <u>drops</u>.
2) In <u>cool</u> conditions, the resistance goes <u>up</u>.
3) Thermistors make useful <u>temperature sensors</u>, e.g. <u>car engine</u> temperature gauges and electronic <u>thermostats</u>.

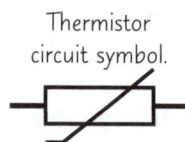

Thermistor circuit symbol.

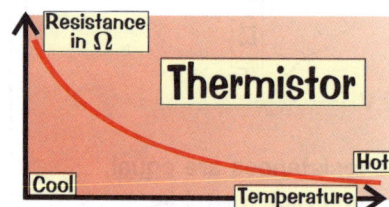

A Thermistor in a Potential Divider Makes a Temperature Sensor

1) Using a <u>thermistor</u> and a <u>fixed resistor</u> in a potential divider, you can make a <u>temperature sensor</u>.
2) You can make a temperature sensor that gives a <u>high voltage output</u> (a 'logical 1' — see page 102) when it's hot and a <u>low voltage output</u> (a 'logical 0') when it's cold. This is how it works...

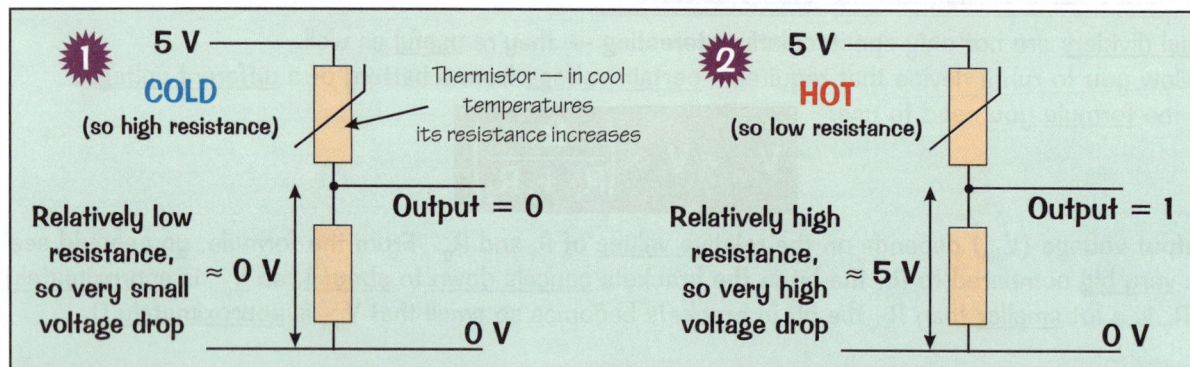

1 5 V — COLD (so high resistance) — Thermistor — in cool temperatures its resistance increases — Relatively low resistance, so very small voltage drop ≈ 0 V — Output = 0 — 0 V

2 5 V — HOT (so low resistance) — Relatively high resistance, so very high voltage drop ≈ 5 V — Output = 1 — 0 V

1 When the thermistor's <u>cold</u> its resistance is <u>very high</u>, so the voltage drop across it is <u>almost 5 V</u>, meaning the voltage of the output is <u>nearly 0 V</u> — a 'logical 0'.

2 As the temperature of the thermistor <u>increases</u>, its resistance <u>falls</u> dramatically. So the voltage across it is <u>almost 0 V</u> and the voltage of the output is <u>nearly 5 V</u> — a 'logical 1'.

3) In the circuit above, the <u>thermistor</u> is in the R_1 <u>position</u> (see previous page). If you switched the circuit <u>around</u> so the thermistor was in the R_2 <u>position</u> and the <u>resistor</u> was in the R_1 position then the <u>output</u> would switch round too. So, the output would be <u>1</u> when it's <u>cold</u> and <u>0</u> when it's <u>hot</u>.

4) If you replace the fixed resistor with a <u>variable resistor</u>, you can make a <u>sensor</u> that triggers an output device at a temperature <u>you choose</u> and can <u>change</u> whenever you like, e.g. in a heating system.

5) You can play around with that circuit to make <u>different kinds of sensor</u>. For example, you could use a similar circuit to make a <u>light sensor</u> — just replace the thermistor with an <u>LDR</u>.

How can this stuff be light-dependent if it's so dull...

Thermistors are used in computers as well. When you first turn the power on, the thermistor's cold, so its resistance is high. The high resistance prevents a surge in the current that could damage a silicon chip. Clever.

Transistors

Things you take for granted in the modern world couldn't exist without <u>transistors</u> — mobile phones, <u>laptops</u>, digital watches... so it's probably best that you learn a <u>bit more</u> about them.

Transistors <u>are</u> Electronic Switches

Transistors are the basic <u>building blocks</u> of electronic components.
Transistors can be made so <u>small</u> that the circuits of a modern <u>computer</u> may contain <u>billions</u> of them.

1) In transistors, a <u>small</u> amount of <u>current</u> is used to <u>control</u> the flow of a much <u>larger</u> current. This means that they can be used as <u>electronic switches</u>.

2) Transistors can be much <u>smaller</u> than mechanical switches, so they can be <u>integrated</u> into circuits, such as logic gates.

Circuit symbol for a transistor

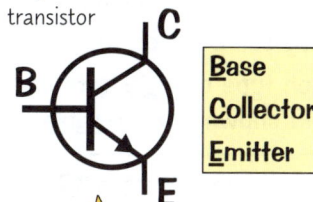

Base
Collector
Emitter

This is an <u>npn</u> transistor. There are other types of transistor but you don't need to know about those.

3) All transistors have <u>three</u> parts:

   a) <u>Base</u> — The '<u>switch</u>' that controls the flow of current. If <u>no current</u> is applied to the base it <u>stops</u> current flowing through the rest of the transistor. When a <u>small</u> current is applied to the base a <u>larger current</u> can flow through the collector and emitter. A <u>large</u> current passing through the <u>base</u> would <u>damage</u> the transistor.

   b) <u>Collector</u> — Current flows <u>into</u> the transistor through the collector.

   c) <u>Emitter</u> — Current flows <u>out</u> of the transistor through the emitter.

4) The currents in <u>each part</u> of the transistor are <u>related</u> by this handy <u>equation</u>:

$$I_E = I_B + I_C$$

Current in emitter = current in base + current in collector

EXAMPLE:
A current of 0.1 A is applied to the base of a transistor. This allows a current of 2 A to flow through the collector. Calculate the current which flows through the emitter.
ANSWER:
Use the equation $I_E = I_B + I_C$. $I_E = 0.1\,A + 2\,A = \underline{2.1\,A}$.

Example — Switching <u>an</u> LED

<u>LED</u>s (see p. 104) are just <u>fancy light bulbs</u>. You can make a circuit to <u>control</u> one using a <u>transistor</u>. You need to be able to <u>complete</u> this circuit for the exam:

1) When the <u>switch</u> is <u>closed</u> a current <u>flows</u> from the power supply into the <u>transistor circuit</u>.

2) The <u>high resistor</u> before the transistor <u>base</u> means only a <u>small current</u> flows through the base.

3) The current through the base '<u>closes</u>' the transistor and lets current flow through the <u>LED</u>, turning it <u>on</u>.

4) If the switch is <u>opened</u>, <u>no</u> current flows through the base, so it turns the LED <u>off</u>.

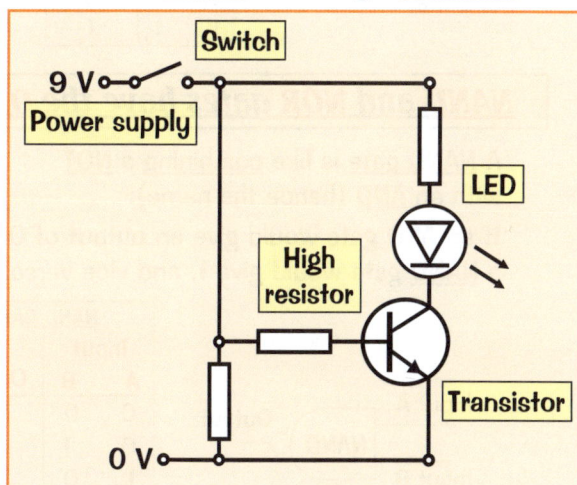

Switch
9 V
Power supply
LED
High resistor
Transistor
0 V

E.g. You could use this system to <u>turn on</u> an LED when the <u>temperature</u> in a room drops <u>too cold</u>. You'd just have a <u>potential divider system</u> with a thermistor in the circuit too. When temperature drops, V_{out} increases, the transistor is <u>switched on</u>, so the LED comes on too.

From a tenement window a transistor [radio] blasts...

Transistors can also be used to <u>amplify</u> a signal, so the first common devices to use transistors were <u>radios</u>. Before transistors, radios used bulky and fragile <u>vacuum tubes</u>. Transistors made radios <u>portable</u> and <u>cheap</u>.

Logic Gates

Transistors can also be <u>combined</u> to make <u>logic gates</u>, which <u>process</u> information and make computers work.

Digital Systems are Either On or Off

1) Every connection in a digital system is in one of only <u>two states</u>. It can be either ON or OFF, either HIGH or LOW, either YES or NO, either 1 or 0... you get the picture.

2) In reality a 1 is a <u>high voltage</u> (about 5 V) and a 0 is a <u>low voltage</u> (about 0 V). Every part of the system is in one of these two states — nothing in between.

A Logic Gate is a Type of Digital Processor

<u>Logic gates</u> are small, but they're made up of really small components like <u>transistors</u> and <u>resistors</u>.

They can be used to <u>process</u> information, giving <u>different outputs</u> depending on the <u>input</u>(s) they receive.

Each type of logic gate has its own set of <u>rules</u> for converting inputs to outputs, and these rules are best shown in <u>truth tables</u>. The important thing is to list <u>all</u> the possible <u>combinations</u> of input values.

NOT gate — sometimes called an Inverter

A <u>NOT</u> gate just has <u>one</u> input — and this input can be either <u>1</u> or <u>0</u>, so the truth table has just two rows.

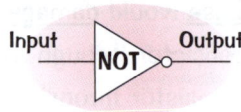

Input ── NOT ── Output

NOT GATE	
Input	Output
0	1
1	0

Some AND and OR gates have more than two inputs, but you don't have to worry about those.

AND and OR gates usually have Two Inputs

<u>Each input</u> can be 0 or 1, so to allow for <u>all</u> combinations from two inputs, your truth table needs <u>4 rows</u>. There's a certain logic to the names...

An <u>AND</u> gate only gives an output of 1 if both the first input <u>AND</u> the second input are 1.

Input A ── AND ── Output
Input B

AND GATE		
Input		
A	B	Output
0	0	0
0	1	0
1	0	0
1	1	1

An <u>OR</u> gate just needs either the first <u>OR</u> the second input to be 1.

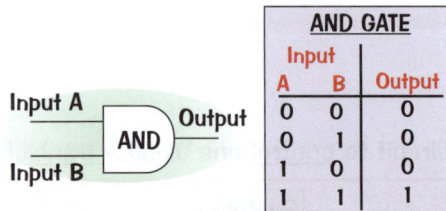

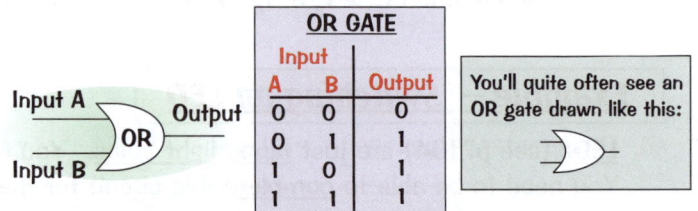

Input A ── OR ── Output
Input B

OR GATE		
Input		
A	B	Output
0	0	0
0	1	1
1	0	1
1	1	1

You'll quite often see an OR gate drawn like this:

NAND and NOR gates have the Opposite Output of AND and OR gates

A <u>NAND gate</u> is like <u>combining</u> a <u>NOT</u> with an <u>AND</u> (hence the name):

If an AND gate would give an output of 0, a <u>NAND</u> gate would give 1, and vice versa.

Input A ── NAND ── Output
Input B

NAND GATE		
Input		
A	B	Output
0	0	1
0	1	1
1	0	1
1	1	0

A <u>NOR gate</u> is like <u>combining</u> a <u>NOT</u> with an <u>OR</u> (hence the name):

If an OR gate would give an output of 0, a <u>NOR</u> gate would give 1, and vice versa.

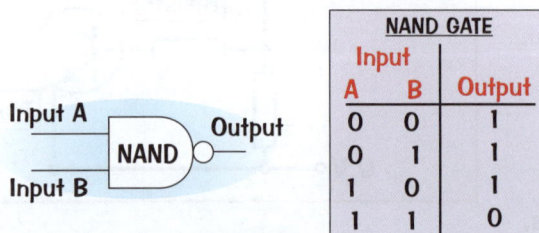

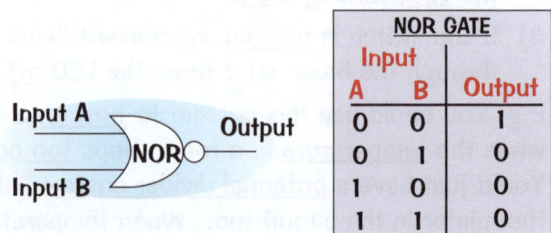

Input A ── NOR ── Output
Input B

NOR GATE		
Input		
A	B	Output
0	0	1
0	1	0
1	0	0
1	1	0

I like physics, NAND chemistry, NAND biology...

Well at least there aren't that many <u>facts</u> to learn on this page — it's more a question of <u>understanding</u> the inputs and outputs for the <u>five</u> types of gate. It's a good idea to be familiar with the circuit symbols of the gates too though. And practise writing out all the <u>different tables</u> — it's the <u>quickest</u> and <u>bestest</u> way to learn.

Using Logic Gates

You need to be able to construct a truth table for a combination of logic gates.
Approach this kind of thing in an organised way and stick to the rules, and you won't go far wrong.

'Interesting' Example — a Greenhouse

Once the gardener has switched the system on, he wants to be warned if the greenhouse gets too cold or if someone has opened the door. He only wants the warning system to work when the greenhouse gets dark.

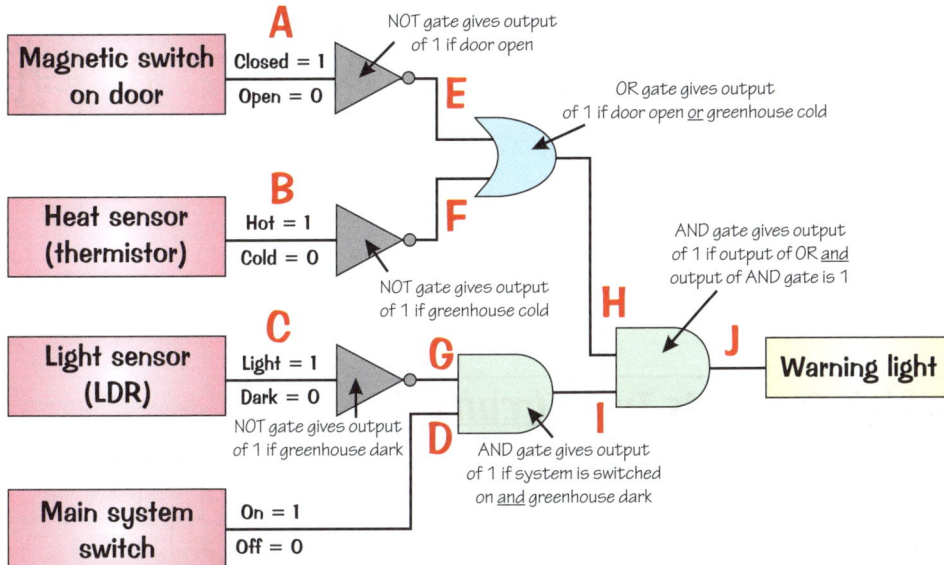

Magnetic switch on door
Closed = 1
Open = 0

A

NOT gate gives output of 1 if door open

E

OR gate gives output of 1 if door open or greenhouse cold

Heat sensor (thermistor)
Hot = 1
Cold = 0

B

F

NOT gate gives output of 1 if greenhouse cold

AND gate gives output of 1 if output of OR and output of AND gate is 1

H

Light sensor (LDR)
Light = 1
Dark = 0

C

G

J

NOT gate gives output of 1 if greenhouse dark

D

I

AND gate gives output of 1 if system is switched on and greenhouse dark

Warning light

Main system switch
On = 1
Off = 0

Inputs									Output
A	B	C	D	E	F	G	H	I	J
0	0	0	0	1	1	1	1	0	0
0	0	0	1	1	1	1	1	1	1
0	0	1	0	1	1	0	1	0	0
0	0	1	1	1	1	0	1	0	0
0	1	0	0	1	0	1	1	0	0
0	1	0	1	1	0	1	1	1	1
0	1	1	0	1	0	0	1	0	0
0	1	1	1	1	0	0	1	0	0
1	0	0	0	0	1	1	1	0	0
1	0	0	1	0	1	1	1	1	1
1	0	1	0	0	1	0	1	0	0
1	0	1	1	0	1	0	1	0	0
1	1	0	0	0	0	1	0	0	0
1	1	0	1	0	0	1	0	1	0
1	1	1	0	0	0	0	0	0	0
1	1	1	1	0	0	0	0	0	0

The warning light will come on if:

i)   it is cold in the greenhouse OR if the door is opened,

ii) AND the system is switched on,

iii) AND the greenhouse is dark.

1) Each connection has a label, and all possible combinations of the inputs are included in the table.

2) What really matters are the inputs and the output — the rest of the truth table is just there to help.

3) An LDR or thermistor combined with a resistor makes a light or temperature sensor (see page 100), the output of which can produce an input signal for a logic circuit (as used above).

4) The resistance changes the 'threshold voltage' (i.e. how bright or hot it needs to be to produce a signal).

5) Using a variable resistor makes the threshold voltage adjustable — e.g. the gardener can adjust the temperature the warning light comes on at.

AND Logic Gates are Made From Two Transistors

1) AND logic gates give an output of 1 if both inputs are also 1.

2) AND gates are made using a series of two transistors.

3) Each input is connected to the base of a transistor.

4) If the signal of either input is 0, no current flows through the base of the transistor it's connected to. The transistor stays open, so no current can flow through the rest of the circuit and the output of the gate will be 0.

5) If both inputs are 1 then both transistors will be closed, current will flow through the gate and the output of the gate will be 1.

6) Other logic gates can be made from different combinations of two transistors.

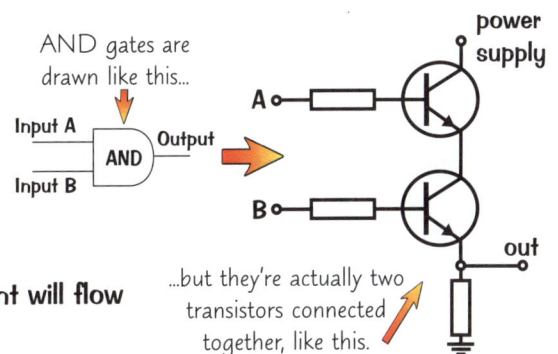

AND gates are drawn like this...

Input A

Input B

AND

Output

power supply

A

B

out

...but they're actually two transistors connected together, like this.

Now we can all sleep easy knowing the cucumbers are safe...

More hard stuff to get your head around here. Try copying out the diagrams of the greenhouse warning system and writing in the different inputs. Then follow them through to find the outputs. It's almost fun. Almost.

LEDs and Relays in Logic Circuits

Two main points on this page: 1) An LED can be used to display the output of a logic gate. 2) Logic gates don't usually supply much current, so they're often connected to a more powerful circuit using a relay switch.

LEDs — Light-Emitting Diodes

1) An LED is a diode (see page 112) which gives out light.

2) Like other diodes, it only lets current go through in one direction. When it does pass current, it gives out a pretty coloured light.

3) You can use a light-emitting diode (LED) to show the output of a logic gate. If the output is 1, enough current will flow through the LED to light it up.

4) An LED is a better choice to show output than an ordinary incandescent bulb because it uses less power and lasts longer.

5) The LED is often connected in series with a resistor to prevent it from being damaged by too large a current flowing through it.

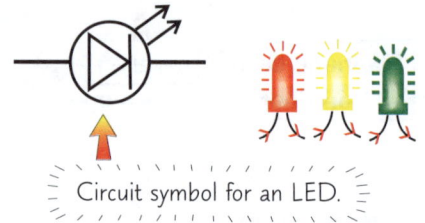

Circuit symbol for an LED.

A Relay is a Switch Which Connects Two Circuits

1) A low-power logic gate would be damaged if you plugged it straight into a high current mains power supply.

2) But an output device like a motor requires a large current.

3) The solution is to have two circuits connected by a relay.

4) The relay isolates the low voltage electronic system from the high voltage mains often needed for the output device.

5) This also means that it can be made safer for the person using the device — you can make sure that any parts that could come into contact with a person are in the low-current sensing circuit. For example, a car's starter motor needs a very high current, but the part you control (when you're turning the key) is in the low-current circuit — safely isolated by the relay.

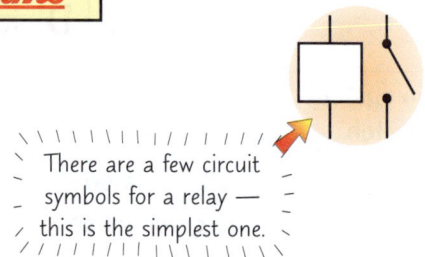

There are a few circuit symbols for a relay — this is the simplest one.

Here's How a Relay Works...

1) When the switch in the low-current circuit is closed, it turns on the electromagnet (see page 105), which attracts the iron contact on the rocker.

2) The rocker pivots and closes the contacts in the high current circuit — and the motor spins.

3) When the low-current switch is opened, the electromagnet stops pulling, the rocker returns, and the high current circuit is broken again.

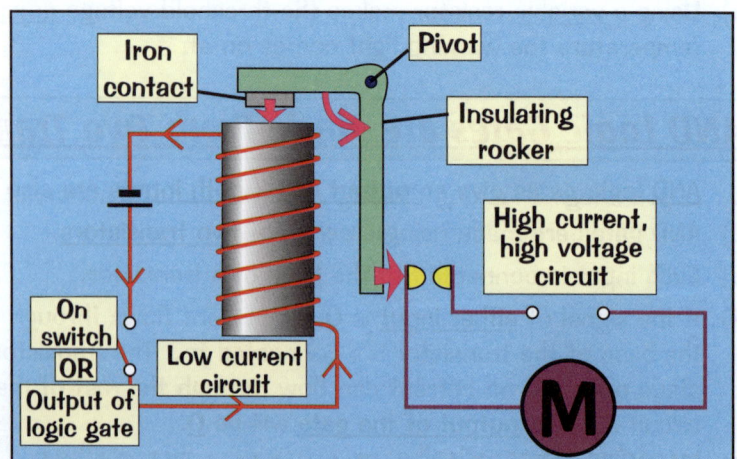

Iron contact

Pivot

Insulating rocker

High current, high voltage circuit

On switch OR Output of logic gate

Low current circuit

M

You should now be relay proud of yourself...

...'cos you've managed to get through all those pages on logic gates. I know it isn't always a barrel of laughs. There's a lot of tricky stuff here — a lot to learn, and a lot that's hard to understand. It's definitely a good idea to learn each page thoroughly before moving on, otherwise it'll all turn into a big tangled mess in your brain.

Magnetic Fields

Loads of electrical appliances use <u>magnetic fields</u> generated by <u>electric currents</u>.

> A <u>MAGNETIC FIELD</u> is a region where <u>MAGNETIC MATERIALS</u> (like iron and steel) and also <u>WIRES CARRYING CURRENTS</u> experience a <u>FORCE</u> acting on them.

Magnetic fields can be represented by <u>field diagrams</u>.
<u>The arrows on the field lines always point **FROM THE NORTH POLE** of the magnet **TO THE SOUTH POLE**.</u>

A Current-Carrying Wire Creates a Magnetic Field

1) There is a magnetic field around a <u>straight</u>, <u>current-carrying wire</u>.

2) The field is made up of <u>concentric circles</u> with the wire in the centre.

3) Changing the <u>direction</u> of the <u>current</u> changes the direction of the <u>magnetic field</u> — use the <u>Right-Hand Thumb Rule</u> to work out which way it goes.

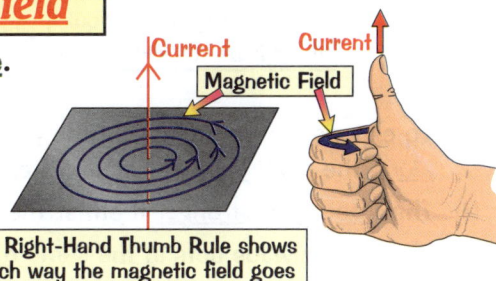

The Right-Hand Thumb Rule shows which way the magnetic field goes

A Rectangular Coil Reinforces the Magnetic Field

1) If you <u>bend</u> the current-carrying wire round into a <u>coil</u>, the magnetic field looks like this.

2) The circular magnetic fields around the sides of the loop <u>reinforce</u> each other at the centre.

3) If the coil has lots of turns, the magnetic fields from all the individual loops <u>reinforce</u> each other <u>even more</u>.

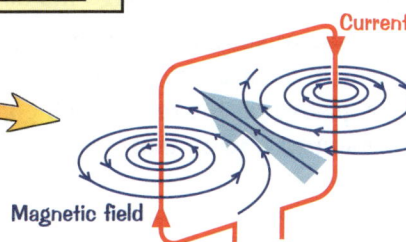

The Magnetic Field Round a Solenoid

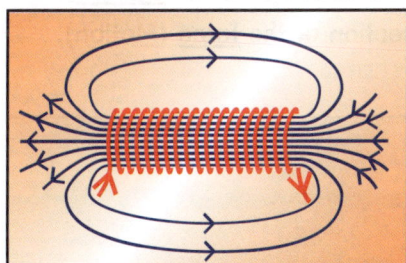

1) The magnetic field <u>inside</u> a current-carrying <u>solenoid</u> (a coil of wire) is <u>strong</u> and <u>uniform</u>.

2) <u>Outside</u> the coil, the field is just like the one round a <u>bar magnet</u>.

3) This means that the <u>ends</u> of a solenoid act like the <u>north pole</u> and <u>south pole</u> of a bar magnet.

4) Pretty obviously, if the <u>direction</u> of the <u>current</u> is <u>reversed</u>, the N and S poles will <u>swap ends</u>.

5) If you imagine looking directly into one end of a solenoid, the <u>direction of current flow</u> tells you whether it's the <u>N or S pole</u> you're looking at, as shown by the <u>two diagrams</u> opposite.

6) If you <u>stop</u> the current, the magnetic field <u>disappears</u>. A magnet whose magnetic field can be turned <u>on</u> and <u>off</u> with an <u>electric current</u> like this is called an <u>ELECTROMAGNET</u>.

7) You can increase the <u>strength</u> of the magnetic field around a solenoid by adding a magnetically <u>"soft"</u> iron core through the middle of the coil.

8) By adding <u>more turns</u> to the solenoid <u>coil</u> you can <u>further increase</u> the strength of the solenoid.

N-Pole   S-Pole

Current-carrying wires always get the thumbs up from me...

...and it's always my <u>RIGHT</u> thumb. <u>Not</u> my left, but my <u>RIGHT</u> thumb. <u>Don't get them mixed up.</u> You'll use your left hand on the next page, though, so it shouldn't feel too left out... (pun intended).

The Motor Effect

If you put a current-carrying wire into a magnetic field, you have <u>two magnetic fields combining</u>, which puts a force on the wire. The force can make the wire move — which can be quite handy, really.

A <u>Current</u> in a <u>Magnetic Field</u> Experiences a <u>Force</u>

When a current-carrying wire is put between magnetic poles, the two <u>magnetic fields</u> affect one another. The result is a <u>force</u> on the wire.

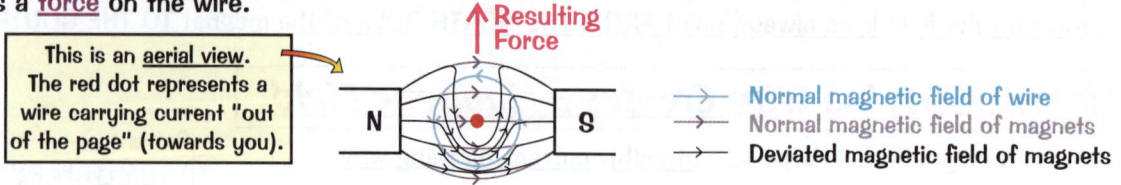

This is an <u>aerial view</u>. The red dot represents a wire carrying current "out of the page" (towards you).

↑Resulting Force

N S

→ Normal magnetic field of wire
→ Normal magnetic field of magnets
→ Deviated magnetic field of magnets

1) To experience the <u>full force</u>, the <u>wire</u> has to be at <u>90°</u> (right angles) to the <u>magnetic field</u>. If the wire runs <u>along</u> the <u>magnetic field</u>, it won't experience <u>any force at all</u>. At angles in between, it'll feel <u>some</u> force.

2) The <u>force</u> gets <u>stronger</u> if either the <u>current</u> or the <u>magnetic field</u> is made stronger.

3) The force always acts in the <u>same direction</u> relative to the <u>magnetic field</u> of the magnets and the <u>direction of the current</u> in the wire. So changing the <u>direction</u> of either the <u>magnetic field</u> or the <u>current</u> will change the direction of the <u>force</u>.

N S F

4) A good way of showing the direction of the force is to apply a current to a set of <u>rails</u> inside a <u>horseshoe magnet</u> (as shown). A bar is placed on the rails, which <u>completes the circuit</u>. This generates a <u>force</u> that <u>rolls the bar</u> along the rails.

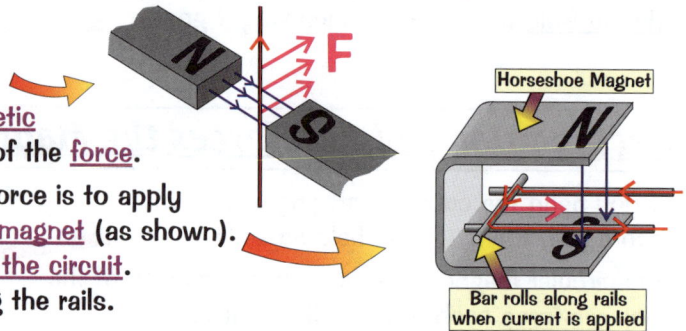

Horseshoe Magnet

N

S

Bar rolls along rails when current is applied

Fleming's Left-Hand Rule Tells You Which Way the Force Acts

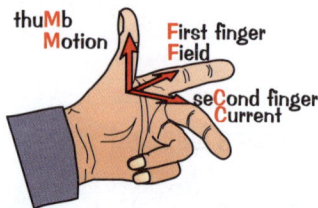

thuMb Motion
First finger Field
seCond finger Current

1) They could test if you can do this, so <u>practise it</u>.

2) Using your <u>left hand</u>, point your <u>First finger</u> in the direction of the <u>Field</u> and your <u>seCond finger</u> in the direction of the <u>Current</u>.

3) Your <u>thuMb</u> will then point in the direction of the <u>force</u> (<u>M</u>otion).

<u>EXAMPLE</u>: Which direction is the force on the wire?

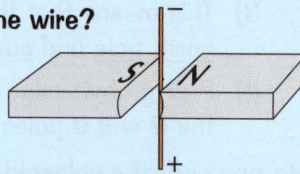

S N

<u>ANSWER</u>:

1) Draw in current arrows (+ve to −ve).

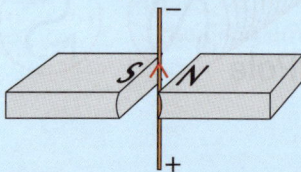

S N

2) Fleming's LHR.

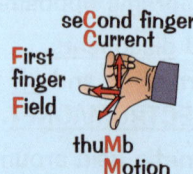

seCond finger Current
First finger Field
thuMb Motion

3) Draw in direction of force (motion).

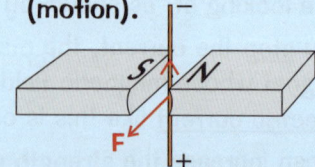

S N
F

Remember the Left-Hand Rule for Motors — drive on the left...

See, I told you you'd need your left hand for this page. Learn the rule and <u>use it</u> — don't be scared of looking like a muppet in the exam. <u>Learn all the details</u>, diagrams and all, then cover the page and scribble it all down from memory. Then check back, see what you've missed, and try again (and again until you get it right).

The Simple Electric Motor

Aha — one of the favourite <u>exam topics</u> of all time. Read it. Understand it. Learn it.

The Simple Electric Motor

4 Factors which Speed it up

1) More <u>CURRENT</u>
2) More <u>TURNS</u> on the coil
3) <u>STRONGER MAGNETIC FIELD</u>
4) A <u>SOFT IRON CORE</u> in the coil

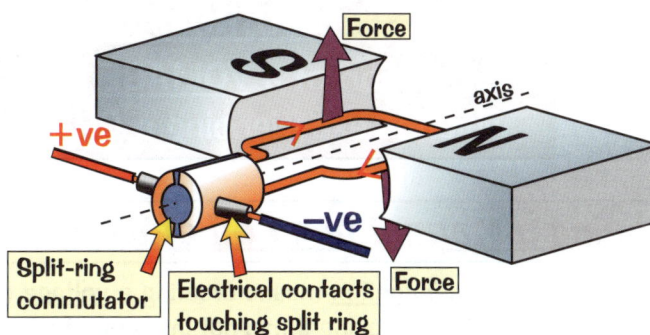

Force

axis

+ve

–ve

Force

Split-ring commutator

Electrical contacts touching split ring

1) The diagram shows the <u>forces</u> acting on the two <u>side arms</u> of the <u>coil</u>.

2) These forces are just the <u>usual forces</u> which act on <u>any current</u> in a <u>magnetic field</u> (see previous page).

3) Because the coil is on a <u>spindle</u> and the forces act <u>one up</u> and <u>one down</u>, it <u>rotates</u>.

4) The <u>split-ring commutator</u> is a clever way of "<u>swapping</u> the contacts <u>every half turn</u> to keep the motor rotating in the <u>same direction</u>". (Learn that statement because they might ask you.)

5) The direction of the motor can be <u>reversed</u> either by swapping the <u>polarity</u> of the <u>DC supply</u> or swapping the <u>magnetic poles</u> over.

EXAMPLE: Is the coil turning clockwise or anticlockwise?

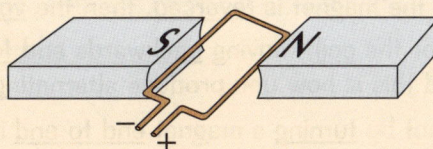

ANSWER: 1) Draw in current arrows (+ve to –ve).

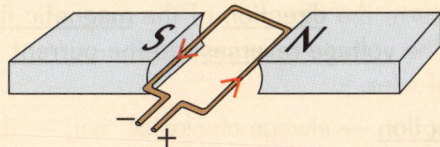

2) Fleming's LHR on one arm (I've used the right-hand arm).

SeCond finger Current

First finger Field

thuMb Motion

3) Draw in direction of force (motion).

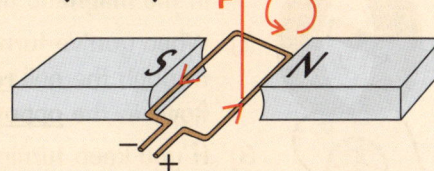

F

So — the coil is turning <u>anticlockwise</u>.

Practical Motors Have Pole Pieces Which are Very Curved

1) Link the coil to an <u>axle</u>, and the axle <u>spins round</u>.

2) If you can make your motor powerful enough, that axle can <u>turn</u> just about anything.

3) The problem is that the type of motor shown in the diagram at the top of the page is pretty useless. It's too <u>inefficient</u> to power anything big and heavy.

Curved pole pieces of magnet

N   S

coil

4) Instead, practical motors use <u>pole pieces</u> which are <u>so curved</u> that they form a <u>hollow cylinder</u>. The coil spins inside the cylinder.

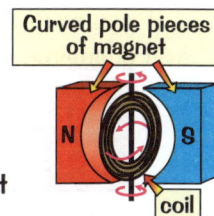

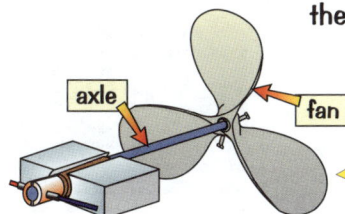

5) The curved pole pieces have a <u>radial</u> magnetic field which <u>increases</u> the magnetic field strength around the coil, so the motor is more <u>efficient</u>.

axle   fan

In this diagram there's a <u>fan</u> attached to the axle, but you can stick <u>almost anything</u> on a motor axle and make it spin round.

Hello Motor...

<u>Loudspeakers</u> demonstrate the <u>motor effect</u>. <u>AC electrical signals</u> from the <u>amplifier</u> are fed to the <u>speaker coil</u> (shown red). These make the coil move <u>back and forth</u> over the poles of the <u>magnet</u>. These movements make the <u>cardboard cone vibrate</u> and this creates <u>sounds</u>.

Electromagnetic Induction

Electricity is generated using <u>electromagnetic induction</u>. Sounds terrifying, but it isn't that complicated.

> ## ELECTROMAGNETIC INDUCTION:
> The creation of a <u>VOLTAGE</u> (and maybe current) in a wire
> which is experiencing a <u>CHANGE IN MAGNETIC FIELD</u>.

(You'll sometimes hear it called the "<u>dynamo effect</u>".)

Moving a Magnet in a Coil of Wire Induces a Voltage

1) <u>Electromagnetic induction</u> means creating a <u>voltage</u> (and maybe a <u>current</u>) in a conductor. You can do this by <u>moving a magnet</u> in a <u>coil of wire</u> OR moving a conductor (wire) in a magnetic field ("cutting" magnetic field lines). Shifting the magnet from <u>side to side</u> creates a little "<u>blip</u>" of current.

A few examples of electromagnetic induction:

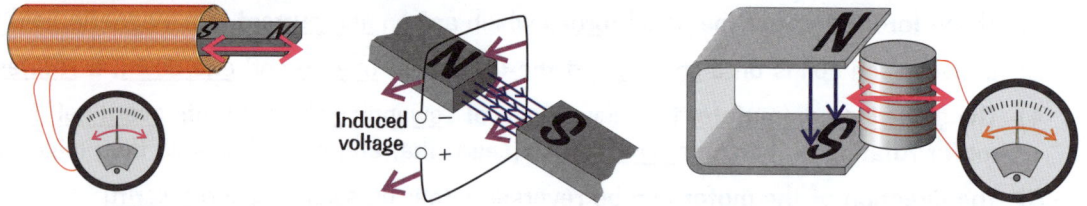

Induced voltage

2) If you move the magnet (or conductor) in the <u>opposite direction</u>, then the <u>voltage/current</u> will be <u>reversed</u>. Likewise if the <u>polarity</u> of the magnet is <u>reversed</u>, then the <u>voltage/current</u> will be <u>reversed</u> too.

3) If you keep the <u>magnet</u> (or the <u>coil</u>) moving <u>backwards and forwards</u>, you produce a <u>voltage</u> that <u>keeps swapping direction</u> — and this is how you produce <u>alternating current</u> (<u>AC</u>).

You can create the same effect by <u>turning</u> a magnet <u>end to end</u> in a coil, to create a current that lasts as long as you spin the magnet. This is how generators work (see next page).

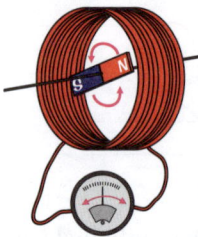

1) As you <u>turn</u> the magnet, the <u>magnetic field</u> through the <u>coil</u> changes — this <u>change</u> in the magnetic field induces a <u>voltage</u>, which can make a <u>current</u> flow in the wire.

2) When you've turned the magnet through half a turn, the <u>direction</u> of the <u>magnetic field</u> through the coil <u>reverses</u>. When this happens, the <u>voltage reverses</u>, so the <u>current</u> flows in the <u>opposite direction</u> around the coil of wire.

3) If you keep turning the magnet in the <u>same direction</u> — always clockwise, say — then the voltage will keep on reversing every half turn and you'll get an <u>alternating current</u>.

Four Factors Affect the Size of the Induced Voltage

1) If you want a <u>different</u> peak voltage (and current) you have to change the rate that the <u>magnetic field</u> is <u>changing</u>. For a <u>bigger</u> voltage you need to <u>increase</u> at least one of these four things:

> 1) The <u>STRENGTH</u> of the <u>MAGNET</u>   2) The <u>AREA</u> of the <u>COIL</u>
> 3) The <u>number of TURNS</u> on the <u>COIL</u>   4) The <u>SPEED</u> of movement

2) To <u>reduce</u> the voltage, you would <u>reduce</u> one of those factors, obviously.

3) If you <u>turn</u> the magnet <u>faster</u>, you'll get a higher peak voltage, but also a <u>higher frequency</u> — because the magnetic field is reversing more frequently.

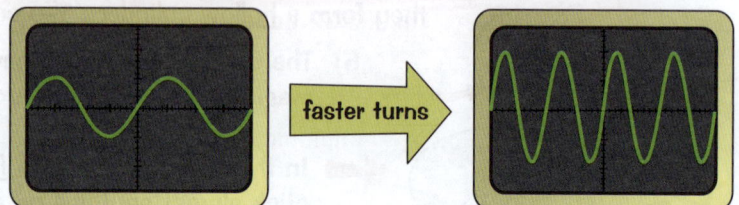

faster turns

EM Induction — works whether the coil or the field is moving...

"Electromagnetic Induction" gets my vote for "Definitely Most Tricky Topic". If it wasn't so important maybe you wouldn't have to bother learning it. The trouble is, this is how <u>all our electricity</u> is generated, so it's important.

Generators

Think about the simple electric <u>motor</u> — you've got a current in the wire and a magnetic field, which causes movement. Well, a <u>generator</u> works the <u>opposite way round</u> — you've got a magnetic field and movement, which <u>induces a current</u>.

AC Generators — *Just Turn the Coil and There's a Current*

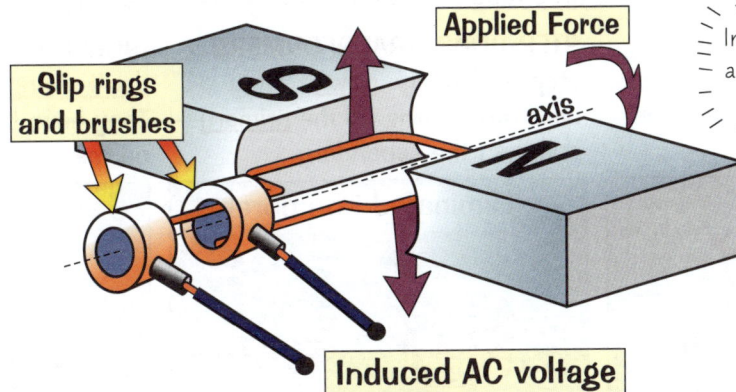

Slip rings and brushes

Applied Force

S

N

axis

Induced AC voltage

In an exam, they could give you a diagram like this and ask you to explain how it works.

1) Generators <u>rotate a coil</u> in a <u>magnetic field</u> (or a magnet in a coil... see below).

2) Their <u>construction</u> is pretty much like a <u>motor</u>.

3) As the <u>coil</u> (or <u>magnet</u>) <u>spins</u>, a <u>current</u> is <u>induced</u> in the coil. This current <u>changes direction</u> every half turn.

4) Instead of a <u>split-ring commutator</u>, AC generators have <u>slip rings</u> and <u>brushes</u> so the contacts <u>don't swap</u> every half turn.

5) This means they produce <u>AC voltage</u>, as shown by these <u>CRO displays</u>. Note that <u>faster revolutions</u> produce not only <u>more peaks</u> but <u>higher overall voltage</u> too.

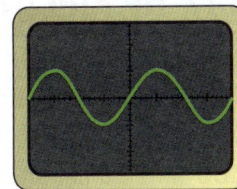

original

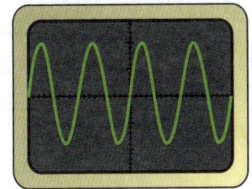

faster revs

Dynamos and Power Stations — *Turn the Magnet Instead of the Coil*

1) <u>Dynamos</u> are a slightly different type of <u>generator</u>. They rotate the <u>magnet</u> instead of the coil to produce alternating current.

2) This still causes the <u>field through the coil</u> to <u>swap</u> every half turn, so the output is <u>just the same</u> as for a generator.

3) This means you get the <u>same CRO traces</u> of course.

4) In a <u>power station</u>, electricity is generated by rotating an <u>electromagnet</u> in a coil of wire.

5) The <u>size</u> of the <u>output voltage</u> can be changed by adding <u>more turns</u> to the electromagnet coil.

6) The <u>size</u> and <u>frequency</u> of the output voltage can be changed by <u>rotating</u> the electromagnet coil <u>faster</u>.

<u>Dynamos</u> are sometimes used on <u>bikes</u> to power the <u>lights</u>. The <u>cog wheel</u> at the top is moved so that it <u>touches</u> one of the <u>bike wheels</u>. As the wheel moves round, it <u>turns</u> the cog which is attached to the <u>magnet</u>. This creates an <u>AC current</u> to power the lights.

Dynamo Kiev — they like a bit of squad rotation...

The National Grid is fed by hundreds of <u>generators</u>. These are usually driven by <u>steam turbines</u> (and the steam usually comes from burning things). You can get small portable petrol generators too, to use where there's no mains electricity — on building sites, say.

Transformers

Transformers use electromagnetic induction to connect two circuits together.
Transformers mean that one circuit can power another circuit with a different voltage and current.

There are Three Types of Transformer

Transformers are basically two coils of wire wound round an iron core. They're used to change the size of an alternating voltage. There are three types — you need to know the differences between them.

STEP-UP TRANSFORMERS step the voltage up. They have more turns on the secondary coil than the primary coil.

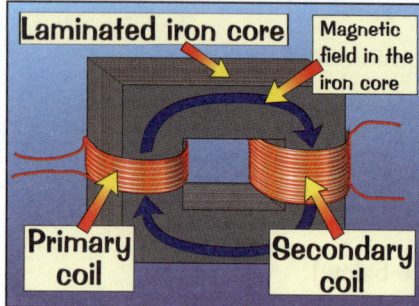

STEP-DOWN TRANSFORMERS step the voltage down. They have more turns on the primary coil than the secondary.

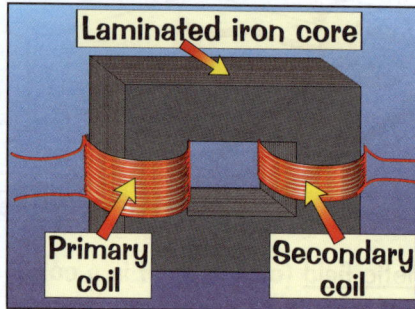

ISOLATING TRANSFORMERS don't change the voltage at all. They have the same number of turns on the primary and secondary coils.

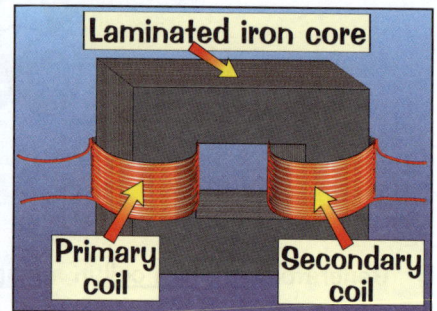

Laminated iron core | Magnetic field in the iron core

Primary coil | Secondary coil

Laminated iron core

Primary coil | Secondary coil

Laminated iron core

Primary coil | Secondary coil

Transformers Work by Electromagnetic Induction

1) The primary coil produces a magnetic field which stays within the iron core. This means nearly all of it passes through the secondary coil and hardly any is lost.

2) Because there is alternating current (AC) in the primary coil, the field in the iron core is constantly changing direction (100 times a second if it's at 50 Hz) — i.e. it is a changing magnetic field.

3) This rapidly changing magnetic field is felt by the secondary coil.

4) The changing field induces an alternating voltage in the secondary coil (with the same frequency as the alternating current in the primary) — electromagnetic induction of a voltage in fact.

5) The relative number of turns on the two coils determines whether the voltage induced in the secondary coil is greater or less than the voltage in the primary.

6) If you supplied DC to the primary, you'd get nothing out of the secondary at all. Sure, there'd still be a magnetic field in the iron core, but it wouldn't be constantly changing, so there'd be no induction in the secondary because you need a changing field to induce a voltage. So don't forget it:

> **Transformers only work with AC. They won't work with DC at all.**

Transformers are Nearly 100% Efficient So "Power In = Power Out"

The formula for power supplied is: Power = Voltage × Current or: P = V × I.

So you can rewrite power in = power out as:

$$V_p I_p = V_s I_s$$

V_p = primary voltage $\quad V_s$ = secondary voltage
I_p = primary current $\quad\quad I_s$ = secondary current

You can use this equation to find the output current when the voltage has been changed. As both sides need to balance, for a fixed input power, the higher the voltage, the lower the current will be.

You have to assume the transformer is 100% efficient though.

EXAMPLE: The primary voltage and current into a transformer are 200 V and 5000 A. Find the secondary current, if the voltage is stepped up to 20 000 V.

ANSWER: $V_p I_p = V_s I_s$, so 200 × 5000 = 20 000 × I_s. I_s = (200 × 5000) ÷ 20 000 = <u>50 A</u>.

More on Transformers

The <u>ratio</u> between the primary and secondary <u>voltages</u> is the same as the <u>ratio</u> between the <u>number of turns</u> on the primary and secondary coils. You can either learn it that way, or learn the formula below.

The Transformer Equation — Use it Either Way Up

You can <u>calculate</u> the <u>output voltage</u> from a transformer if you know the input voltage and the number of turns on each coil.

$$\frac{\text{Primary Voltage}}{\text{Secondary Voltage}} = \frac{\text{Number of turns on Primary}}{\text{Number of turns on Secondary}}$$

$$\frac{V_P}{V_S} = \frac{N_P}{N_S}$$

or

$$\frac{V_S}{V_P} = \frac{N_S}{N_P}$$

Well, it's <u>just another formula</u>. You stick in the numbers <u>you've got</u> and work out the one <u>that's left</u>. It's really useful to remember you can write it <u>either way up</u> — this example's much trickier algebra-wise if you start with V_s on the bottom...

EXAMPLE: A transformer has 40 turns on the primary and 800 on the secondary. If the input voltage is 1000 V, find the output voltage.

ANSWER: $\frac{V_s}{V_p} = \frac{N_s}{N_p}$, so $\frac{V_s}{1000} = \frac{800}{40}$. $V_s = 1000 \times \frac{800}{40} = \underline{20\ 000\ V}$

Or you can say that 800 is 20 times 40, so the secondary voltage will also be 20 times the primary voltage.

Transformers Are Used on the National Grid

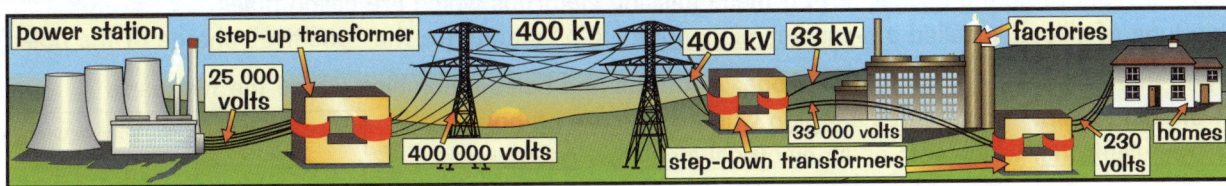

power station | step-up transformer | 400 kV | 400 kV | 33 kV | factories | homes
25 000 volts | 400 000 volts | step-down transformers | 33 000 volts | 230 volts

1) To transmit <u>a lot of power</u>, you either need <u>high voltage</u> or <u>high current</u> ($P = VI$).

2) The problem with <u>high current</u> is the <u>loss</u> (as <u>heat</u>) due to the <u>resistance</u> of the <u>cables</u> (and <u>transformers</u>).

3) The formula for <u>power loss</u> due to resistance in the cables is:

$$\text{Power Loss} = \text{Current}^2 \times \text{Resistance}$$

$$P = I^2R$$

4) Because of the I^2 bit, if the current is <u>10 times</u> bigger, the losses will be <u>100 times</u> bigger.

5) So it's much <u>cheaper</u> to boost the voltage up to <u>400 000 V</u> and keep the current <u>very low</u>. This requires <u>transformers</u> as well as <u>big pylons</u> with <u>huge insulators</u>, but it's still <u>cheaper</u>.

6) The transformers have to <u>step</u> the voltage <u>up</u> at one end, for <u>efficient transmission</u>, and then bring it back down to <u>safe, usable levels</u> at the other end.

Isolating Transformers are Used in Bathrooms

1) <u>Isolating</u> transformers have an <u>equal</u> number of <u>turns</u> in the primary and secondary <u>coils</u>, so also have equal primary and secondary <u>voltages</u>. They can be found in some <u>mains circuits</u> in the <u>home</u>, such as in a <u>bathroom shaver socket</u>.

2) Isolating transformers are there for <u>safety</u>. The <u>mains</u> circuit is connected to the <u>earth</u>, so if you <u>touch</u> the <u>live parts</u> and are <u>also touching the ground</u>, you will <u>complete a circuit</u> with you in it. <u>NOT good</u>.

3) The isolating transformer inside the shaver socket allows you to use the shaver without being <u>physically connected</u> to the mains. So it minimises the risk of the <u>live</u> parts <u>touching</u> the <u>earth</u> lead and likewise <u>minimises your risk</u> of getting <u>electrocuted</u>. Phew.

National Grid — heaven for noughts and crosses fans...

In most power stations, <u>fuels</u> are burned and the energy from this powers a massive <u>generator</u>. Not all the heat can be converted into mechanical power, though, so heat is often <u>lost</u> to the environment. What a waste.

Diodes and Rectification

Mains electricity supplies alternating current (AC), but many devices need direct current (DC).
So we need a way of turning AC into DC. That's where diodes come in.

Diodes Only Let Current Flow in One Direction

1) Diodes only let current flow freely in one direction — there's a very high resistance in the other direction.

2) This turns out to be really useful in various electronic circuits.

3) You can tell which direction the current flows from the circuit symbol.

   The triangle points in the direction of the current.

Here the current flows from left to right.

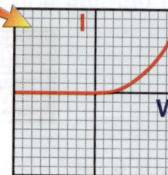

Diodes are Made from Semiconductors Such As Silicon

1) Diodes are often made of silicon, which is a semiconductor.
This means silicon can conduct electricity, though not as well as a conductor.

2) Silicon diodes are made from two different types of silicon joined together at a 'p-n junction'.
One half of the diode is made from silicon that has an impurity added to provide extra free electrons
— called an n-type semiconductor ("n" stands for the "negative" charge of the electrons).

3) A different impurity is added to the other half of the diode so there are fewer free electrons than normal.
There are lots of empty spaces left by these missing electrons which are called holes.
This type of silicon is called a p-type semiconductor ("p" stands for the "positive" charge of the holes).

4) When there's no voltage across the diode, electrons and holes recombine where the two parts
of the diode join. This creates a region where there are no holes
or free electrons, which acts as an electrical insulator.

5) When there is a voltage across the diode the direction is all-important:
Applying a voltage in the RIGHT direction means the free holes
and electrons have enough energy to get across the insulating
region to the other side. This means that a CURRENT FLOWS.
Applying a voltage in the WRONG direction means the free holes
and electrons are being pulled away from the insulating region,
so they stay on the same side and NO CURRENT FLOWS.

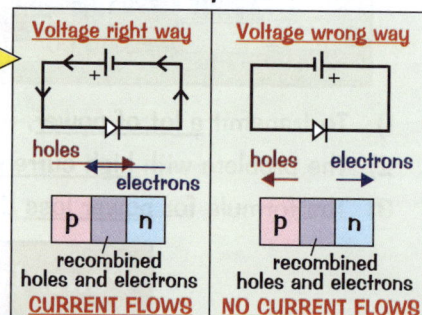

Voltage right way | Voltage wrong way

holes | electrons | holes | electrons

p | n | p | n

recombined holes and electrons
CURRENT FLOWS

recombined holes and electrons
NO CURRENT FLOWS

Diodes Can be Used to Rectify Alternating Current

1) A single diode only lets
through current in half of
the cycle. This is called
half-wave rectification.

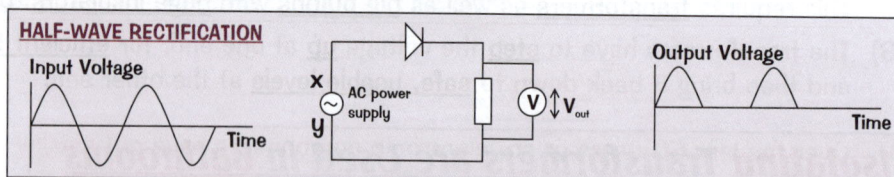

HALF-WAVE RECTIFICATION

Input Voltage

Time

x
y

AC power supply

V ↕ V_{out}

Output Voltage

Time

2) To get full-wave rectification,
you need a bridge circuit
with four diodes.
In a bridge circuit, the
current always flows
through the component in
the same direction, and
the output voltage always
has the same sign.

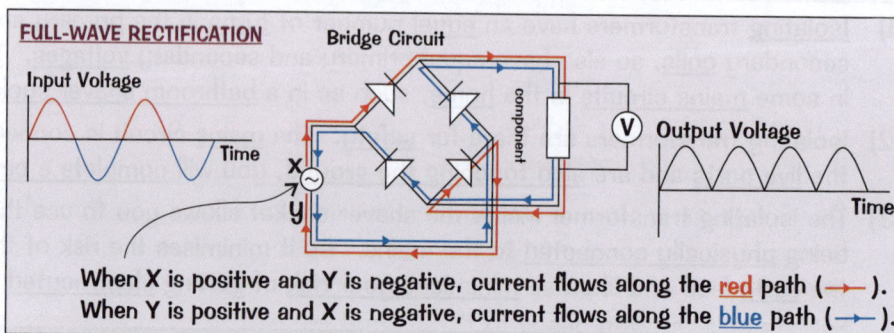

FULL-WAVE RECTIFICATION

Input Voltage

Time

Bridge Circuit

x
y

component

V

Output Voltage

Time

When X is positive and Y is negative, current flows along the red path (—→).
When Y is positive and X is negative, current flows along the blue path (—→).

Yep, it's all just common sense really...

Only joking — this stuff's flippin' hard. At least you've made it through to the other side though, well done.

Capacitors

AC voltage that has been <u>rectified</u> is not all that useful in its <u>raw form</u>. For example, computer chips are very sensitive to input voltage, and won't work with a voltage that looks like this: ∧∧∧∧∧. They need a <u>smoother</u> voltage like this: ∼∼∼∼. This is where <u>capacitors</u> come in handy.

Capacitors Store Charge

1) You <u>charge</u> a capacitor by connecting it to a source of voltage, e.g. a battery. A <u>current</u> flows around the circuit, and <u>charge</u> gets <u>stored</u> on the capacitor.

Circuit symbol

2) The <u>flow of current decreases</u> as you charge for longer periods of <u>time</u>.

3) The <u>more charge</u> that's stored on a capacitor, the <u>larger the voltage</u> across it.

4) When the voltage across the capacitor is <u>equal</u> to that of the <u>battery</u>, the <u>current stops</u> and the capacitor is <u>fully charged</u>. The voltage across the capacitor <u>won't rise above</u> the voltage of the battery.

5) If the battery is <u>removed</u>, the capacitor <u>discharges</u> — the <u>flow of current</u> is the <u>same</u> for <u>discharging</u> as for charging (see shape of graph above) but the current flows in the <u>opposite</u> direction round the circuit.

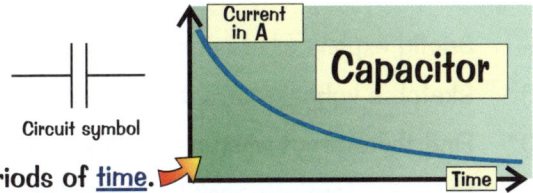

<u>CHARGING</u>:
Current flows until capacitor is fully charged
Voltage rises as capacitor charges

<u>DISCHARGING</u>:
Current flows in opposite direction until capacitor is fully discharged
Voltage falls as capacitor discharges

Capacitors are Used in 'Smoothing' Circuits

The output voltage from a rectified AC power supply can be '<u>smoothed</u>' by adding a capacitor in <u>parallel</u> with the output device. A component gets current <u>alternately</u> from the power supply and the capacitor.

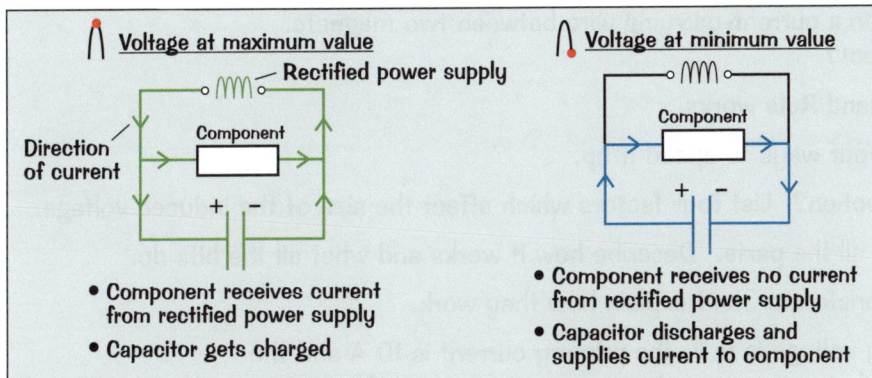

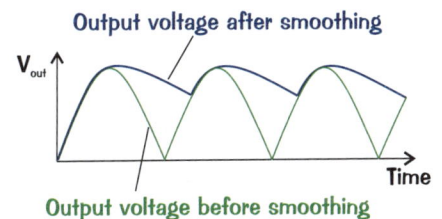

Voltage at maximum value
Rectified power supply
Component
Direction of current

- Component receives current from rectified power supply
- Capacitor gets charged

Voltage at minimum value
Component

- Component receives no current from rectified power supply
- Capacitor discharges and supplies current to component

Output voltage after smoothing
V_{out}
Output voltage before smoothing
Time

Electronic Components Are Getting Smaller

1) Over the last 50 years or so, electronic components have got <u>smaller</u> — it's known as miniaturisation.

2) This has both <u>benefits</u> and <u>drawbacks</u> for <u>makers</u> of electronics, and for the people <u>using</u> them:

Makers
<u>Benefits</u>: Smaller devices use less raw material. Most customers like smaller devices.
<u>Drawbacks</u>: It can be more complex to produce small devices, and more expensive.

Users
<u>Benefits</u>: More portable electronic devices available. More powerful and feature-filled devices produced.
<u>Drawbacks</u>: Smaller devices can be more expensive. They're easier to lose down the back of the sofa.

3) Computers have become smaller, cheaper and more <u>powerful</u> too. As <u>more people</u> have access to more <u>computing power</u> (e.g. computers and phones) <u>society</u> needs to decide how this should, or should not, be allowed to be <u>used</u>.

For example, society needs to think about controlling <u>hacking</u>, <u>piracy</u> and <u>access</u> to personal data.

Current never flows through a capacitor...

Capacitors just <u>store charge</u>, and then send current back the <u>other way</u> when the voltage falls. Handy.

Revision Summary for Module P6

Electricity and magnetism. What fun. This is definitely physics at its most grisly. The big problem with physics in general is that usually there's nothing to "see". You're told that there's a current flowing or a magnetic field lurking, but there's nothing you can actually see with your eyes. That's what makes it so difficult. To get to grips with physics you have to get used to learning about things you can't see. Do these questions to see how you're getting on. Then you can relax, it's the end of the book. Ace.

1) Briefly explain what causes resistance in a metal conductor.

2) Sketch a voltage-current graph for: a) a resistor, b) a filament lamp.

3)* Find the current when a resistance of 96 Ω is connected to a battery of 12 V.

4)* Four resistors with resistances of 2 Ω, 4 Ω, 6 Ω and 3 Ω are connected in a circuit in parallel. Calculate the total resistance of the circuit.

5) Explain how potential dividers work.

6) State the formula for potential dividers. Do your own worked example, including a sketch.

7) Write down two facts each about: a) LDRs, b) thermistors.

8) Draw and label the circuit symbol for a transistor. Describe what happens in each part of the transistor.

9) Draw truth tables for AND, OR, NAND and NOR gates.

10) What are AND gates made from?

11) Explain how an LED can be used to show the output of a logic gate.

12) Make a sketch of a relay.

13) Give a definition of a magnetic field.

14) Sketch magnetic fields for: a) a current-carrying wire, b) a rectangular coil, c) a solenoid.

15) Make a sketch of the force on a current-carrying wire between two magnets. What is the name of this effect?

16) Explain how Fleming's Left-Hand Rule works.

17) Sketch a motor and list the four ways to speed it up.

18) What is electromagnetic induction? List four factors which affect the size of the induced voltage.

19) Sketch a generator, labelling all the parts. Describe how it works and what all the bits do.

20) Sketch the three types of transformer, and explain how they work.

21)* In a transformer, the primary voltage is 6 V, the primary current is 10 A and the secondary voltage is 3 V. What is the secondary current in the transformer?

22)* A transformer has an input voltage of 20 V and an output voltage of 16 V. If there are 64 turns on the secondary coil, how many turns are there on the primary coil?

23) Explain why power is transmitted at such a high voltage.

24) Write down three facts about isolating transformers.

25) Explain briefly how a diode works. What semiconducting material are diodes often made of?

26) Explain the two ways in which an AC current can be rectified. Include circuit diagrams and voltage/time graphs in your explanation.

27) What is a capacitor? How can it be used to smooth rectified voltage?

28) Electronic components are getting smaller. Explain why this could be a bad thing for:
   a) manufacturers of electronic devices,   b) users of electronic devices.

29) Go and read up on quantum theory... no wait, I mean... go and put the kettle on.

Index

Index and Answers

Answers

Bottom of page 48

1) a) CH_2 b) CH_2O c) $AlCl_3$

2)
C	H
2.4	0.8
$2.4 \div 12 = 0.2$	$0.8 \div 1 = 0.8$
2	8 So the empirical formula is CH_4

Bottom of page 52

number of moles of $H_2SO_4 = 0.2 \times (25 \div 1000) = 0.005$
$H_2SO_4 + Ca(OH)_2 \rightarrow CaSO_4 + 2H_2O$
So for every mole of H_2SO_4 there is one mole of $Ca(OH)_2$
So the number of moles of $Ca(OH)_2 = 0.005$
concentration = moles ÷ volume = $0.005 \div (40 \div 1000)$
= $0.005 \div 0.04 = 0.125$ mol/dm³

Revision Summary for Module C5 (page 62)

2) M_r of $Na_2SO_4 = (23 \times 2) + 32 + (16 \times 4) = 142$
moles = mass ÷ M_r = 284 ÷ 142 = 2

3) M_r of Cl_2 in $MgCl_2 = 35.5 \times 2 = 71$
mass = moles × M_r = 2 × 71 = 142 g

5) Number of moles of $Na_2O = 108.2 \div 62 = 1.745$
4 moles of Na produce 2 moles of Na_2O.
So number of moles of Na = 1.745 × 2 = 3.49
mass = moles × M_r = 3.49 × 23 = 80.3 g

6)
Mg	S	O
21.9	29.3	58.3
$21.9 \div 24 = 0.9$	$29.3 \div 32 = 0.9$	$58.3 \div 16 = 3.6$
9	9	36
1	1	4

So the empirical formula is $MgSO_4$

7) a) 7.5 g/dm³   b) 7.5 ÷ 2 = 3.75 g/dm³

8) $0.2 \times (500 \div 1000) = 0.1$ moles

9) Take 50 cm³ of the 1 mol/dm³ sulfuric acid solution,
and dilute it with 200 cm³ of water.

14) a) $0.15 \times (25 \div 1000)$
= 0.00375 (3.75 × 10⁻³) moles of KOH
$HNO_3 + KOH \rightarrow KNO_3 + H_2O$
1 mole of nitric acid reacts with
1 mole of potassium hydroxide
concentration = $0.00375 \div (22.5 \div 1000)$
= 0.167 mol/dm³
b) mass = moles × M_r = 0.167 × (1 + 14 + (16 × 3))
= 10.5 g/dm³

18) a) 50 cm³   b) about 13 s

Revision Summary for Module C6 (page 78)

11) $Q = I \times t = 2 \times 3 = 6$ C

24) permanent hardness

Refraction (page 91)

Refractive index of sapphire
= speed of light in a vacuum ÷ speed of light in sapphire
= $3 \times 10^8 \div 1.7 \times 10^8 = 1.76$
Light speeds up going from sapphire into air so the light would bend away from the normal.

Revision Summary for Module P5 (page 96)

2) 0.2 m/s north   0.5 m/s south

Vectors are directly opposite so overall velocity is (taking
south as positive): 0.5 m/s – 0.2 m/s = 0.3 m/s south

3) 5 mph west   θ   12 mph north

Use Pythagoras's theorem to find the speed:
speed² = 5² + 12² = 169
speed = √169 = 13 mph
Find direction using trigonometry:
tan θ = 5 ÷ 12 = 0.417   θ = 22.6°
So, the bird is flying 13 mph at 22.6° west of north

4) u = 0 m/s, v = 14 m/s, t = 0.4 m/s, s = ?
using s = ½(u + v) × t
s = ½(0 + 14) × 0.4 = 2.8 m

5) Make velocity upwards positive.
u = 13.4 m/s, a = –10 m/s², s = 7 m, v = ?
using v² = u² + 2as
v² = 13.4² + (2 × –10 × 7) = 179.56 – 140 = 39.56
v = √39.56 = 6.3 m/s

7) a) Taking the vertical motion: u = 0 m/s, t = 10 s,
a = 10 m/s², s = ?
using s = ut + ½at²
s = (0 × 10) + ½(10 × 10²) = 500 m
b) speed = distance ÷ time
rearrange to find distance = speed × time
distance = 1.5 m/s × 10 s = 15 m

9) Momentum before = momentum after
so, momentum after the collision = 0.

11) The force will increase by a factor of nine.

19) a) Refractive index = speed of light in a vacuum ÷
speed of light in a medium. Rearrange to find
speed of light in a medium = speed of light in a
vacuum ÷ refractive index.
So, speed of light in jet = 3×10^8 m/s ÷ 1.66
= 1.81×10^8 m/s
b) The light would bend away from the normal.

24) Magnification = image height ÷ object height
= 4.5 cm ÷ 1.5 cm = 3

Revision Summary for Module P6 (page 114)

3) I = V ÷ R = 12 ÷ 96 = 0.125 A

4) Resistors in parallel, so use $\frac{1}{R_T} = \frac{1}{R_1} + \frac{1}{R_2} + \frac{1}{R_3} + \frac{1}{R_4}$.
$\frac{1}{R_T} = \frac{1}{2} + \frac{1}{4} + \frac{1}{6} + \frac{1}{3} = 1.25$
so, R_T = 1 ÷ 1.25 = 0.8 Ω.

21) $V_pI_p = V_sI_s$, so 6 × 10 = 3 × I_s, so $I_s = \frac{60}{3} = 20$ A.

22) $\frac{V_p}{V_s} = \frac{N_p}{N_s}$, so $\frac{20}{16} = \frac{N_p}{64}$. $N_p = 64 \times \frac{20}{16} = 80$ turns